FROM THE BOOKS OF

P. Padgett.

Those Amazing RINGLINGS and their CIRCUS

By

GENE PLOWDEN

ILLUSTRATED WITH PHOTOGRAPHS

Introduction by Roland Butler

BONANZA BOOKS · NEW YORK

In Fond Memory
of
R O L A N D   B U T L E R
Longtime friend, noted raconteur,
And the greatest circus press agent
of the century
This book is
Affectionately Dedicated

Introduction

By Roland Butler

To me this book is just tops from start to finish and by far the best story of the Ringlings ever done by anyone.* It improves as it unfolds. Without plastering his subject with the goo-goo common to circus books, Gene Plowden gives us the fantastic facts and the real lowdown on a most extraordinary family.

Gene Plowden is the only person on earth I know of who is qualified to tell the full, authentic story of the Ringling Circus and its main character—John Ringling. In this book he has done just that—clearly, concisely, and completely in a refreshingly simple, straightforward manner.

Gene had an unusual opportunity to know John Ringling, and he was close enough to look behind the scenes. He had access to a gold mine of material not available to others and was free to write what he saw.

Gene first met John Ringling one winter night in 1927 when he went to the El Vernona Hotel in Sara-

---

* Roland Butler was general press representative of Ringling Bros. and Barnum & Bailey Combined Circus for more than thirty years, until June, 1954. He was widely known and generally recognized as one of the greatest circus press agents of our time until his death on October 20, 1961.

Butler worked closely with the author for nearly thirty years, on newspaper and magazine material and in the preparation of this manuscript. This is what he wrote shortly before his death.

sota, Florida, to take part in a radio broadcast. John was just leaving the studio. He shook hands and stopped to talk a few minutes as he nibbled on his cigar and spat on the thick velvet carpet at his feet. This intrigued Gene Plowden, the young reporter, who had yet to learn about John's habits.

"Even if he did own the hotel," Gene said to me later, "that wasn't any excuse for him to ruin a costly floor covering like that. I figured a man as big as he was would be housebroken, at least."

For several years Gene was sports editor of the *Sarasota Daily Tribune* and he knew the workings of the fight game as well as the doings of promoters, managers, and boxers by the hundreds, from champions to club contestants. John liked to win small bets and he relied on Plowden for his dope.

The sports editor called the turn so often in his daily column, "Fan Fare," that John thought he was a second-sight artist. He made it a point to contact the sports editor before laying his money on a fight, and he usually won. This pleased him immensely, whether he'd risked ten dollars or a hundred. Money appealed to John. Gene became his friend.

Magazine writers and newspapermen from New York City often used to comment and ask me, "What is Plowden's drag with J. R.?" Many circus stories that made the front pages throughout the nation first appeared in Sarasota under Gene's by-line.

John told me to keep Plowden in mind for our press department, "if you can get him," he said. "That guy knows how to get news, and how to dish it out. I wish he was heftier, but I think he'll fill out and make a hell of a good agent for us."

Although John went in for men of poundage and preferred heavily-built six-footers to represent the show, Gene was an exception at five foot seven. John said he'd go in for smaller agents if he could get them as smart as Plowden, and as energetic.

While Gene would never seriously consider traveling with the circus as a regular thing, he did considerable writing for us. John confided in him, trusted him, and told him things no other writer ever got him to say.

For thirty years Gene knew the circus as intimately as it was possible to know it. He made trips with it, ate in the cookhouse, and traveled in the show's sleepers. But the glitter and glamor of the Big Top never dazzled him. Always he remained the reporter, alert and observant.

He had the time, energy, and patience to dig into all the records and follow the ramifications of the circus operation. This he has done with all the thoroughness of the top-flight reporter that he is; gathering all the facts, diligently sifting them for the more salient; searching through mountainous stacks of musty court records and old newspapers; interviewing hundreds of persons in many parts of the country to double-check details; and supplementing it all with his own personal knowledge of the subject and remarkable memory for names, dates, and places.

In many instances he was there—when Gargantua was christened and when he "married" M'Toto, and when the Big Top came home for the last time. He was free to roam through winter quarters, which he did hundreds of times, and through the art museum and Ringling home. Court records were open to him as a reporter.

Thus this is the true, unbiased chronicle of the Ringling Circus from the day it was born until the night it died—accurate beyond question, interestingly written, and entertaining throughout. It is on-the-spot reporting; nothing is concealed, nothing glorified.

It is the first completely authentic history of the Ringlings and their circus ever put on paper.

ROLAND BUTLER

PALMETTO, FLORIDA

Contents

Illustrations

Ringling's Pygmy Elephants Were Presented with Tremendous Fanfare

In 1953 the Circus Featured Master Mistin, a Child Prodigy, on the Xylophone

CHAPTER ONE

This Way to the Big Top

THE GOLDEN AGE of the American circus was beginning. For more than a hundred years menageries, and then circuses, had exhibited in such cities as New York, Philadelphia, Baltimore, Boston, and Hartford.

Gradually these routes spread out to include Washington, Richmond, Charleston, and Savannah; circus groups sailed down the Ohio and Mississippi rivers to Memphis and New Orleans; moved overland to reach such settlements as Mobile, Pensacola, Dothan, Apalachicola, and Tallahassee, then up to Thomasville and Augusta.

By the middle of the nineteenth century circuses had more or less absorbed menageries so that the public was being entertained by such traveling organizations as Barnum's Asiatic Caravan, Museum & Menagerie, E. F. and J. Mabie, Seth B. Howes, Levi J. North, John Robinson, Spalding & Rogers, Stone & Madigan, Isaac Van Amburgh, and others.

Thirty years later most circuses still traveled by horse and wagon over rutty, dusty, or muddy roads and were lucky to make ten or fifteen miles a day. But they managed to reach even the rural districts and gave isolated communities an occasional bit of entertainment, with a look at some wild animals. It must be observed that some of these visits were without invitation or welcome, but merchants generally approved because the circus brought people to town.

Most circuses employed advance men, had experienced managers, and gave first-rate performances at moderate prices. They had to because competition was fierce and even family-type shows such as those of George L. Whitney, Mat Wixom, and Miles Orton included blackface comedians and novelty acts, acrobats, riders, tumblers, clowns, and an abundance of band or orchestra music.

By the early 1880's, more than seventy thousand miles of railroads had threaded their way through the forests and across the plains of America, linking all important cities from coast to coast. Thus a train could go from the Atlantic to the Pacific in less time than it took a horse and wagon to cross one state.

Onto rails went P. T. Barnum with his Greatest Show on Earth and Howes' Great London Circus and Sanger's Royal Menagerie. This was all one enterprise, with three advance cars, each carrying a calliope to play at every stop and whip up enthusiasm. These recent inventions were big and brassy, and they drew crowds.

A stereopticon brigade preceded the show, with pictures of the coming attractions to whet the public's appetite. The circus itself followed, giving afternoon and evening performances in two rings and on a hippodrome track, and concluding with a concert or aftershow.

Barnum's wasn't the only circus to go on rails. William Washington Cole traveled by train, and so did Adam Forepaugh and John Robinson. The Sells brothers had two shows—the Great European Seven Elephant Circus—to compete with Barnum's six elephants —on rails, and Anderson & Company's Great World's

Circus and Menagerie, which moved by horse and wagon.

There were others, too—Buffalo Bill's Wild West, Coup's Equescurriculum, Harris' Nickel Plate, Van Amburgh, Dan Rice, Lucky Bill Newton, Yankee Robinson, and the notorious John V. (Pogey) O'Brien's Circus Royale.

Those traveling by rail rented or owned cars thirty to forty feet long, with sleeping accommodations for officials and top performers. Workingmen stretched out under the wagons on flatcars, or wherever they could find room to curl up and catch a nap between towns.

The typical tented circus of the 1870's and 1880's provided the highlight of the year for many a town and village. If it was big enough to come in by train and give a two-mile-long street parade, thrills and excitement were multiplied a hundred times.

Day was breaking when the long circus trains pulled in, their silver sides glistening in the soft, yellow light of swinging lanterns and gas streetlamps. As the engines rolled to a stop and sighed with a loud hissing of steam, men hopped down and began the task of unloading and moving to the lot.

Elephants and horses were led from the cars and wagons were pulled off the flats and onto the street. The men worked smoothly, rapidly, and with noticeable efficiency. There was no loafing or lost motion— the whole gang pitched in as if every one had done the same thing a thousand times, and more than likely he had.

Soon there was a procession of people and horses and wagons and elephants and cages of wild animals streaming toward the lot where stakes marked the location of every tent and wagon. Here burly hammer gangs swung and hummed in unison as they drove stakes to anchor the massive sheets of canvas that would house the show for the day.

Elephants pulled the center poles into place and dragged the great rolls of canvas up and up until the big top was an immense brown shell surrounded by smaller tents and wagons. It was a fascinating sight to see a weed-covered lot transformed into a fairyland of lights, music, and a hundred displays of ferocious beasts from foreign lands. There were strange people, games, and barkers everywhere.

By now it was eleven o'clock and people began gathering on sidewalks up and down Main Street and clustering at intersections, for here came the street parade, heralded by the distant echo of a brass band and the clopping of horses' hooves on cobblestones.

First came the outriders, their steeds prancing nervously against the curbs, the uniformed men shouting: "Hold your horses; the elephants are coming!"

Youngsters hunkered down to get a better view, or shinnied up trees and telegraph poles along the line of march so as not to miss a thing. There was scarcely a window or a door that did not frame one or more faces.

There was the owner himself, or the equestrian director, wearing a tall, stovepipe hat; big, shiny gloves, and a boutonniere. He was driving matched horses and they fairly danced along as they toyed with the light, high-wheeled buggy or two-wheeled cart and allowed the driver plenty of liberty with the lines.

The parade marshals, banner bearers, and buglers, all

mounted on sleek, spirited horses, came next with flags flying and trumpets glistening in the sunlight.

There was a string of horses, two abreast, pulling the gigantic bandwagon, and it was crammed with musicians. The horses had red, white, and blue plumes over their ears and their harness was decorated with rosettes and huge brass medallions.

The driver was astride the last horse on the left, or he perched on a tiny seat that stuck out in front of the wagon, lines stretching to the ten or twenty steeds he was driving.

The cavernous bandwagon was a riot of color, heavily carved and with sunburst wheels, and it was filled with twenty or thirty uniformed musicians playing at the tops of their lungs to whip up enthusiasm.

There were tandems with stylishly-dressed ladies and gentlemen, even to the latest in hats, gloves, and parasols. There were wagons of every size, frames and wheels decorated with glossy enamel and side panels painted in jungle scenes. Inside were lions, tigers, leopards, panthers, and other wild beasts, pacing and snarling or lying stretched on the floor, panting, barely visible through the thick plate glass.

There were high school horses, tableaux wagons, and open cages of animals such as seals and sea elephants. Finally there were the real elephants, trunk to tail, with their ornate blankets covering rubbery old sides, and wearing huge silver nameplates above the eyes.

And there were clowns everywhere, walking with dogs, ducks, or perhaps a rooster; riding in a tiny cart drawn by a pony or a goat, or almost hidden in a huge cluster of balloons.

Bringing up the rear was the calliope, panting out an

invitation to follow the parade and visit the circus, now about to start. Hundreds quickly fell into line, making the procession even longer and more impressive, so it seemed that everyone was chatting and laughing and heading for the circus.

Among those who walked with quick and easy strides toward the lot where the Great Inter-Ocean Circus had erected its tents for afternoon and evening performances on that hot, muggy July day in 1883 was young John Ringling, fresh out of Baraboo, Wisconsin.

He could hear the noise and high-pitched voices on the circus grounds five blocks away—there seemed to be music and merriment everywhere, and the very atmosphere was charged with excitement.

John Ringling liked lively music and he scarcely noticed the collar-wilting heat as he walked briskly to join the throng now swarming around the first calliope many of them had ever seen or heard.

The music ended on a tinny whine and a man with a neat waxed mustache mounted a small platform. He wore a derby perched on the back of his head and white cuffs dangling from the sleeves of his dark gray linen jacket. He carried a slender, gold-headed cane which he alternately twirled and leaned upon as he surveyed the growing assemblage through piercing black eyes set deep in his flamingo-colored face.

"My friends." He began his spiel in a clear, crisp voice that penetrated the grounds. "You have just heard this modern marvel of musical mechanism—the only gen-u-wine vaporic calorophone, perfected at a cost of over one hundred thousand dollars in glittering gold!"

He paused to let the words fall like raindrops upon the eager crowd, then continued:

"I might remind you, la-deez an' gen-tul-men, that the tones of this incredible instrument are so powerful they can be heard five miles away and yet are as sweetly soft as a lover's lute!

"And now, my friends, if you will kindly give me your attention for just a moment, I shall endeavor to tell you about some of the outstanding attractions of our enormous double annex or sideshow department, brought to your fair city and exhibited exclusively throughout America by that master showman of the age, Mister John B. Doris."

John Ringling pressed forward to have a closer look at the calliope, then sauntered along with the crowd to pause in front of the freak tent where the sideshow grinder was going into his spiel, gesturing with his cane toward a square of canvas that pictured Flora, the fat girl, considerably larger than life size.

Surrounding Flora's picture were likenesses of a strong man, a fire-eater, an armless man writing with a pencil stuck between his toes, a bearded lady, a girl whose head came to a sharp point, and a calf with two heads. Entwined among arms and legs and stretching across the entire twenty feet of canvas was what appeared to be a very pregnant python, breathing flames.

"Now, my friends," the grinder said, lowering his voice into a serious and confidential tone, "to prove to you that each and every attraction of the Great Inter-Ocean Circus is exactly as represented, we are going to show you, ab-so'-lute-ly free, some of our many outstanding exhibits awaiting your inspection.

"And, don't forget, you have ample time to see them

before the big show commences one hour from now."

A tall, skinny man scissored his way through folds of canvas and mounted the platform behind the talker's stand. He towered like two telegraph poles joined together near the middle, wearing a big cowboy hat and waving his arms as if to balance himself on his stiltlike underpinnings.

"Here you see the world's tallest living skeleton," the grinder said. "This man is eight feet six and a half inches, without his boots, and weighs a mere one hundred and fifteen pounds."

The crowd stared in open-mouthed disbelief—a patch of faces gaping at the human splinter tottering above them—and the talker continued.

"Now, la-deez an' gen-tul-men, inside there you will see the most fascinating display of human beings in the entire world," and he stabbed his cane toward the canvas. "The smallest man alive is here—only thirty-one inches tall and weighing only twenty and one-half pounds.

"There's the pin-headed girl, the armless wonder, the strongest man in all the world, and many, many more odd, strange, and unique features you may never see again."

John Ringling turned and walked away, his eyes and ears striving to assimilate and absorb the vast and changing picture—carriages, wagons, saddled horses and trolley cars rimming the grounds, spilling their loads of eager children; the throb and hum of the crowd blending with the noise, heat, and confusion of a great symphony of color and sound.

John's nostrils caught the heady odors of fresh sawdust and frying onions, sweating humans and tobacco smoke, lemonade and licorice sticks, plus the smell of wild animals and horse manure.

Up and down the midway he watched young bucks try their skill and strength at the games, listened to the pitchmen, and studied the faces of the crowd, enthralled. Even the canvas tops and sidewalls, the lines, stakes, and poles; stout wagons and cages, their red and gold paint glittering in the sunlight, made an appealing picture.

Young John Ringling had been steeped in circus history. He had heard or read about the Mabie Brothers, who started over at Delavan in 1847; the Buckleys, Hollands, Herr Driesbach, Phillips & Babcock, Dan Castello, Haight & Chambers, the Orton Brothers, William C. Coup and many more, down to the days of Burr Robbins and P. A. Older, all of whom originated in Wisconsin.

He had heard of old Yankee Robinson, who wintered in the state; and of course he had read of such giants as Phineas T. Barnum, the Sells Brothers, John Robinson, and Van Amburgh. But this was the biggest circus he had ever seen, and the most exciting.

For long minutes he stood and looked around, drinking in the atmosphere with undiluted pleasure, feeling the presence and the thrill of the crowd as only a born entertainer can experience it.

His reverie was interrupted by the sharp whinny of a horse, and from over near the Big Top came the throaty, rasping roar of a lion. John Ringling turned and walked toward the entrance to the main tent, but a canvas wall caught his eye and he stopped to read this message:

"To the public: I shall always endeavor to conduct

a very high class, pure and moral circus. Nothing in the speech or manner of the attaches of my vast organization that will in any way be offensive to the most fastidious will be tolerated under any circumstances."

Above the printed message was a life-size painting of John B. Doris with his name in fancy lettering underneath. The proprietor of the Great Inter-Ocean, with an assist from the artist, was a downright handsome man with a round, expressive face; rosy and full in the prime of life. His thick, wavy black hair was parted on the side; he wore a batwing collar and a black cravat, and on the knot of his necktie was a stickpin with a diamond as big as a hickory nut.

Doris seemed to be peering down at the crowd with a twinkle in his eyes that were brown and foxy. A slight but assuring smile played around his lips.

Clever, John Ringling discovered, that the stretch of canvas used to convey Doris' message of sanctimony shielded an open trench being used as a latrine by a steady stream of men and boys.

Three men stood in the shade of the bandwagon, near the entrance to the Big Top, and John sidled closer to hear their discussion. One wore a black derby, white shirt and black cravat. He was showing the other two some printed matter and roasting old Adam Forepaugh in vitriolic language, calling him "a rotten, side-whiskered son-of-a-bitch."

The speaker looked like Doris and according to his discussion, John Ringling was certain it was the proprietor of the Great Inter-Ocean. He was not to learn until years later, however, that the two men with him were Bennie Keith and Ed Albee, who at that very moment were planning their "great variety circuit."

By the time Doris concluded his appraisal of Forepaugh, John Ringling had heard enough and he moved through the main entrance in a daze, stopping to buy a program that extolled the virtues and many attractions of the Great Inter-Ocean Circus in pictures and text. He was amazed at the size of the circus Doris had been able to put on the road after he dissolved partnership with Batcheller and came out with his own show.

The program opened with the Royal Japanese Troupe of acrobats and jugglers, followed by Billy Showles, the bareback rider; James Ward and Willie Turnour on the bars and trapeze; Sally Marks and Millie Elizie in their riding act; the Rice brothers in their novelty number, and a dozen others. John Patterson and George Drew were the featured clowns.

The final act, the human cannonball, was one of the most sensational of the time. Rosa Richter, an English actress, had performed the feat in London, using the professional name of "Mlle Zazel, the human cannonball," and toured this country with the Barnum show in 1879 or 1880. This gave rise to similar acts by other performers, most of whom were propelled upward and outward by springs, and a few who even used the name "Zazel."

As a climax to the "Great Inter-Ocean Circus" program, workmen dragged an enormous cannon into the tent. The wheels apparently had come from a great cart or Civil War field piece and the barrel was like a giant hollow log. The whole was braced and anchored so that it resembled a gigantic grasshopper.

A woman wearing a white quilted suit came skipping

into the ring, climbed between the wheels and tiptoed along the barrel to its mouth, where she stood for a moment, looking over the crowd.

"La-deez an' gen-tul-men!" the announcer bellowed. "Mister John B. Doris and his Great Inter-Ocean Circus proudly present the most sensational, death-defying act ever seen in America.

"This little lady will be shot from the cannon—yes-s-s; she will actually fly through the air in the most daring and dangerous act ever performed anywhere."

The slender figure in white dropped into the mouth of the cannon so that only her head and one arm were showing, waved briskly to the audience, and disappeared as the muzzle began to tilt slowly.

Workmen swarmed around the mechanism, turning screws and twisting knobs, adjusting straps and tightening and testing lines and stakes. The crowd waited expectantly, with scarcely a breath or a blink to interrupt the tenseness.

"Are you ready, Mam'zel Zazel?" the announcer shouted. There was no reply, only a stiffening silence. Then the whole tent seemed to explode in a jarring, shocking, deafening "ker-bloom-oom!"

Women screamed and swooned, children whimpered and stirred, men stood up and applauded, uncertainly.

Cries of "Where is she?" "What happened to her?" and "Did she make it?" rippled through the crowd. One man near John, the points of his mustache dancing nervously, said, "The whole contraption exploded." Another agreed, and in a knowing attitude announced, "She's been blown to smithereens!"

A cloud of thick, black smoke billowed around the cannon, filling the tent with choking fumes that set off a siege of coughing and eyewatering. At the same time the white-clad figure bounded to her feet in a long net about twenty yards away, and the band broke into a lively tune.

The crowd surged out, as if anxious to find fresh air. Bodies sagged from the heat and excitement, arms were heavy with tired and sleepy children, and hands clutched programs and souvenirs.

John Ringling stopped and stood aside at the exit to watch the people stream past him and spread out along the midway, now alive with chanting grinders and eager concessionaires, the whole scene like a living, stirring rainbow.

He picked up a discarded eight-page pink herald and studied it briefly, then stuffed it into his pocket, along with the program he had saved. Then he walked slowly down the midway, his alert brown eyes taking in the vast panorama of happiness.

Thus John Ringling, six weeks past his seventeenth birthday, took his first positive steps along the road that would lead him to the throne as king of the circus.

CHAPTER TWO

Five Fingers on a Hand

THE SAGA of the Ringlings actually began with the arrival of one Gottlieb G. Gollmar from Germany with his parents in the early 1800's. He grew up in Ohio, became a blacksmith and went to work in Chicago where he met and married Mary Magdalene Juliar.

The Juliar family, which included several daughters, had come from Colmar, in France, and settled near Milwaukee.

A few years later, in 1847, young August Rüngeling arrived in Canada from his native Alsace, worked his way across the country and landed in Milwaukee. There this round-faced, stocky and stubborn young man met and married Marie Salome Juliar, who was Mary's sister.

The wedding took place in 1850 and August Rüngeling went with his bride to Chicago, where he went to work in a wagon factory with his brother-in-law, Gottlieb Gollmar. It was in Chicago, in 1852, that the first of the August and Marie Salome Rüngeling brood was born, a son christened Albrecht C.

At that time young August Rüngeling was amazed at the constant stream of people going West and it inspired him to seek his fortune in that direction. By now another child was on the way and the young couple returned to the Juliar home in time for it to be born there in the summer of 1854. The boy was named August G., and the family called him Gus.

August Rüngeling did not wish to live with in-laws on a farm, nor to impose on the family, so he struck out for Baraboo, in south-central Wisconsin, where he went into business in what historians refer to as a "one-horse harness shop."

The description may have been apt, and it laid good groundwork for the family's success story, but some who grew up with the boys have pointed out that August Rüngeling's operation was in keeping with the size of the community, and they were quick to add that, while the family did have modest beginnings, and the usual ups and downs as fortunes fluctuated, none of the children ever missed a meal or lived in any degree of poverty.

Actually, August Rüngeling did very well from the start, and soon sent to Milwaukee for his wife and two sons. They settled in a comfortable house on the corner, and down the street was the shop where he made and repaired harness, and offered for sale such other necessities of the time as saddles, bridles, brushes, currycombs, and buggy whips.

He Americanized his name and advertised his establishment in the newspaper as owned and operated by "A. Ringling." Some say the name originated when a printer spelled it that way and the owner liked it and let it stand. Chances are August Rüngeling himself changed it, with the help of his wife, who was a clever and imaginative person.

Anyway, business was promising and soon Marie Salome's sister, Helena Catherine Juliar, and her husband, Henry Moeller, came from Milwaukee to join the Ringlings. Henry opened his own commercial establishment, the Moeller Wagon Works.

About this time a depression swept the country and by 1857 it had grown into a financial panic. A third son, Otto, was born to the Ringlings in the midst of the money drought.

August Ringling decided to give up in Baraboo and packed his growing family off to the town of McGregor, on the Iowa side of the Mississippi and on one of the main routes between Chicago and the West. McGregor was something of a teamsters' headquarters and a thriving community. It had been a river port for years and a trade center for several counties in Iowa, Minnesota, and Wisconsin.

There a fourth son, christened Alfred Theodore but commonly known as Alf T. to distinguish him from his older brother, Al, was born in 1863, followed the next year by Karl Edward, whose first name was later Americanized to Charles.

Two other harness shops in McGregor offered more competition than August Ringling could stand, so he finally gave up and went to work in one of them, making harness.

Eventually he opened another shop, however, and his family was living in rooms above it when Johann was born on May 30, 1866. He was christened in the German spelling and his mother called him Johann as long as she lived, but no one outside the family ever used the name. To his classmates in school and later in the entertainment and business world he was John Ringling, and he signed his name that way.

Some chroniclers of the Ringling story have said flatly that John was the seventh son but, actually, he was the

THE
RINGLING
FAMILY

*Front row,
left to right:*
John, Marie
Salome and
August
(parents),
Ida, and
Henry.
Back row:
Al, Alf. T.,
Gus, Charles,
and Otto.
This
photograph
was taken
about 1895.

THE CIRCUS KING, JOHN RINGLING, AT THE HEIGHT OF HIS CAREER

MERLE EVANS, RINGLING CIRCUS BANDMASTER

He is one of the most renowned exponents of circus music and a leading authority on the subject.
He has played at over twenty-five thousand performances with the Ringling Bros. and Barnum &
Bailey Circus.

CONFERRING ON DETAILS

Circus producers Richard Barstow, director-choreographer, and Robert Dover, performance director, standing, confer with Antoinette Concello, aerial ballet director, and Pat Valdo, general director, on production details of the 1964 edition of "The Greatest Show on Earth."

sixth. The seventh and last was named Henry, and he arrived in 1868. John's astounding good luck, coupled with his flair for flamboyancy in everything he undertook, may have fathered the impression, and on that premise he should have been the seventh son of a seventh son.

Two daughters followed the succession of sons. One died in infancy and the other was named Ida Lorraine Wilhelmina, born in 1874. By this time young Al Ringling was working with his father in the shop and Gus had gone out on his own, in McGregor.

Papa Ringling could no longer make a go of it, and he looked to the town of Prairie du Chien, two miles up the river from McGregor and on the Wisconsin side. A railroad had recently been built there from Milwaukee, and the town showed promise.

A carriage factory was built there and the Ringling family left McGregor after a dozen years. Young Gus Ringling, now twenty years old, was working in a harness shop and elected to stay in McGregor, over the objections and tears of Mama Ringling, who said she felt like the family was splitting up.

Papa Ringling and Al, now twenty-two, went to work as trimmers in the carriage factory in Prairie du Chien, and for a time life moved smoothly for the Ringlings.

They lived in a large house on the northern edge of town where rent was cheap and there was plenty of land on which to raise potatoes, cabbage, beans, onions, and other foodstuffs, and keep a flock of chickens.

By now Al was becoming quite proficient as a balancer and juggler. He went to work on the horizontal bars and trapeze, and practiced in every spare moment. He stretched a rope between two trees, made a balancing pole, and learned to walk a tightrope.

But after only a few months, fire destroyed the carriage factory; August Ringling and his son Al were out of work.

Al went to Brodhead and got a job in Williams & Ballou's carriage shop. His father opened a little harness repair shop and moved his family into a log house east of Prairie du Chien, where there was land enough for a garden.

Gus and Al sent a little money home to help out, but when Papa Ringling heard that Stillwater, Minnesota, was growing and needed a harness shop, he moved the family there.

By now Otto was big enough to help in the shop, but business was bad and they moved back to Baraboo, where August Ringling went to work for his brother-in-law and Otto got a job in Racine.

John often said that the first thing he could remember about his boyhood, aside from moving frequently, was climbing onto the backs of farm wagons and over the sides of open railroad cars to cut off the tails of pigs en route to the market in Chicago.

He liked to relate how he'd slip over the tailgate of a wagon piled high with frozen pigs, snip off a handful of tails and scurry away, undetected by the driver. Then he would join his brothers and cousins at their rendezvous, where they'd cook the tails over an open fire and have a feast.

Because of his youth and daring, John said, his playmates encouraged such forays, leaving to him also the risk of being caught and paddled. That he seldom had to pay the penalty was a tribute to his cunning and resourcefulness. In those days, he boasted, he could run faster than any boy his age in Baraboo, and get those pigtails off in jig time.

Such escapades must have had tremendous influence on young John Ringling, because all his life he liked to outsmart the other fellow, whether it involved the price of drinks and dinner or a fifty-thousand-dollar deal.

All the Ringlings were normal, healthy, and husky youngsters and they managed well in the public schools but none of the boys finished the grades. Ida graduated from Baraboo High in 1892.

The boys showed unusual talent for music, both instrumental and vocal, and Mama Ringling encouraged them to play and sing. Soon there was an orchestra within the family. Some of the children formed a singing group, clowned and told stories as they entertained at church suppers and socials.

All were leaders, including Ida, who showed it during an incident at Baraboo High. An old man wandered onto the school grounds and collapsed among a group of children at play. Ida saw what had happened, ran over to him, folded her coat to make a pillow, and sent two boys to get help while she tried to comfort him. School authorities commended her for her initiative and kindness.

Mama Ringling had motherly pride in her offspring, recognized their talents, and gave them all the encouragement she could in music, art, and literature. The house was never without musical instruments and reading material.

On the other hand Papa Ringling believed in honest toil and he attempted to direct his sons' energies in that direction. He had little training in music or the arts and lacked imagination for such things. Even when five of his sons showed serious interest in show business, he thought they were wasting their time and warned them that the public would not pay for such "foolishness."

Had not Herr Ringling left Chicago, his sons might have become tycoons of the mail order or meat packing business. As it happenaed, the family meanderings gave them an appetite for travel and a knowledge of the area where they lived.

They liked to make music and mimic, and drew inspiration from the many circuses that originated in Wisconsin and from a steady stream of visiting entertainers.

It has been recorded that John Ringling got his inspiration for a circus one bright spring morning when he sat on the banks of the Mississippi and watched Dan Rice's Showboat tie up for a stand at McGregor.

John no doubt would have readily agreed to the legend, but he couldn't twist time. He was never opposed to gilding the pill, but he was far too clever to be caught in a web of historical facts, and he was only two years old at the time!

Charles Ringling wrote that they watched Dan Rice come up the river that morning in May and he noted that Al had to carry little Johnny most of the way from their house to the river to keep his new shoes from getting muddy.

Al was sixteen years old at the time, and Dan Rice may have fathered his ambition to become an entertainer. Dan danced, clowned, and made speeches much along the line of Will Rogers many years later. He exhibited his performing horse, Excelsior, and was tremendously popular. He was even mentioned as a candidate for the Republican presidential nomination in 1868, and drew scattered support from small-town editors.

Dan Rice's presidential boomlet never reached national proportions, however, and his chief claim to fame was that circus folk considered him one of the greatest of American entertainers and clowns. At the height of his career, Adam Forepaugh paid him the munificent sum of one thousand dollars a week—enough to inspire many a boy.

Five of August Ringling's robust sons were like fingers on a hand, each separate but pertinent to the whole; each supporting the other in a remarkable display of coalescence.

Each was strong and versatile but all were apposable and endowed with more connatural capabilities than any other five brothers in America. Stubborn as jackasses, they often argued vociferously and at great length, but once they reached agreement, differences were forgotten and they carried on in complete accord and with enthusiasm.

They could blow horns, stroke strings, or press keys to make music which, likely as not, one of them had composed. They could be clowns or lay out the circus lot, do a Risley act or man the ticket booth, walk a tightrope or route the show. They could write advertising, put up posters, or talk contracts with merchants and politicians.

Together they formed a powerful fist that could drive their opposition to the wall and smash it, or, with fingers extended, grasp it like an octopus and strangle the life out of it.

Occasionally rivals referred to them as the "ruthless Ringlings," but that was for public consumption, and more a compliment than an insult, for every circus man of the time had to admire the bold and bullish brothers for their ability and versatility.

While he might have felt the sting of their competition, he profited by their example and devoutly wished for their strength and resourcefulness.

Circuses were individual operations, large and small. They did not cooperate and each went his way to battle fires and floods, blowdowns and train wrecks, diseases and depressions; heat, cold, mud, and sometimes political or public displeasure.

The Ringlings experienced all of these, and because of the magnitude of their operation, troubles came to them in giant doses. There had been brother groups in the circus field before them, and afterwards, but never five active as performers and operators, and none as prominent and successful.

Actually there were seven sons but only five figured in the circus empire. Eventually the other two went to work in the organization, but they owned no part of it and had no influence while the five were at the helm. The Ringlings needed no partners, just as the hand needs no extra fingers.

Albrecht C., or Al, was the oldest and he could be compared to the middle finger, for he led the way from the time he learned bareback riding as a boy of ten, using an old gray mare loping around in a garden patch.

Various theatrical groups and circuses provided the inspiration and experience he needed to become an actor and clown, but natural ability and determination made him the guide and commander, as an older brother should be.

Al was the showman of the group and he dressed in the height of fashion, with Prince Albert coat, silk top hat, and gold-headed walking stick. His boots were always shiny and his Ascot tie had not a wrinkle in it.

Al was qualified both by training and temperament to blow the whistle on the show and when the time came, he led his contumacious brothers to the pot of gold.

He was the only member of the family who continued to act like a performer all his life, whose very presence on the lot sent a feeling of confidence and well-being to all hands, and who was one of the most capable and respected men in circus history.

Alfred Theodore, or Alf T., was the second son and producer of the group—the ring finger. His artistic ability made the Ringling show well and favorably known and his productions were the most lavish ever seen in the tented arena.

Working with horses, dogs, doves and pretty girls on swings, pedestals and revolving stages, he designed and executed magnificent displays which were a feature of the Ringling Brothers Circus for more than thirty years.

Alf T. wrote special music for the ballets and tableaux, which filled all three rings and intervening stages —spectacular productions of great beauty—with as many as 1,200 people in the cast.

Alf T. would watch the performance for a few days, make suggestions to improve it, then slip away to plan the next season's spectacle, often spending days and

weeks in museums to find authentic costumes and background material for the new theme.

Otto was the third brother and the tight-fisted banker
of the clan—balance wheel of the organization. Born in
the depression, he was the man who watched dollars
and pennies. He became the master of logistics and
arithmetic, the index finger of the hand.

In the early days it was Otto's frugality that made it
possible for the brothers to keep their show on the road,
and turn a neat profit. His stinginess showed them how
to cut corners and save money.

Otto spurned ostentatiousness all his life, never married, and never owned a home. His brothers rode in
chauffeured limousines and relaxed in private railroad
cars, maintained spacious homes, and traveled extensively, even to weekend fishing trips, but not Otto.

He shunned luxury and made his way by horse and
buggy even after automobiles came into fairly general
use. If business forced him to make a trip into town
from the circus grounds he went by streetcar rather
than by taxicab or rented hack. Usually the only reason for him to make such a journey was to save money
on a contract, or to check up on the street parade and
criticize it.

Employees despised him and called him "King Otto"
or "The Little King." He kept a sharp and distrustful
eye on everyone connected with the circus, attacked
waste and inefficiency wherever he found it, and suspected everyone of being a wastrel or a thief. Nobody
ever made a dime off of Otto.

Then there was Karl Edward, whose first name was
Americanized to Charles. He typified "Charles"—soft
and gentle as one's little finger but just as essential to

the hand. A kind and understanding man, Charles spent most of his life in the backyard. He knew all the performers by name and had a personal interest in their problems.

He was a sober, industrious individual who went to bed early, got up early, and generally had a steadying influence on his more volatile brothers.

While Charles lacked some of their drive and determination, he was tremendously popular with circus personnel generally, and he always had time to stop and exchange a word or two with the workingmen or to join in friendly conversation with the cookhouse gang.

He could be sarcastic but he also could be appreciative, and he could be generous. It is said by many that never in his life did Charles make a promise that he didn't keep.

Finally, there was John—apart from the others, thumb of the hand. Youngest of the five, he also was the most flamboyant, most daring, and by far the most widely known. He was a big, handsome fellow and his very presence inspired men and excited women. He personified the slogan, "The Greatest Show on Earth."

John was a manipulator and a diplomat who could give opportunity a bear hug. He was a foxy fellow who wouldn't hesitate to close a deal involving thousands of dollars over a poker table at three o'clock in the morning, and quibble over last month's milk bill. He'd spend a fortune for a painting, and swear he was being overcharged for an order of groceries.

He would buy beer by the boatload, expensive cigars by the dozen boxes, and complain bitterly over the price of gasoline for his Rolls-Royce.

When the Ringling Brothers Circus had swallowed

all its rivals, reached the peak of its magnitude and splendor, and entertained some four million spectators in a season, only John was left to rule as king.

Call him also gourmet and art connoisseur, promoter and front man, raconteur and poker player par excellence, night operator and gormandizer. A man of Herculean achievements and magnificent extravagances—that was John Ringling.

CHAPTER THREE

The Show Is About to Commence

WHILE AL was still working in Brodhead, he joined a marching club and took part in a Fourth-of-July parade. He practiced juggling and balancing, learned to spin plates on the tips of his fingers, and took up acrobatics.

It called for a lot of time, patience, and practice, but Al kept at it. He even swung a trapeze from a beam in the Ringling barn so he wouldn't miss his training when he visited in Baraboo, and his brothers could practice, too.

Al liked music and one of his cherished possessions while he was still a teen-ager was a battered old cornet which he learned to play. Soon he was doing a high wire act between the roofs of buildings on the main street in Brodhead, advertising various enterprises and entertaining Saturday shoppers.

He was always trying something new to vary his routine, and he gained considerable notoriety when he learned to balance a heavy hand plow on his chin!

Alf T. and Charles studied music and practiced regularly; soon the whole family was playing and singing. Charles was something of a child prodigy and by the time he reached high-school age he could play the violin very well. In later years he liked to entertain his friends with violin solos.

Alf T. and Charles also learned to walk the tightrope and do some tumbling routines, following the admonitions and examples set by their older brother.

John drew ideas and inspiration from the others but he had a mind of his own and often acted independently. He liked good music, had a fair singing voice and could dance and recite monologues and poems.

Thus four of the Ringling boys had ambitions to become entertainers and every one of them was full of ham. Soon after the family moved back to Baraboo from Stillwater, they put on their first program—a kid show in the barn.

Al came from Brodhead to direct it and he had a leading part. He did a turn on the horizontal bars, appeared in a high wire act, and gave his exhibition of juggling and plate spinning. Alf T. and Charles played a duet and did a tumbling routine. John was the boy clown, in a red and white costume, with his brothers as straight men for his antics and jokes. All provided vocal and instrumental music. Soon Al left his job in the carriage factory and joined Fred White, who owned a Punch and Judy show. He received special billing as "Alphonse Ringling, juggler and balancer," and he toured with White for two winters through Wisconsin, Minnesota, and parts of Iowa and Illinois.

Al raised a bushy, black mustache, forerunner of the famous Ringling lip adornments that were to be the brothers' trademark for more than thirty years. It gave him an appearance of maturity and was the fashion of the times. When he stopped in to visit the family, the mustache and accounts of his travels charmed his younger brothers.

Al left Fred White to manage a little wagon outfit called the "Big 4 Show." It was then that he met and married a lively, attractive, and intelligent widow named Eliza Morris, to whom they gave the name Louise.

She was a busy, energetic young woman and, in addition to her job of snake handler, she doubled at collecting tickets, washing and mending clothes, and doing other chores that went with trouping in those days. Louise became a rudder not only for Al Ringling but an inspiration for all the brothers.

The Big 4 Show couldn't compare in size with most other entertainment ventures of the day and its identity appears to have been lost among the myriad wagon or "mud" shows that roamed the country. It lasted only one summer.

Showboats were in their prime and the American circus was commencing to flower. James E. Cooper and James A. Bailey, operating as Cooper & Bailey, had become serious rivals of P. T. Barnum and a merger was arranged in 1881 whereby Cooper retired and Bailey went into partnership with Barnum and his brother-in-law, James L. Hutchinson.

Other circuses which traveled exclusively by rail included John Robinson, Adam Forepaugh, Sells Bros., and John B. Doris. Many had expanded to two rings and a hippodrome track, a menagerie and one or more sideshows, plus the concert or afterpiece.

About this time Barnum bought the huge African elephant, Jumbo, for ten thousand dollars and brought it to this country from London amidst tremendous fanfare.

With all this to encourage and inspire, the Ringling brothers plunged into the amusement field, although they had no money and no financial backers.

They polished up their musical instruments, spent hours running through all the popular songs, and bought cloth which Mama Ringling and Louise made into uniforms for the musicians and costumes for performers.

Alf T. drew some window cards and handbills, with help from Al; the brothers practiced dancing, clowning and juggling, rehearsed a couple of one- and two-act plays, and put their show together. From the beginning they were determined to entertain and amuse, to generate as much laughter as possible.

They called the first venture the "Ringling Bros. Classic and Comic Concert Co., and billed it as a "refined and high class entertainment of the most prominent features of the musical and comedy world."

Even with Al's experience and the others' hours of practice, they were amateurs, and there were only four. John took part in the early rehearsals with Al, Alf T., and Charles, but at sixteen years of age he was a big, bullheaded boy with a mind of his own. He fell out with his father, quit school, and ran away from home. Even at that age he was as independent as a young bear, with a restless and absorbing mind.

John's three brothers loaded all their props, costumes, and musical instruments into two spring wagons and set out on tour. A white frost covered fences and fields when the Ringlings rode off into the crisp sunrise of that Monday, the twenty-seventh of November, 1882. With Al, Alf T. and Charles went another young musician and entertainer, Ed Kimball, who later was to father Clara Kimball Young, a noted actress of her time.

Four others—Ed S. Weatherby, Fred Hart, William Trinkhouse, and M. A. Young—joined the party at Sauk City and they drove nine more miles to Mazomanie, Wisconsin, for their first performance.

Charles Ringling later wrote that there were fifty-nine people in the audience and the show took in thirteen dollars. It wasn't much but it generated enough heat to warm their enthusiasm and solidify their determination to stay in show business.

"It was a cold night and a pitiful performance," according to Charles. "From the very beginning, the show seemed to fly to pieces, but we kept going and got better as we went along. The people applauded our efforts and this was like a tonic, giving us confidence and encouragement, which of course we needed."

Young, who had the title of "boss hostler," went ahead to Spring Green where he rented a hall, put up window cards, and passed out some handbills advertising the performance. The troupe followed and at Richland Center played in a real theater for the first time and took in over thirty-five dollars. Then they turned south and went to McGregor and Prairie du Chien.

"Going to McGregor and Prairie du Chien was a smart move for us," Charles said. "We had friends in both places and they not only came to see the show but warmly applauded. Some even invited us to their homes for meals, and we accepted, of course.

"We had very little cash from day to day and none in reserve, spending nearly all we took in on hall rentals, advertising matter, food, and what little lodging we had to have. We barely made expenses that first week or two, but we kept going, gaining experience and making friends in every town we played."

From Prairie du Chien they headed west into Iowa. At the same time, back in Baraboo, John Ringling stuffed his belongings into a hand satchel, tucked a pair of big wooden shoes under his arm, and set out to join them.

The Ringling Bros. Classic and Comic Concert Co. was in Sanborn, Iowa, on that Sunday, the seventeenth of December, 1882, when John arrived. He found them at the hotel, sitting around a potbellied stove trying to keep warm, and talking up the show among the guests.

That night they rehearsed in the dining room, after the dishes had been cleared away, going over some humorous skits and brushing up on a one-act play they had run through several times.

Next morning they were up early greeting townspeople and spreading word of their show in stores, barbershops, and livery stables; making special mention of the latest member to join their troupe—John Ringling. They were optimists—talkative, friendly, and persuasive, and they described their show as one of the finest and funniest on the road.

When the curtain went up, Charles Ringling, the interpolator, introduced his younger brother as "The newest member of our troupe; a real live dude who will give dudish delineations, songs and sayings."

John wore a dark blue jacket, white shirt, black string tie, tight-fitting pants and shiny patent leather shoes. He had on a black derby set at a jaunty angle, which he lifted in acknowledgement of applause, nodding and bowing to the audience.

He was the picture of a young man fresh from the big city, with round, boyish face and snappy, stylish clothes; he had thick, black hair parted in the middle,

POSTER OF ABOUT 1900 ADVERTISING THE GREATEST SHOW ON EARTH

Standing beside it is L. Wilson Porch, of Arlington, Virginia, past president of the Circus Fans Association of America. In his hands is a bull hook or elephant goad.

FRED BRADNA, EQUESTRIAN DIRECTOR OF THE CIRCUS FOR NEARLY FORTY YEARS
His wife Ella was a featured performer in the center ring

AN
EARLY-DAY
VIEW OF
THE
CIRCUS
"BACK-
YARD"
Note the
improvised
barber chair
and the
"customers."
The barber
supplies are
on the table
in the center.

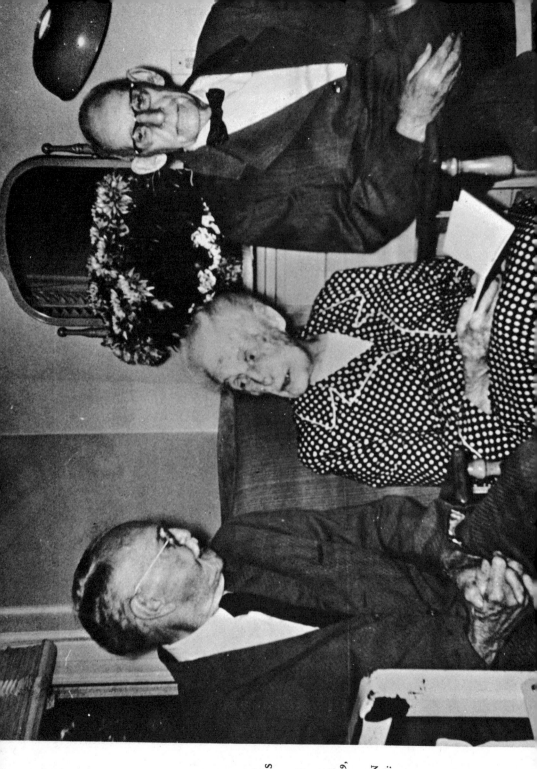

THESE
THREE
ARE
BELIEVED
TO BE
THE LAST SURVIVORS
OF THE
FIRST
RINGLING
BROS.
CIRCUS
AUDIENCE
OF MAY 19,
1884, AT
BARABOO,
WISCONSIN

Left to right:
Dr. Samuel
G. Barker,
Jefferson,
Iowa; Mrs.
Ida Potter
and John M.
Kelley, both
of Baraboo.
The photo-
graph was
taken in
1961.

slicked down and glossy. The months he had spent practicing with his brothers had given him confidence, and
he showed no signs of nervousness as he went through
his routine. John was by all standards the best actor in
the family.

In addition to his first brief skit, the program included:

"Just a few minutes with America's cornet virtuoso,
rendering Levy & Arbuckle's difficult solo—Alf T.
Ringling; the great plate spinner, gravity-defying manipulator and balancer—Al Ringling; Charles Ringling,
introducing his motto and comical songs."

Then John appeared on stage following this introduction by the interpolator:

"Now we will have fifteen minutes in Ireland—songs,
dances, sayings; Irish witticisms and so forth, by John
Ringling, the funny Irish comedian of the period. John
will introduce his original parody version of 'Over the
Garden Wall,' so everybody prepare to laugh."

In the next offering John played the role of Pat Mul-
len, "A bad man," in a skit, "our roaring comedy play
called, 'Ki-Ko-Kan-Kum.'"

A minstrel overture followed but the crowd wanted
John and shouted, "Bring on the dude; bring him back!"
Charles responded with this announcement:

"Again by popular request, we have John Ringling,
the emperor of Dutch comedians, in his very funny ma-
neuvers creating roars of laughter with every move and
expression. You'll laugh as you never laughed before.
John will introduce Dutch songs, positions, jokes and
sayings, hiby-dibdy faces, and his roaring comedy song
and dance in big wooden shoes."

The program concluded with what was called "The

funny afterpiece, entitled 'Room 35, or Trouble in a Hotel.' " John had the lead role, of course, playing the part of Ferdinand Kline, "A Dutchman in search of lodgings."

John summed up those early days this way:

"The performance was crude but the people loved it. They didn't have much to entertain 'em in those days. I guess I surprised everybody on the show but I'll say one thing for Al and the rest—by God, they made me earn my keep!"

Al's balancing and juggling acts were as good as any of the day, but they belonged in a circus and not a hall show. Alf T. and Charles were musicians but John was the actor, and he had crowd appeal.

His youth, energy, and enthusiasm gave the show a lift. Soon he had a sizable following, especially among young people. The brothers realized he was by far the best thespian in the family and gave him special billing. It paid off at the ticket window.

John and his brothers did practically all the entertaining, while others helped bill and publicize the show, played in the orchestra, doubled as stage hands, sold tickets, and looked after props, scenery, and costumes. They drew increasing crowds and made some money during the Christmas holidays.

Feeling expansive, they sent for Otto, who quit his job in Racine and joined them early in January, replacing M. A. Young as advance man. Now the Ringling hand had all its fingers.

Otto's job was to arrange bookings, put up window cards, and pass out handbills advertising the performance. He was a novice but he was also thorough and thrifty, and he tackled his assignment with rugged determination. He went about with a package of yellow window cards, a supply of lithographs done up in a stout strap, and carried a small hand satchel. He also had five dollars.

Otto, a stodgy man with a black derby and a bushy mustache, was a picture of individual enterprise in action as he roamed the countryside proclaiming the virtues of the Ringling Bros. Classic and Comic Concert Co. He walked from the depot to his hotel and nearly everywhere else around town, carrying the satchel and his lithographs like a peddler. He saved all the cash he could and usually managed to pay for his meals and often his lodging and laundry with passes to the show.

The Ringlings were in full command from the very first, and they ruled the operation. They kept a tight rein and if an employee missed a parade or for any reason showed dissatisfaction, they reprimanded him sharply, or paid him off. From all hands they demanded, and got, full allegiance and productivity.

Al's age and experience made him the leader, and his brothers gave soldierly support. With all five of them working like willing horses, each pulling his load, success was assured although there were early disappointments and hardships.

Bitter cold the latter part of January dealt them staggering blows. Blizzards and snowstorms often halted trains or delayed them for hours, and blocked what few roads there were. The people stayed home.

By February, the brothers realized it was futile to try to carry on under such miserable conditions, so they paid off the help and went home to Baraboo, discouraged but still determined to make a go of it in the entertainment world.

In less than a month the weather moderated, so they tried again, having practiced and rehearsed new acts. After giving a hometown performance, they went on the road with what they advertised as "An entirely new show."

Not all the show was new, of course, and the slim crowds would have discouraged men of lesser fortitude and determination, but it only made the Ringlings work the harder. Besides, they had sent Otto ahead and must live up to his billing.

Al, Alf T., Charles, and John were the entertainers, and they followed Otto to Viroqua, Wisconsin, on the twenty-seventh of April. He had finished his job of booking and billing, so he went home. They hired Ed Kimball and the five-man troupe played a dozen more stands, until they reached Waunakee on the eleventh of May.

They arrived in Baraboo with nearly four hundred dollars, which was more than Papa Ringling had earned in three months, and they promptly invested nearly all of it in evening clothes and high top silk hats. By now they were known all over southern Wisconsin and parts of Illinois and Iowa, and figured they ought to dress up.

"I've got the offer of a job with the Parson-Roy Circus over in Illinois and I believe I'll take it," Al announced. "Not much spondulix but it's a start. You fellows pick up what you can playin' for dances and entertain' at lodge meetings and picnics. That way we can keep our hand in and our name before the public. In the fall we'll go out again."

Otto booked a few engagements for Alf T., Charles, and John but now farmers were busy in the fields and there was little time or cash to spend on sociabilities.

Some of them found occasional work and John got a

job in a hardware store in Baraboo. It was galling drudgery for the restless, ambitious boy of seventeen who had never relished manual labor and disliked waiting for or on customers in a store. The job lasted less than a month.

Even at that age, John could not abide confinement, dullness, and monotony. He was anxious to be out where things were going on, not cooped up and taking orders from someone else.

He was big for his age, with a broad, expansive chest and shoulders like a growing young bull. He was nearly six feet tall and downright handsome at a hundred and seventy pounds. He had a round, pleasant face, easy and disarming smile, and artistic hands unblemished by the scars of toil.

He had the boundless energy and absorbing curiosity of a boy blended with the independence and determination of a man. His alert, eager, and inquisitive mind soaked up information like a sponge and his sharp brown eyes missed nothing. He liked crowds and bright lights; to entertain gave him an emotional thrill and the heady feeling of fine wine. To be applauded and paid for it was the clincher.

He already had traveled far more than most men twice his age and had acquired some polish along with experience. His vocabulary had been enriched, or at least flavored with many new and expressive words picked up outside the schoolroom.

Determined not to seek sparrows in the meadow when there was big game on the mountain, John quit his job in the hardware store and went to Minneapolis, where he visited his brother Gus and spent a couple of days looking around. Then he headed east to see the Doris circus.

CHAPTER FOUR

At the Bottom of the Ladder

JOHN WAS PROUD of the circus billing matter he had brought home from the Doris show and went over it with Alf T., Charles, and Otto, describing in detail every act and attraction.

"How much does he charge?" asked Otto, his mind on finances.

"Fifty cents a head, and he's rakin' it in; probably clears a thousand dollars a day. No reason why we can't do the same thing. Ja! A circus is a moneymaking thing. It's for us."

"Maybe next year," they agreed. "We make some money, talk it over with Brother Al, and maybe start in the spring."

By now most crops had been laid by, county fairs were being held, and the Ringlings felt the time was ripe to hit the road again. Al was out with the Parson-Roy Circus, so the others put their heads together to organize an entertainment group.

Al knew many professionals and helped his brothers contact the best of those available. They hired eight in all, for the "Ringling Bros. Grand Carnival of Fun."

Their wardrobe, with the help of Mama Ringling and Louise, was part new but mostly left over from the previous season, with the same musical instruments but some new songs.

Alf T. was manager, assisted by Charles and John. Otto was advance man and it was his job to route the show, rent halls and auditoriums, put up window cards and advertise the attraction. Their first program was at Ironton in mid-August.

The troupe included Ed Kimball, Barry Stanwood, George Rowan, Jack Kernan, F. Taylor, James Blainey, Harry and Lottie Hormoyne, the first woman besides Louise ever to tour with the Ringlings.

Alf T. was twenty-two years old at the time, hardly one to inspire confidence among troupers who had spent years on the road and played in some of the outstanding theaters in the country. Charles was only nineteen and John had only recently celebrated his seventeenth birthday.

The brothers consulted on policy matters and always included Otto in their discussions before reaching a decision. But they formed a tight ring of management and some older members of the troupe resented this. They regarded the Ringlings as "greenhorns" in the entertainment world and once or twice referred to them as "novices," which they were.

There was loud and long grumbling about distances between one-night stands, miserable traveling accommodations, and the fact that nearly all performances were given in poorly-lighted and badly heated halls and vacant storerooms, with no dressing rooms on the premises.

They also were sharply critical of Otto's bookings, but mostly they disliked the way the show was managed and the rigid Ringling control.

They looked upon Alf T. as an artist and dreamer rather than a practical showman; Charles, a musician but no performer; and John, just a brash young man. The fact that he had three turns on the program did not set well with some older, more experienced performers.

Discord had been building up for days and the blow-up came at Campbell, Minnesota, where the crowd was small. All but two refused to parade in the cold and mud, so only the band appeared on the street before the show.

The brothers decided they had reached the end of their patience and must take drastic action. The next day was payday, but there was enough on hand to pay off everybody, so they decided not to wait but to close the show on Thursday.

"It's the only thing to do," Alf T. said. "Pay 'em all off and start with a clean slate. That way we'll be rid of the troublemakers."

The troupers suspected nothing and reasoned the Ringlings were paying off early that week to appease them. The brothers took into their confidence the proprietor of the hotel where they were staying, and left with him enough cash to pay for the troupers' breakfasts.

They tiptoed out of the hotel at three o'clock in the morning, telegraphed Otto to meet them in Sedan on Friday, and swore the station agent to secrecy as to their destination.

"The rascals," Otto commented when they told him all their troubles. "You should have done it sooner. Now we can cut expenses to the bone and make some money. You don't need me to route the show, so, if

you want, I'll go home and try to find work, but I'd
rather stay."

"You stay and beat the drum," they said.

The four brothers moved on to Starbuck, where they
passed out hastily-printed handbills advertising a performance that night—admission twenty-five cents; ten
cents for the children.

That afternoon they put on a little entertainment in
the town square for a cluster of farmers and dairymen
who had come in to do their weekly shopping and talk
crops and politics.

Alf T. played the cornet, John alto and Charles baritone. Otto made his first appearance as a performer,
beating the drum. Charles played a couple of violin
solos and John told some jokes.

They reminded their listeners there would be a two-
hour show that night, "entirely new from start to
finish."

Of course they kept Al informed by telegram and
letter. He ended the season with Parson-Roy in mid-
November and came on to join them. Now the hand
had all its five fingers. From now on the brothers, all
robust and rugged, would work as a team, striving for
the benefit of the Ringlings.

They toured all the small towns in Minnesota and
parts of Iowa, Nebraska, and Wisconsin, playing practically all one-night stands and no nights off. On such
holidays as Thanksgiving, Christmas, and New Year's,
they gave two or even three performances.

Their stands included every community boasting a
school auditorium or a lodge hall and, when such facilities were not available, they put on performances in
vacant stores, with borrowed chairs or seats made of

empty boxes and rough planks spread across carpenters' saw horses. Once they even took over a hotel dining room, after the dinner dishes were cleared away.

They caught catnaps in sooty, drafty depots while waiting for trains, or slept in day coaches between towns. Often they exchanged admission tickets for meals, hotel rooms, or rides to the next town, and they did not leave the road until they reached Poynette, Wisconsin, on April 11, 1884.

They went home to Baraboo with more hard cash than they'd ever had before, and they now felt proud, expansive, and experienced.

John had never let them forget the money to be made in a circus and he insisted they have one of their own. His brothers admired his spunk and before the tour ended they commenced to share his enthusiasm for an outdoor entertainment venture.

Al was the last to give his approval. He knew it would take a lot of cash to buy tents and rolling stock, animals and equipment to outfit even a small circus, but he realized it was a popular form of entertainment and he felt the days of the hall show were numbered.

"You've got to be smart to run an outdoor entertainment venture—and lucky," Al said. "It takes a lot of cash to put a show on the road, and keep it there. You're always gambling on the weather and business conditions. All you've got to do is look at the circuses that don't make it from one year to the next. It's not all easy money, I can tell you."

"Sure, it's a gamble," John admitted, "but so's everything else. You'll never get ahead if you don't take a chance. Help yourself or you'll never get helped. We're smart, and we can do it."

They discussed several possibilities and finally Al brought up the name of Yankee Robinson, whom he'd met once or twice but had never worked for, as some historians claim.

Al suggested they go into partnership with the old fellow, who had been a trouper for nearly half a century, owned and lost two circuses, and now was near the end of the line. He was short of wind and cash but a real trouper who was widely known and highly respected.

And so Yankee Robinson came to the Ringlings.

He still had a supply of business cards—small, pink pasteboard with rounded corners and a thumbnail-size picture in the center. Above the tiny photograph of the bewhiskered old showman was the name, "Fayette Lodawick Robinson," and the title, "Big Show Manager, &C." Across the bottom, in square, black letters, was the name, "Yankee Robinson."

He handed one of the cards to each of the brothers as they escorted him into the Ringling parlor.

CHAPTER FIVE

The Wagons Roll

THE RINGLING BROTHERS showed unusual resourcefulness in organizing their first circus. Through Yankee Robinson's connections and with his advice they were able to get the show ready for the road with a minimum of time and expense.

Yankee contacted some performer friends and helped the Ringlings fit their acts into a program that ran an hour and a half. He helped Al lay out a route that would start at Baraboo and take them into Iowa, a section Yankee knew as well as he knew the back of his hand.

The Ringlings worked day and night, assembling what circus properties they could; buying, building and renting tents, seats, sidewalls and wagons; polishing up their own acts and signing others.

They cut a tree and peeled it to make a center pole. They bought a spring wagon from their Uncle Henry Moeller and painted it a fiery red, lettering their name on the sides and calling it their advance wagon.

Lou Ringling designed costumes for the band and leading performers. She took over the job of wardrobe mistress and found time to practice bareback riding. Al and Alf T. wrote advertising copy and, upon Yankee's recommendation, had a supply of posters printed

in bright red and blue, with space at the bottom for
the name of the town and the date the circus would
appear, to be filled in with marking crayon—another
job for Lou.

The billing matter read: "Yankee Robinson and Ringling Bros. Great Double Shows, Circus and Caravan."

Yankee Robinson, born in Avon, Livingston County,
New York, in 1818, knew the value of publicity, and
sought it. He had with him a clipping from a newspaper which he took to the editor of the Baraboo *Re-
public*. It appeared in full in that paper on May 14,
1884, as an interview with the old trouper, as follows:

"I first started with a little show of paintings representing 'The Raising of Lazarus,' with a young printer
who played the violin. We traveled from New York
State to St. Louis in a one-horse buggy and were from
August to December making the trip.

"At that time an ex-Mormon preacher named Adams
was running a little theatre in St. Louis at the corner of
Third and Pine streets, which building is still standing.
I made his acquaintance and after the holidays he wanted
to produce Richard III and was compelled to resort to
amateur volunteers, and accepted the part of Radcliffe.

"Nobody could have made a worse failure than I did,
and it was my first and last experience in tragedy. It
was terrible, I completely paralyzed them. Kate Mea-
dows, now on the stage as Mrs. Harry Ryner, is the only
one of the players now alive. She was a little bit of a
girl at that time.

"The next thing I did in the way of show business
was to get up a nigger band or variety show, called the
'Olympic Serenaders,' which I believe was the first ven-

ture of the kind ever made. This was in the winter of 1845-46. We played in St. Louis a week, then started off on a trip with a two-horse wagon and made quite a success.

"I appeared as 'Lucy Long' in the nigger band and made as decided a hit in that character as I had previously made a failure in Radcliffe. This experience showed that my talent ran in my heels and not in my head.

"In the summer of 1846, I met June & Turner's Circus at Galena, Ill., and traveled with them for two years. Aaron Turner is the man with whom Barnum traveled for a while. At the end of two seasons I organized a little family-room show, as in those days there were no halls.

"In 1848 my wife and I joined Lennox's Floating Show at Evansville, where we made our first public appearance together. The city in those days was a little, insignificant-looking hamlet, squatted down on the banks of the river. We played the drama of the 'Idiot Witness,' and a pantomime.

"I was the clown in the pantomime. This was, perhaps, the first show that was ever given in Evansville. We went down the river and at almost every place we stopped, the throttle valve was taken out and the boat tied up for debt, but we managed to fix it up every time and finally got to Memphis, and 'busted.' At Cairo there wasn't anybody left on shore when we gave an exhibition; every man, woman and child came on board to see it.

"The boat was tied up at Memphis but we managed to steal the scenery and got hold of a little unoccupied church building—now known as the Zoo-Zoo Theater,

in Memphis—and fixed it up as a theater and played
stars there all winter.

"The elder Booth, Cornelius Logan, his daughter,
Eliza; Plunkett and Mulholland, the Irish comedians;
Rachel Cantor and other actors and actresses subsequent-
ly known to fame, played there during that season.

"Old Dan Bennett, the author of 'Dixie,' was the
leader of the orchestra. My next move was in the
spring, when I came back up the river to New Albany
and started out again until I had saved up money enough
to build a canvass, which I did in 1857, and gave my
first tent show that year in Quincy, Ill. I continued to
enlarge my canvass and increase my attractions each
year until I got to be the 'boss.'

"I showed in Evansville on the river bluff with my
circus in 1857. We showed there two days and had a
big crowd at every performance. The place had grown
to be considerable of a city at that time. We picked up
a young man here whose professional name is Don San-
tiago DeGibbonois, who afterwards became the most
celebrated contortionist in the ring.

"When in Charleston, in 1850, the John Brown excitement made things so hot that I had to run away
and leave a show outfit which cost me $40,000. It was,
in fact, the finest that had ever been seen up to that
time. That broke me all up and I had to fall back on
the drama again.

"I had, every winter, however, kept up my connection with the stage, while the circus was in winter quarters. I got on top again at last and made my next visit
to Evansville in 1875, with a hippodrome. This was
the second hippodrome ever organized in the country.

"That season my partner died, and I closed out the

concern, and have since been principally on the stage, starring in my own pieces. I am now playing principally the dramas, 'The Days of '76,' in which I take the parts of Darious Dalton, and the 'F.F.V.s' in which I take the part of Uncle Asa Bassett."

The editor added that: "Mr. Robinson has produced his comedy drama 'Days of '76,' alluded to above, over 5,000 times and has played in all principal cities of the United States."

Monday, the nineteenth of May, 1884, was a gala day in the little town of Baraboo. Buds were bursting, birds were singing, flowers blooming; the sky was clear and bright; the air clean, crisp, and fresh—an ideal day for the circus.

Around the long dining table at the Warren House down the street, five young couples talked about the circus the Ringlings were about to launch and agreed to attend the first performance in a body. Several others joined them on the walk from the boardinghouse to the north end of the jail yard, where the tents had been erected.

Yankee Robinson, greeting patrons and friends at the entrance, was happy to be back in business and when the party of eighteen young people, most of them women, arrived he made note of it.

"What is this, a female seminary turned out for the circus?" he boomed, then motioned to an usher and said, "Show them to our best reserved seats."

This display of magnanimity was good for the show and although reserved seats were only boards set close to the ground and covered with rag carpeting, the girls giggled with delight at such attention while the band played and the tent filled rapidly.

Admission was only a quarter and the show was worth it. John had argued for fifty cents, contending that people would expect that much entertainment from any circus, but Yankee Robinson advised against it until they could establish a reputation, and the brothers agreed.

Doubtless the old circus man realized their little outfit could not match other circuses in size and performance, no matter how ambitious, for there were a number of old and creditable shows in the field, some in the Midwest at that very moment.

The sideshow, in a tent thirty by forty-five feet, was run by a combination barker and magician and it boasted such "strange people" or freaks, as a woman with frizzled hair billed as the "Circassiun Princess."

There also were a pet pig, some snakes, and a few other attractions to lure the curious for a dime.

In addition to the five Ringling brothers—Al, Alf T., Otto, Charles, and John—there were seventeen others in personnel, not counting Yankee Robinson. These included Al's wife, who was snake handler, bareback rider, and wardrobe mistress.

Every person on the show had multiple duties, hurrying through one task so he could get at another, doubling as musician, clown, rider, usher, ticket seller, and workingman.

The main tent, forty-five by ninety feet, was filled with nearly six hundred patrons for the first show. So unexpectedly large was the turnout that the brothers had to go up and down Third Avenue, borrowing chairs

from the undertaker and from neighbors to accommodate late arrivals.

At last the band came marching in from the backyard, walking two abreast and spread out to make an
impression, playing loud enough to be heard all over
town. It was followed by all the others in personnel in a
quick walk-around.

Yankee Robinson strutted to the center of the ring,
doffed his Lincolnesque hat, bowed low to the audience,
and made a little speech. He declared that he had traveled in every state of the Union and had been associated
with or competed against every circus man of prominence in America, concluding with a tribute to the
Ringlings as "rising young showmen."

Al did his juggling and plate-spinning act, then re-
lieved Alf T. as bandleader. John, in clown costume,
took over for a comedy routine, followed by acrobatic
riding, a trained dog act, and more clowning. A high
wire act climaxed the program.

The first performance over, they tidied up the lot,
restocked the concession wagon, and smoothed out rough
spots on the program, aiming for a tighter, livelier show.

They gave two performances in Baraboo and after
the night show they struck tents and packed everything
into the two property wagons they owned and the five
others they'd rented, piling them high with canvas,
poles, stakes, seats, props, and costumes.

They collected all the refuse—discarded wrappings,
torn paper, and other "lot litter"—into a neat pile and
burned it. Yankee Robinson took out his gold watch,
snapped open the face and bent to the firelight, squint-
ing to see the time. It was a quarter to twelve.

Al boosted his wife onto the seat of the lead wagon

and walked back to check on the others. Otto and John got into the second wagon and Alf T. and Charles into a third.

Al saw that everything had been loaded, fires out and flares put away, then went back to the front wagon, climbed up beside Louise and called out, "All right; let's go!"

Drivers clucked to their horses and the sturdy animals swung into action. Wagons creaked and whined under their burdens, gaining momentum as hooves began to clop in unison and wheels started turning. The little caravan headed south into the night. Sauk City, fifteen miles away, was its destination.

CHAPTER SIX

Circus and Carnival

THEY ROLLED into town shortly after sunup and by midmorning had tents up and seats installed, then fanned out over the community to pass out handbills and talk up the show.

From Sauk City they went to Black Earth, Spring Green, and other communities, playing a chain of small towns and villages in southern Wisconsin before turning west into Iowa. Crowds were only fair but the Ringlings pumped encouragement into the others and kept the enterprise moving.

This was not the rosy circus business John had visualized, and the brothers soon realized that it cost considerable to keep a company of twenty-three persons, and a few animals, on the road. However, as treasurer, Otto watched every penny and managed to put aside some cash at practically every stop they made.

Each stand over, strong willing hands loaded canvas and equipment onto wagons, hitched up freshly-fed horses and drove the rest of the night over sticky black prairie roads to reach the next town in time to set up and, usually, hold a street parade.

Often that had to be canceled on account of late arrival, bad weather, or other drawbacks, but the show went on as advertised, "Two performances daily, rain or shine. Four great clowns—something new under the sun."

The clowns were the brothers Ringling—juggling, balancing, performing on the bars and high wire; clowning, playing in the band and running the show, virtually carrying the entire enterprise on their broad and willing shoulders.

They slept when and where they could but never all at once, usually dozing while the wagons jostled over stony or rutty winding roads. They ate at odd hours— upon arrival, between performances or after the show, but often they were pressed for time and took quick snacks, driving themselves and everyone in personnel to the limit of endurance.

In those days the brothers were young, strong, and muley in their determination to gain a foothold in the entertainment field. They had an indivisible zealotry and Teutonic tenaciousness seldom found among members of one family. Thus they compensated for lack of experience and financial support.

In that first season they advertised in newspapers, with window cards and by word of mouth in every village and town they could reach, proclaiming their circus "A combination of resources unparalleled in the history of tented expositions."

Actually, it was a puny little outfit that could not compare with such enterprises at Adam Forepaugh, John B. Doris, W. W. Cole, John Robinson, Sells Bros., Buffalo Bill's Wild West Show, Anglo-American, Gus Bailey and others, to say nothing of a recent consolidation called P. T. Barnum's Greatest Show on Earth, Howes' Great London Circus and Sanger's Royal British Menagerie, owned by P. T. Barnum, James A. Bailey, and James L. Hutchinson.

The Ringlings owned but three horses and two wagons, hiring farm boys with teams to help move the show and using them as workingmen on the lot. This was a satisfactory arrangement to all concerned, since many young men were anxious to "see the world" and were happy to be on the road with the Ringlings.

Often they could spend only a few days away from their chores but the brothers found replacements. They preferred farm boys because they not only were strong and husky but could provide a team and wagon, which was even more important.

The brothers made up for their inexperience and lack of cash by initiative and enthusiasm, and they never passed up a town, no matter how small, if it offered a chance to pick up a few dollars.

Many a time, that season and later, they played settlements with little more population than they had in personnel, but people came from miles around, and the Ringlings made new friends and built a solid reputation.

Yankee Robinson stood by with timely suggestions and sound advice but he could do little actual work on account of his age and physical condition. He gave the show prestige, however, and he appeared at every performance as long as he was able.

His health failed rapidly as the summer wore on, and the Ringlings realized the gallant old showman was near the end of the trail. Al Ringling persuaded him to ride the train rather than endure the discomfort of a circus wagon for the forty miles to Lake City, then went with him to the railroad station at Bayard, Iowa, on August 27, and saw him aboard a passenger coach.

Yankee Robinson became so ill he had to be removed from the train at Jefferson, twenty miles from Bayard, and was put to bed in Charlie Dean's hotel.

For some reason the old showman concealed his identity but word went around town that a brother Mason was ill and needed help. Members of Morning Star Lodge No. 159, A. F. and A. M., went to see him and tended to his needs until he died a week later. Then they arranged to bury him in their cemetery on a hill near town.

It was pouring rain at the time for the services but thirty lodge brothers walked the three miles behind Jim May's team and wagon that bore the casket to the grave. After services, the lodge arranged to pay burial expenses, and did. Al Ringling traced Yankee to Jefferson and went there to see him, but arrived the day after the funeral.

Over the grave in the center of Jefferson Cemetery stands a tall, brown marble monument erected by the Ringlings and Sells Bros. in 1890. It bears this inscription:

"Fayette L. Robinson, born May 2, 1818; died Sept. 4, 1884. Yankee Robinson."

The passing of the old entertainer and circus man was genuinely mourned, but it did not seriously affect the Ringling enterprise, which from the beginning had been the brothers' undertaking and was built by their energies and talents. Yankee Robinson had influenced their decision to enter the circus business that spring and had helped them get started, but now they were on their way.

They played six days a week without an interruption, and went home in late September with more cash than they had anticipated, and with valuable experience from that first season as performers and circus operators.

Cramming their tents, wagons, and props into a barn, they rehearsed some plays and went on the road again as "Ringling Bros. Carnival of Fun." Otto was advance agent and the other four formed the backbone of the troupe.

Rain and snow plagued them and often kept them indoors for days but they stuck with it until after Christmas and made some money, which Otto hoarded.

Al and Otto went home to work on circus equipment, for already they were planning another season under canvas. The others hired Rich Dialo and Fred C. Hall, the latter a contortionist. They saved all they could and sent it home to be invested in new canvas and rolling stock.

When they ended the tour in May, the circus was almost ready for the road. Through the efforts of Al, Otto, and their uncle Henry Moeller, new canvas had been bought, including an eighty-foot round top and a sideshow tent thirty by fifty feet. More wagons had been built and now they owned a dozen, not including sideshow or privilege wagons.

They put John's name first, and advertised as "John, Charles, Alf T., Otto and Al Ringling, proprietors and managers." From the beginning the show was a partnership, share and share alike. There was no company or corporation but a simple combination of initiative and determination. They wanted to have the biggest and best circus in the land.

That spring they offered brother Gus a chance to go

with them but he was not a performer and, being entirely without foresight or imagination, turned it down. Henry was still at home, a growing boy.

Besides the five brothers, they had only a dozen others in personnel, including Louise, when they took the road in 1885. They dropped Yankee Robinson's name from the title and billed as "Ringling Bros. Great Double Shows, Circus, Caravan and Trained Animal Exposition."

On posters and broadsides they proclaimed it "A most gigantic and tremendous aggregation of acrobatic equestrians, performing feats of breathless wonder."

Henry Moeller built for them an ornate, hand-carved body on the frame of a sturdy wagon and they painted the sides bright red and gold, the wheels a sunburst. Otto complained about the cost, but the others argued it would be worth far more than it cost, and would pay for itself in a single season in advertising and prestige.

From one of the five heads came an idea that proved to be a stroke of genius, an innovation that gave them a tremendous boost and stunned the opposition.

They had cards printed which they passed out sparingly and judiciously among acquaintances in the traveling gentry known as drummers. A card would admit the holder to any performance, without charge.

Thus every traveling man who owned a card became a booster for the Ringlings, spreading word that the circus was coming and often arranging his route to attend the performance, with a party of guests.

This created lasting good will among the men whose jobs kept them on the road and who were in a favorable position to give the Ringlings word-of-mouth advertising and praise neither they nor their rivals could buy at any price.

It was one of the best ideas the Ringlings ever hatched, but they were always thinking and scheming, often matching good business judgment with human fancies and foibles.

John fathered a plan, in the midst of the 1885 season, that was to turn into one of the most profitable of them all, not alone for his brothers and the circus but for him personally.

It grew out of his realization that many cities and towns did not roll out the welcome mat for circuses. Officials, knowing full well the feeling of merchants and certain religious groups, sometimes looked with disfavor on traveling amusement enterprises.

"I ought to go ahead, scoutin' for the best stands," John told his brothers. "It can mean real cash for us. We've got to pass up these dead towns. A good front man ought to keep his eyes open and ears tuned so he'd know where to put the show to make money; learn where there's a celebration we might tie in with, or if we ought to pass up the town entirely.

"I could work on the town officials, too, and maybe do something about these high licenses they're votin' against us. We've got to fight 'em."

The brothers gave it thought. They realized John was an extrovert; that he knew when to act the smart buffoon, or the simpleton. He continued to propound his theory while they listened.

"I'm the youngest one and they'll have a softer feelin' for me. It'll be a lot easier to get the show into a town after I've been there and done some sweetenin' than to pull in and set up cold, like we've been doin'.

"They'll have some sympathy for a young fellow try-in' to match these big outfits. They can be lenient as the devil collectin' these taxes and license fees, if we do a little talkin' and sweetenin' up.

"I can tell 'em how little the show is; how we're just a bunch of kids, and get licenses and lots cheaper. Then we can advertise the show big as we please. They'll understand. We've got to work on them from all angles, don't you see?"

"He's absolutely right," Otto agreed. "I can see where we need a good front man, not to lay out routes particularly, but fix it so we can get into a town without havin' to lay out so much cash. They keep slappin' heavy taxes on us. Johnny ought to get us some concessions along that line, and save us money."

"If we don't do something, they'll put us out of business," John continued. "Some places want as much as a hundred dollars just to come in. We've got to put up a scrap, and I know how to do it. Old Yankee is dead now and we can't keep goin' on his reputation and connections. We've got to make some of our own."

He spread a map of Iowa across the lid of a trunk and used his forefinger to point out the route he proposed to take. The brothers looked and listened.

"I'll start at Linville," he said. "We never played it as a circus, so we'll need to get fixed up there. We've got to get our permits cheap as possible, and we'll need supplies. We have to patronize local merchants, so we'll sell 'em on the idea we're bringing people to town, and spendin' money with them even before the circus gets in.

"I can work Linville while you're playin' Monroe. By the time you get in Sunday, I'll have it all set up.

We're billed there, but we'll need supplies on the lot, and make some arrangements. I can have everything done before you get in."

The brothers debated it briefly, then agreed it could benefit the organization in more ways than one. With their blessing, John rode off into the Iowa night. The date was July 25, 1885, and it marked a significant milestone in his career. From then on, he was out on his own, operating for the benefit of the circus and himself.

CHAPTER SEVEN

The Ringling Circus Grows Up

THE RINGLING CIRCUS played six days a week for twenty weeks without a break or a single missed performance in that 1885 season—a different stand every day for one hundred and twenty days.

The tour ended at Randolph, Wisconsin, on October 3 and as soon as the tents and animals were put away in the barns at Baraboo, the brothers hired Tom Nichols and Vic Richardson and went out again as the "Ringling Bros. Carnival of Fun."

They wanted not only to make money but to keep their name before the public. All during the tour they talked up the circus, reminding everyone to watch for it in the spring, "bigger and better than ever."

They had plenty of time to talk and plan during one of the most severe winters that section ever had. They were snowed in for eight days at Odell, Nebraska; snow and rain stopped them again at Aurelia, Iowa, and at Alta it was so cold they not only missed the performance but couldn't get out of town.

At Fort Dodge they gave up and went to Janesville, Wisconsin, where they bought two cages, a wagon and a wardrobe. They added a thirty-foot middle piece to the ninety-five-foot round top and now could count eighteen wagons in their caravan.

While the brothers were shopping in Janesville, John went to Milwaukee where he bought the first trick animal act they ever exhibited—a donkey named January and a Shetland pony called Minnie.

That spring, when the circus went out, it listed thirty-four in personnel, not including Henry Ringling, who joined in September as an employee on salary. He was eighteen years old.

The season was a short and not very profitable one. The tour covered only Wisconsin, Iowa, and Minnesota. Bad weather prevailed at many stands and when glanders hit the stock, killing fourteen head, the brothers cut short the tour and went home.

They returned to the road as the Ringling Bros. Carnival of Fun and Specialty Co., toured until March and went home to plan another circus season, coming out as "Ringling Bros. United Monster Shows, Great Double Circus, Royal European Menagerie, Museum, Caravan and Congress of Trained Animals."

By the sound of it, their show should have been the biggest thing on wheels and it actually was the largest the Ringlings had ever put on the road. It included two advance wagons, one elk, a camel, one bear, two lions, a kangaroo, hyena, deer, monkeys, four Shetland ponies and sixty horses.

Admission was only a quarter, as it had always been, although John argued for fifty cents. He contended the show was worth it and the people would pay, but the brothers wouldn't hear of it.

John, who spent the season ahead as usual, met the show for its last couple of stands and announced he had arranged to get it home without making the long overland journey. It would go by boat.

Accordingly, they drove to the Mississippi, loaded the show aboard the steamboat *Libby Condor* and a barge, and sailed for East Dubuque. From there they drove overland to Baraboo, arriving home ten days after the final performance.

The trip had taken longer, cost more, and was more disagreeable than even John anticipated. The brothers gave him a tongue-lashing for making such a boner and reminded him that if they'd stayed on land and played their way home, they'd at least have made expenses.

That winter the brothers put together not one troupe but two for their indoor tour. One included Alf T., Charles, John, and Henry, along with six others. Al organized his own unit with Louise's help, hired six performers and went out as "Ringling Bros. Carnival of Fun, Company No. 2."

Al's was a specialty company featuring a new play he had written called "The Dude," and a Negro comedian.

After Christmas John wanted to end the tour and go home, or merge with Al's company and travel as one, but the others would not approve. Through his friend, the sheriff, at Frankfort, Illinois, John heard of a stranded riverboat show and went there to look over the property. About all he could see was a boat and two elephants.

"I got no use for a boat," John assured the sheriff, who was offering the property for sale, but he did buy, for a thousand dollars, the elephants named Babylon and Queen—the first elephants the Ringlings ever owned.

That afternoon he met his brothers at Pleasant Hill and told them they were in luck, that he'd been able to get two elephants for the price of one because the owner was broke and had to raise cash.

"You're a trader, all right," Alf T. agreed, "but what're we going to do with two elephants, and it January? Couldn't you wait 'til we finished the season?"

"No," John shot back. "I'm going to take 'em home. We've got to have elephants to make our circus respectable. Why, they'll mean an extra fifty dollars a day in the till. You wait and see. They can help move the show and be an added attraction, too. They'll put us in the big time."

"You not going to finish the tour with us?" Charles asked.

"No; I'm a circus man. Do as you like, but I'm through troupin' with concerts and hall shows. Too much work for what you get out of it. I'm goin' home and help Otto get ready for the season."

Bullheaded John Ringling was showing rare ability and leadership for a youngster not yet twenty-one, but the brothers couldn't argue with him. Though he seldom raised his voice, if he wanted a thing badly enough, he would cajole and plead until he had his way.

Alf T., Charles, and Henry played out their bookings, which kept them on the road for a week, then went home to join Otto, John, and the elephants. Al and Louise followed them into Baraboo.

Thus ended the Ringling Bros. Carnival of Fun, the undertaking that had kept them busy for five winters and led the way to their circus.

John's idea of going ahead to handle routes and transportation affairs worked well from the beginning. He could choose the best routes and get the show into the most profitable territory with a minimum of expense.

Being the youngest of the brothers had its advantages, too, and John always had his wits working. Once he met a crusty old fellow who owned a choice block right downtown which was an ideal location for the circus. He had visions of big rental money but John was cagey.

He told the old man they had nothing but a little mud outfit run by three or four kids trying to get started, a "little bitty thing" that probably wouldn't take in more than ten or twenty dollars, and couldn't afford to pay rent on a lot.

The owner agreed to let the Ringling "boys" use his property, but when he saw the size of their circus, he was furious.

He claimed he had been swindled, but there was nothing he could do about it for young John, not yet of age, had drawn up the agreement which both signed, and now he was miles away, in the next county.

When they opened the next season at Baraboo on May 6, billed as "Ringling Bros. Stupendous Consolidation of Seven Monster Shows," nobody knew what shows they were but the brothers had a big main tent, menagerie, sideshow, two horse tents and a dressing tent—largest spread of canvas they had up to that time.

On the lot were six cages of wild animals, a tableaux wagon, ticket wagon, band wagon, three lions, two camels, and the elephants, Babylon and Queen. There were eighty head of horses and ponies, many only recently off the farms or out of livery stables in the area, but all well fed, a fetish with the Ringlings.

They started with admission up to fifty cents for the first time, but snow halted the tour a week after it began. They headed south into Iowa, where they ran into heavy rains, and cut the price of admission to a quarter. John dropped in for a visit, heard about the price reduction, and raised a ruckus.

"My God," he whined, "it's costin' us like hell to run the show; licenses and contracts higher than ever, and you cut the price in half? We've got a tremendous nut [overhead]. If you don't make money at fifty cents, how can you make it chargin' a quarter? All you're doin' is cheapenin' the show."

The price went back up to fifty cents and John was satisfied. He left the show just in time to avoid a stretch of trouble.

Rain and cold harassed them and for weeks they didn't see the sun. Advance wagons bogged down and some had to be abandoned when billers couldn't hire farm teams, now busy with spring plowing. Often they could bill only by rail, missing many small towns and playing to slim crowds when they played at all.

On June 23 at Webster City, Iowa, James Richardson was shot and killed by a fellow employee, Thomas Baskett, who was sentenced to fifteen years in prison. The Ringlings knew that such things were normal in the course of human emotions but they also realized they must do all they could to counteract unfavorable publicity and improve the public image.

They were well aware that some circuses and other traveling amusement enterprises had mottled reputations—infested with pickpockets who worked on a commission; ticket sellers and others who shortchanged patrons or even passed counterfeit money; "Monday men" who stole clothes off lines or burglarized homes while occupants stood out front watching the parade, or attended the performance.

"Fixers" bribed officials to wink at petty crimes. They settled claims, when they must, in the quickest and easiest way possible, with glib promises. Often a complaining patron would be shuttled from one man to another until his patience wore out, or be told that "the man who handles that is not here, but he will be here tonight."

With typical boldness and initiative, the Ringlings stressed in all their publicity and advertising, "A strictly clean, highly moral performance," and even banned profanity on the lot. They drew up a set of fifty-one rules of conduct governing behavior of employees, not only on the lot but in the cars, in the street parade and in all public places "in conducting our institution in a business-like, high-standard manner."

Special rules were made "to protect" the Ringling girls and all females on the circus were cautioned as to proper dress and conduct at all times. Girls were told not to dress in a flashy, loud style but to be neat and modest in appearance; to register in the sleeping car not later than eleven o'clock, and not to leave the car after registering.

They must not stop at hotels at any time; not visit with relatives in cities where the show appeared without special permission from the ballet master, and never talk or visit with male members in personnel, except the management.

"The excuse of accidental meetings will not be accepted," the Ringlings said. "Men in personnel are forbidden to visit with the ballet girls and the excuse of accidental meetings, even on Sundays, in parks, theaters and restaurants, will not be accepted."

The Ringlings refused to show on Sunday and publicized their intention to "remember the Sabbath day to keep it holy." Soon the opposition began calling them "The Sunday School Boys."

The tag stuck, and brought favorable reaction. The brothers were proud to be known as righteous young men and made much of their intentions to give the people clean, wholesome entertainment.

They ordered ticket sellers and ushers to don smart blue and gold uniforms, stand erect and walk with military bearing, to bow politely to customers and say, "yes, sir," and "this way, sir."

The Ringling show became known throughout the Midwest as the most courteous and moral on the road. The public had long felt that it would not be amiss to clean up most of the traveling amusement enterprises and now they were being constantly reminded that the Ringlings were showing the way. The people liked "The Sunday School Boys."

John, who kept thinking and talking of combining and consolidating, felt the need of another established name to go with their own and mentioned several possibilities to his brothers. He wanted to tie in with whatever other circuses he could get for a reasonable price, not only to eliminate as much competition as possible but to expand and gain prestige.

He kept in touch with other showmen and abreast of what was going on in the amusement world. He heard that the Van Amburgh show was not going on the road and the title might be for sale. He contacted Hyatt Frost, the proprietor, who was broke, saw no chance of taking the show out, and let John have the title at a nominal figure.

It was the Ringlings' first consolidation since they

started out with Yankee Robinson, and they went on the road in 1888 as "Ringling Bros. and Van Amburgh's United Monster Circus, Museum, Menagerie, Roman Hippodrome and Universal World's Exposition."

They were not unmindful of the approaching World's Fair in Chicago, plans for which were already in the making. Their growth had been remarkable and they now had a first-rate circus, with a large collection of animals in a big menagerie tent and a sideshow equal to any on the road.

They still traveled by horse and wagon and their itinerary was limited to Wisconsin and the states adjacent. Often their wagons bogged down to the axles in the black prairie mud and the elephants had to free them.

The next year they dropped the Van Amburgh title but still traveled by horse and wagon. They played only two states that season, but they made a hundred and forty-one stands in Wisconsin and Illinois between the first day of May and the middle of October, avoiding Milwaukee, Madison, Chicago, and Springfield but showing in every other community of any consequence in the two states.

They made more money than they'd ever made before and were able to come out with a railroad show in the spring of 1890. They had two advance cars and sixteen for the circus. These included one performers' sleeper, one workingmen's sleeper, one elephant car, five stock cars and eight flatcars piled high with canvas, stakes, and wagons.

The show was billed as "Ringling Bros. United Monster Railroad Shows, Great Triple Circus, Museum, Menagerie, Roman Hippodrome and Universal World's Exposition."

Brother Gus had come on from Minneapolis to go aboard one of the advance cars while John was still out ahead, buttering up town officials.

They played parts of Wisconsin, Illinois, Iowa, Nebraska, and Minnesota, then went into Ohio, Pennsylvania, Maryland, and Virginia.

It marked their first invasion of the East and it proved to them that there were far more cash customers in that thickly-populated area than in the West. Rails, too, enabled them to travel many times farther than they ever had before.

It was not all wiener schnitzel, nor even pigs knuckles and sauerkraut for them. There was opposition from the Wallace show and the Andress & Sells Circus but the Ringlings met it and made some money.

By now they were experienced circusmen, big and resourceful, and their show had attained a status of respectability equal to any on the road.

The five brothers cultivated awning-type mustaches that blended perfectly with their full, round faces; they had large, snappy brown eyes and glowing complexions. The mustaches were black, well-trimmed to match their always well-barbered and combed black hair, so that they looked startlingly alike.

The brothers, with their high, well-shaped foreheads and good grooming, were handsome men and their pictures slanting across billboards, on the sides of barns and in show windows throughout America attracted attention and comment.

The pictures arranged in a row became their trademark. Through this and their circus the Ringlings soon became the most famous five brothers in the country.

Many who grew up with the Ringlings knew them as energetic and completely charming men who worked like mules to attain their goal. The mustaches set them apart as men of distinction and their faces soon became familiar to millions.

Historians have said they often divided a season's profits by stuffing potato sacks with bills of equal denomination. It could have been, in those halcyon days before Uncle Sam dreamed up income taxes and fell into the habit of handing out billions of dollars in subsidies and foreign aid.

Riding the first wave of prosperity they had known, the brothers bought land for winter quarters and made plans to enlarge their circus. They purchased railroad cars, wagons, canvas, and stock; added a hippodrome and hired a brass band and a drum and bugle corps.

Up to now they had used performers in the band, even helping out personally, but now they were spreading out and, having appetites and appreciation for good music, decided to have plenty of it.

In their barns that spring Charles reported, in a privately-printed little volume, they counted 130 head of horses and ponies, 18 cages of wild animals, and an assortment of elephants, camels, zebras, and such little-known critters as a zeba, bovalapus, and a yak.

Surrounded by all the trappings and equipment to outfit a circus as mammoth as any they had seen or heard of, and with all the personnel and rolling stock to move it, they came up with another idea.

John had already spoken to an outstanding press agent before he mentioned the subject to his brothers, and he sold them on the wisdom of a first-rate press department.

"A smart press agent can do a hell of a lot for us," he said with enthusiasm. "He'll take all this advertising and program mess off our hands and leave us more time to run the show. We've got to keep remindin' the people that the Ringling show is the biggest and best on the road."

"Who'd you have in mind?" Otto asked.

"Willard Coxey. He's the best in the business and we can get him."

They agreed and John wasted no time putting Coxey to work. It proved especially beneficial because Coxey was a well-known press agent, recognized the Ringlings as capable showmen, and put many of his ideas into the program.

For the first time the Ringlings presented a historic event in dramatic splendor, which Coxey suggested be called "Caesar's Triumphal Entry into Rome."

"Tremendous idea," John agreed enthusiastically. "Announce it in all the papers as our crowning achievement and make it an eye-poppin' exhibition of pomp and pageantry. It'll top anything ever seen under canvas."

Alf T. promised to write special music for it and the brothers gave the display their support, spending thousands on costumes, props, and scenery; featuring it in advertising and working everybody in personnel; using every available wagon, chariot, cage, and animal in the glittering spectacle.

At the same time they did not neglect their acts and presented a balanced program that pleased the public.

CHAPTER EIGHT

Big Top Troubles and Triumphs

THEY STARTED the 1891 tour in Baraboo on May 2, billed as "Ringling Bros. World's Greatest Railroad Shows, Real Roman Hippodrome, Three Ring Circus and Elevated Stages; Millionaire Menagerie, Museum and Aquarium; Spectacular Tournament, Production of Caesar's Triumphal Entry into Rome."

The title may have come from Coxey, the new press agent, but he no doubt had help from Alf T., who liked to think up high-sounding phrases and devoted most of his efforts to staging the "spec."

They decided to make another tour of the East, where such seasoned circus men as Sells Bros., Barnum & Bailey, Buffalo Bill, and Adam Forepaugh held the stage.

John went ahead, laying out routes and choosing what he regarded as the most profitable stands, hobnobbing with leading politicians and financiers along the way. He soon learned that business was in a slump along the Atlantic seaboard and the opposition already had booked many cities and towns on the Ringlings' projected route.

So John, the strategist, knowing it would be costly to buck such competition, telegraphed his brothers to go west and south, and doubled back accordingly. The show swung through Illinois, Iowa, and down into Missouri where it was scheduled to play Bolivar on Saturday, the twenty-sixth of September.

There was the usual street parade, which stirred the populace into excited anticipation of the program to be presented that afternoon and evening. Farmers from miles around had come to town to sell their cotton and see the circus. Bolivar was jammed with people and it looked like a profitable stand for the Ringlings.

Some said trouble started in the fortune teller's tent —the mitt joint—but others claimed it broke out in the Oriental or "cooch" show. All agreed it originated on the midway and spread like fire through a field of broom sedge in the fall.

When a circus employee was clubbed on the head with a tent stake there was a shout, "Hey, Rube!" It was the battle cry of the hour and quickly boiled into the biggest clem the Ringlings ever had.

The candy stand was wrecked in a flash; the soft drink booth was toppled; lemonade trickled in the dust. The kid top was slashed to ribbons; the dressing tent hung at a crazy angle, half up and half down, stakes pulled up and guy lines cut. Seats were scattered and wagons overturned.

Hundreds of townspeople milled about, screaming and shouting, stomping and running to or from the scene of battle. In their frenzy and confusion, people clubbed their best friends, or smashed into them and sent them sprawling.

Clubs thumped and bloodied the heads of showfolk and towners alike. Screams rent the hot, stifling air and fists and feet churned in utter chaos. The noise was deafening, the dust thick and choking.

The two hundred men and women in personnel had

to fight fiercely to save animals and equipment, and finally themselves. To give a night performance was out of the question.

In the gathering dusk, officials, performers, and workingmen piled aboard the circus' twenty-two railroad cars and headed for Arkansas, glad to be out of Bolivar and the whole state of Missouri.

That they succeeded in saving most of the equipment and their own lives is a tribute to the tenacity and resourcefulness of all troupers. Circus people are a hardy breed and they stick together.

The Ringling Circus never played Bolivar again. Even John avoided the town after that, though he had missed all the excitement and bloodshed.

They finished the season in Texas, added a big chime wagon and a steam traction engine—a departure from horse and elephant power in raising the Big Top. The following spring they went out as "Ringling Bros. World's Greatest Shows; Three Rings, One Stage, Hippodrome."

Actually, the Ringlings were not retrenching, but they had to cut down to load their circus onto twenty-two cars, and they let their cousins, the Gollmar brothers, have some of the wagon-show equipment.

Rain and mud cancelled the Ringling show on the second day out of winter quarters. The brothers missed another stand at Maquoketa, Iowa, and at Topeka, Kansas, it rained so hard they couldn't raise the Big Top and had to call off the performance. Everyone was soaked to the skin and many props and costumes were ruined by mud and water.

There was rain for thirty consecutive days and nights, often of flood proportions. It made life miserable for everyone—slogging through ankle-deep mud and water and wearing drenched clothing day after day, constantly dosing to ward off colds and pneumonia. Even with every precaution, many fell ill.

Opposition from the Barnum & Bailey, Wallace, and John Robinson circuses added to the Ringlings' woes. When the rains finally let up, high winds kept the tents from going up or flattened them and ripped them to pieces on water-logged lots.

Finally there came trouble more costly than wind and rain—train wrecks. The first was at Concordia, Kansas, when two men and twenty-six horses were killed, two score animals injured, and four railroad cars destroyed.

The show managed to play Concordia, putting up sidewalls only for an abbreviated performance. The Ringlings bought eighteen head of stock in the area and ordered twenty more from Chicago, to be delivered at Wichita four days later.

A storm struck at Ponca City, Indian Territory, and the show never got to the lot. Another train wreck at Centralia, Missouri, demolished six cages, damaged some wagons and railroad cars, and cost the day's business.

Like a wounded elephant, the circus limped on, reaching Cape Girardeau, Missouri, in late October, ending the season there and heading for home. Another train wreck, at Centralia, Illinois, left several cages smashed, half a dozen railroad cars wrecked, and dozens of persons injured.

Of course John had missed all the misfortunes that beset the show. He was out ahead and while he knew about the opposition and the wrecks, the wind and rain and mud, they were not bitter, personal experiences to blunt his enthusiasm and sicken his determination. He gave his brothers encouragement and hope, assuring them that their troubles surely were over.

"We've whipped all that now," he said back in Baraboo, where they talked retrenchment. "We're bound to have better sailin' from now on. All the train wrecks and bad luck can't come our way; we've already had more than our share. Holy Jesus! Some of it's bound to hit the other fellow."

He talked on, exuding confidence and quoting business leaders and politicians he had met in all parts of the country. The brothers had no intention of quitting, but John persuaded them to expand rather than simply hold their own.

They discussed how to improve the opening spectacle, what acts to add and how to step up the whole performance, for the Ringlings were first of all entertainers.

"We need a calliope," John said. "You can hear one of them a mile or more. People go for music and a calliope will pull 'em in. Once they're on the lot, we can do the rest, but we've got to draw 'em with a little free entertainment. A calliope will be the ticket."

He bought one, with his brothers' approval, from John Robinson, the old circus man from Cincinnati. They added some elephants and a giraffe to their menagerie, but at the moment the calliope was the main attraction.

It was trimmed in red and gold and the name "Ringling Bros. World's Greatest Shows," was lettered on the sides in Prussian blue with brilliant orange border.

"By God," John beamed, "That's a beaut. It'll be a tremendous attraction; ought to bring in a hundred new customers every day."

John took the liberty of buying and expanding while his brothers were busy with their part of the operation. Al was overall manager and general boss; Alf T. was engrossed in planning spectacles, writing music, and preparing billing matter and other circus literature. Charles kept the big circus family of performers and workingmen contented, and Otto watched the finances.

Carpenters built what the brothers called "eight elegant carved cages," painters applied red and gold trimmings to the gilt panels, lettering in the Ringling name and slogan to match the band and tableaux wagons.

When they opened the 1894 season in Baraboo, they had forty-two railroad cars, including three advance cars. The route led east through Illinois, Indiana, Ohio, Pennsylvania, New York, Connecticut, Vermont, and then into the South.

It stretched into the longest season the Ringlings had up to that time—a hundred and seventy-five days and nights in eighteen states—and the most profitable.

The Ringlings rolled into Chicago and treated the public to an illuminated free street parade for three consecutive nights prior to the opening on Friday, April 5, 1895, at Tattersall's—the first time a circus staged such a feature in the Windy City after dark.

It also marked the first time that a circus, menagerie, and hippodrome were presented in a Chicago building. Signor A. Liberati, one of the leading cornet soloists of the period, was engaged to conduct a band concert for one hour prior to each performance. In the band were fifty musicians, half of whom played only in the concert.

This was another John Ringling innovation. He knew Liberati, liked music and wanted circusgoers to have their share of it. The show still carried the calliope, of course, but John assured his brothers that a fifty-piece band, and a good one, would be appropriate for the Chicago opening, which was one of the most spectacular any circus ever had.

It was the first time the Ringlings exhibited in Chicago, Boston, and St. Louis in a single season and the first time the "Ding-Dong brothers from Baraboo" made an extended tour of the East. A series of events made them anxious to step in, but they never dreamed of the fierce competition they would meet.

Phineas Taylor Barnum, impressario, lecturer, author, flamboyant promoter and proprietor of museums, who had gone into the circus business in 1870 and brought it incalculable publicity, had died on April 7, 1891.

After Barnum passed on, James A. Bailey, the other half of the partnership, expanded his holdings and for the next few years was high mogul of the circus world.

Bailey, generally recognized as the master circus man of the century, introduced a third ring and devised intervening stages; he brought many innovations to the circus and was brilliant as an organizer, originator, and financier. Where Barnum lived and thrived on publicity, Bailey produced.

By 1895 the little showman owned both the Barnum & Bailey and Adam Forepaugh circuses. Of course he had been watching the Ringlings, and when they dared to move into the East, he was ready for them.

Bailey's first move was to give Buffalo Bill rolling stock and other equipment to outfit a twenty-two-car Wild West Show and send the widely known and colorful old Colonel William F. Cody out to fight the Ringlings.

The circus battle was joined when Buffalo Bill just

beat the brothers into Boston, opening a two-weeks' stand on June 22, 1895. The Ringlings played surrounding communities and exhorted the people of Beantown to be patient.

"Wait! Wait and see the big show," they begged in banner lines and on broadsides. "After the minnow comes the whale!"

But a vast majority of the circus-going public in that part of Massachusetts didn't wait. Buffalo Bill had a good show and drew capacity crowds. He moved out after Saturday, the Fourth of July, and the following Monday the Ringlings moved in, but there wasn't much business left for them.

Competition for the Ringlings also came from another old and familiar outfit—the Sells brothers. Ephraim, Allen, Peter, and Lewis Sells had started their show in 1872, a dozen years before the Ringlings, giving impetus to the brother idea in show business.

The Sells Bros. Circus went to Australia late in 1891 and returned to this country on June 9, 1892, at San Francisco. Moving east, it declared war on the Ringlings, who by now had grown up in the corn and wheat belt, which had been Sells territory.

After three seasons of furious competition with the Ringlings and generally unfavorable economic conditions, the Sells Bros. had to look for help. It was not long in coming—from Bailey.

CHAPTER NINE

The Ringlings Roll and Romance

BAILEY LET the Sells brothers have the Adam Forepaugh title and in return held a third interest in the enterprise. So Bailey now had three circuses with which to fight the Ringlings—Barnum & Bailey, Buffalo Bill, and Forepaugh-Sells.

The latter went out in the 1896 season in three sections, with 332 workingmen and 64 performers; 245 horses, 13 elephants, 7 camels, and various other attractions under the title of "Adam Forepaugh and Sells Bros. Great Combined Shows."

It opened in Columbus, Ohio, where it had a thousand acres of land and one of the largest and finest winter quarters in the country. It went out to play the West in competition with the Ringlings.

In that season the Ringlings had opposition at forty-five stands. Not only was business divided four ways, but fighting was bitter. Each tore down the other's billing, or plastered his own gaudy posters over those of his rivals. Dates were changed by simply pasting new ones over old, confusing not only the public and the rival show's advance men but often their own.

Fists, clubs, and tack hammers were used in hand-to-hand combat that left workingmen disabled or jailed, and chicanery was common. One trick that was especially effective worked this way:

An agent would walk into a junction express office, pose as the opposing show's representative, and order shipments of bills, programs, and other supplies sent to another city, perhaps a hundred or five hundred miles away, making them worthless.

Clerks soon became wise to such shenanigans and began demanding identification, but this could easily be faked, or addresses on shipments could be changed while backs were turned. Billers often slipped into advance cars and dumped sand in the gunk (paste used in billposting).

The Ringlings, who by this time knew all the tricks and could match brains and brawn with any circus man or combination in the country, never gave an inch. To the public they were "The Sunday School Boys" but to those who fought them they were shrewd operators, on or off the lot.

John still had his eye on the populous East and he argued that the circus should play that section instead of chasing after business in the sprawling West. He even made a tentative agreement to move winter quarters to Philadelphia, which he knew was nearer the center of population. It was a typical John Ringling deal, made without a written word.

"That way we'll be in the East and won't have to travel so far to get into good payin' territory," he argued when his brothers heard about it and gave him a verbal thrashing. "I can see a hell of a lot of money in it for us. It's a smart move."

The brothers refused to leave Baraboo, and they told John very emphatically he could forget all his high-falutin' plans to move to Philadelphia, or anywhere else. They'd have none of it.

To stifle any further notions he might have for moving winter quarters, they expanded their holdings in the old home town, after spreading rumors that they really might move.

They bought land east of the old Case farm, where they planned to raise feed for the stock, as Forepaugh-Sells did in Columbus; they built additions to the car-shops, a new animal house, elephant house, camel barn, and wagon storehouse. They rebuilt the ring barn and bought what had been the old city pound.

Upon John's recommendation and to appease him, they took the circus into the East after opening at the Coliseum in St. Louis, and played thirty stands in New York and New England in the early months of the tour.

But they didn't leave their western and southern territory uncultivated. They rented the John Robinson Circus, one of the oldest and best known in America, and sent it out with Henry Ringling and John Robinson, Jr., as co-managers. Henry was twenty-eight years old at the time, built like a bull and every inch a Ringling.

Charles joined them for the first three months, then returned to the big one, for by now the John Robinson Circus was doing well.

Forepaugh-Sells provided formidable opposition for the Ringling enterprises at many stands, and boasted thusly in the 1896 season:

"Had the opposition been a really first-class show, the Forepaugh-Sells victory would have been great. An elephant gains little glory in besting an ant."

The battle continued all over Illinois, Wisconsin, Minnesota, the Dakotas, Nebraska, Iowa, and Missouri. The Ringlings made some money but Forepaugh-Sells didn't, and on August 1, Ephraim Sells, the treasurer and ticket supervisor, passed on.

Allen had died four years earlier and now ownership was divided equally among Lewis and Peter Sells, James A. Bailey, and W. W. Cole.

At the end of the 1897 tour, Bailey took his big circus to Europe and left Buffalo Bill and Forepaugh-Sells to fight the Ringlings.

The 1898 season was fairly profitable for the Ringlings and the following spring they spent the first few days on virtually the same route, then made a transcontinental journey to Washington and Oregon.

Enriched and entrenched, they embarked in 1900 on the most ambitious and extensive tour they'd ever undertaken, from coast to coast. They played as far north as Vancouver and south to Mexico, in twenty-two states, two territories, and British Columbia, spending five weeks in California alone.

Thus, when James A. Bailey brought his circus home from Europe in 1902, he found the American circus picture considerably changed. The Ringling show had become a giant, traveling on more than sixty railroad cars and with five hundred in personnel.

The brothers were in the prime of life, vigorous and financially secure, proud and strong, tough and determined, operating collectively for their common good. John was thirty-six years of age and Al was fifty, the others in between. They'd lived and grown up with the circus—their circus—and now they were riding high.

On the other hand, Barnum was dead and Bailey was well past his prime, approaching his sixtieth birthday.

He was still the master circus man and had about all
the personnel and equipment one man could supervise
effectively. He was smart enough to know that no good
would come from constantly fighting for territory,
playing opposition stands all over the country, especially
with the Ringlings.

He realized they would never surrender and he believed it was time to cooperate. Of course it must be
done with a flair, and Bailey was the man who could
do it. He still had winter quarters in Barnum's town
of Bridgeport, Connecticut, and he still opened the
season in New York City, as the Barnum show had
done since 1873.

An event that forced the sale of the Forepaugh-Sells
Circus occurred on October 3, 1904, when Peter Sells
died. Peter's estate had to be settled and Lewis was the
only one of the brothers still alive. He was ready to
quit.

John Ringling wanted his brothers to buy, outlining
what they could do with such a well-known title and
property. To his surprise, they were enthusiastic.

The brothers had been friendly with Bailey and naturally they kept abreast of events in circusdom through
the *Billboard,* newspapers, and word of mouth.

They approached Bailey about the Forepaugh-Sells
property, but he suggested they wait, then announced
that the circus would be sold at public auction, piece
by piece, at Columbus on January 10, 1905. The bewhiskered showman put out a thirty-two-page catalog
listing every item in the sale.

Circus owners from everywhere gathered for the
occasion, carefully studied the catalog, and waited ex-

pectantly. Bailey offered $150,000 for the whole setup, and that was that.

After the sale, Bailey met the Ringlings as he had promised, and sold them the Sells brothers half of the property. Thus the Baraboo brothers became partners with Bailey in Forepaugh-Sells, a most favorable union.

But the Ringlings soon found that the more they expanded the bigger their headaches. Train wrecks, wind, rain, mud, and cold were costly and when a cyclone hit the show at Maryville, Missouri, on Monday afternoon, September 18, 1905, and knocked out the night performance, they decided it was time to act.

What they needed was a full-time legal representative, a qualified lawyer known in circus parlance as "the fixer." That night Charles put in a call to John M. Kelley, a young practicing attorney in Baraboo.

"I want you to come with us and represent us," Charles said. "We're running into a lot of lawsuits and we need some expert help. We have to clean up all these damage claims. Can you come right away, Mr. Kelley?"

Kelley was a farm boy, had graduated at the University of Wisconsin law school in 1901, and had opened an office in Baraboo. He had known the Ringlings most of his life, liked them, and realized that here was a real opportunity. He closed his law office at once.

Kelley quickly determined that sentiment was against the circus in every local courtroom; so he had all but one of the suits against the Ringlings transferred to Federal court.

"We won every one of them," he recalled many years later.

Kelley stayed with the circus for more than a quarter of a century, representing the Ringlings in thousands of cases and settling nearly all claims before they reached the courtroom. He was a smooth and fast operator, knew all the legal loopholes, and proved a real genius in handling damage claims. He knew when to offer a piddling settlement, stall for time, or let the case go to court.

"There never was a contract or so much in writing as you could scribble on a thumbnail," he recalled shortly before his death late in 1963.

With money pouring in, capable staff men in every department, and a legal eagle to look after their interests, the brothers found time for romance and marriage.

Of course, Al had married Louise (Eliza) Morris soon after his first job with a circus and she worked long and hard to help them make a start. Then she presided over the big stone house in Baraboo where she and Al lived.

Alf T. married Della Andrews, daughter of a Baraboo physician, and Charles took as his bride Edith Conway, whose father was a minister. Edith was only eighteen years of age at the time, a schoolteacher, but she soon adjusted to the circus life and, in her later years, became known as "the grand old lady of the circus."

Henry Ringling married Ida Palmer, and the only Ringling girl, Ida Wilhelmina, married Henry Whitestone North, a railroad engineer considerably older than she was.

Henry courted Ida Ringling during long buggy rides out of Baraboo and while the difference in their ages and their courting habits caused tongues to wag, their union lasted long enough to produce three lively and gifted children before he died.

Otto was interested only in the circus and the cash it brought in. He'd never think of spending money on a girl, never took a wife, remained the skinflinty bachelor to the end, and lived at Al's house when he wasn't on the road.

John broadened his activities as the circus grew and his work permitted him to go where and when he chose and to lead the unfettered life. While he kept an eye on the enterprise and claimed his share of the profits, his energies were spent on meeting people in high places and adding to his wealth while indulging his pleasures.

During one of his visits to Chicago he looked twice at a pretty young woman recently arrived from the family farm near Moons, Ohio. Her name was Mable Burton.

Mable—she always spelled it that way although her sisters wrote it "Mabel"—was a striking brunette with soft brown eyes and black glossy hair. Her lips were thin, her chin firm and rather round, and her fingers long and graceful. Mable was a charming person.

Naturally, she was rather excited over meeting the rich and very eligible "Mr. Ringling," but she was old enough at twenty-five not to let his interest turn her pretty head.

One story was that Mable was a rider on the circus but she never was a performer. Another published report made her a telegraph operator, but this had no basis of fact.

One of her sisters, Mrs. Amanda Wortman, a long-time resident of St. Augustine, Florida, described the meeting of John and Mable in these words:

"While she was in Chicago during the World's Fair and worked as a cashier in the largest restaurant, when

John went in for his lunch he looked at her with his admiring eyes, and married her right away."

Most of the Ringlings married early in life, had conventional honeymoons, and went about their business of building the circus, but not John. He made a production out of it.

He bought a private railroad car and had it fitted out to his taste, including sitting room, bedroom, bath, and pantry, plus a well-stocked cupboard of beverages.

Al had a private car and so did Charles, but theirs went with the circus and were utilitarian rather than plush. Subordinates often were called in for conferences and those who had a problem could discuss it with Al, Alf T., Otto, or Charles.

John's friends came aboard his car, which was named the "Jomar," a contraction of "John" and "Mable" with the letter "r" for Ringling. It was one of the finest on rails in those days of plush red velvet and brass trimmings.

His rolling home compared favorably with one owned by his close friend and confidant, Colonel Edward Howland Robinson Green, son of Hetty Green, at that time the richest and one of the most miserly women on earth.

Ned Green was a good match for John—a gargantuan fellow, six foot four and 240 pounds—but he was forced to hobble around on a cork leg because Hetty had been too stingy to provide proper medical care for him when he was a boy.

The title of "Colonel" came from a Texas governor, but Green was proud of it and while he inherited some of his mother's craving for riches, he also used her cash.

Colonel E. H. R. Green was a progressive man with

an inquiring mind and he carried out many experiments on plant and animal breeding in his adopted state of Texas. But he also had an appetite for lusty living.

John had met the colonel in Chicago around the turn of the century and they became fast friends, so that when the circus man and Mable went to St. Louis on their honeymoon in April, 1904, Green and his lady friend, Mabel Harlow, joined them there.

Green and his girl arrived aboard his private railroad car, "Mabel," and it pulled up near the Jomar, where John and Mable were sojourning.

Green's car outshone John's for he had paid George Pullman seventy-five thousand dollars to build this rolling mansion to his specifications. It was one of the most elegant on the road at a time when such richly-furnished transportation was a mark of distinction.

It had extra-heavy suspension springs, the latest type shock absorbers, dining room, kitchen, bedroom and bath, plus an extra large observation platform surrounded by brass railings.

When the circus left St. Louis, John and Mable headed for California to continue their honeymoon in the West, while Green and his Mabel went to Terrell, Texas, where he maintained residence and was president of the Texas Midland Railroad.

The two millionaires met again during the panic of 1907, when John called on Ned Green, now dwelling in a hotel in Dallas. As John told the story to Green, the circus was in bad shape financially, losing money and needing cash to meet operating expenses until it could get into Texas. He offered to sell Green part of the Forepaugh-Sells show.

"Actually," said John, "I was just tryin' him out to see if he would lend me money if I needed it."

"I don't want any part of your circuses," Green told him. "They ramble all over the country and I want nothing to do with any business that don't stay in Texas, where I can keep my eye on it.

"But you're a good friend of mine, so I'll tell you what I'll do—I'll lend you the money. How much you need?"

"Twenty-five thousand dollars."

Green provided the cash with one stipulation—he would put a representative on the Ringling Circus to see that the money was repaid.

"I had gone too far to back out," John recalled later. "I had to go through with the deal, so I took it."

From the day the circus rolled into El Paso from Deming, New Mexico, on October 5, 1907, it began making money. Big crowds, their pockets jingling with cash from cattle and cotton, greeted the show at Abilene, Weatherford, Fort Worth, Dallas, and Sherman, then at Durant, Indian Territory, and on into Oklahoma Territory at Shawnee.

Green's loan was repaid within the month and he was so impressed with the opportunity of making money with the circus that he wanted to buy into it.

"Wouldn't think of sellin' now," John chided him. "We're out of the woods and you've got your money back. You had a chance to buy, but you missed the boat."

CHAPTER TEN

Exit Mr. Bailey

AFTER THE RINGLING show opened its 1906 season in the Coliseum in Chicago on Thursday night, April 5, John headed east to New York City. He craved a bigger slice of the circus pie and was making plans to get it. His first objective was to buy Bailey's share of the Forepaugh-Sells outfit so the Ringlings would own all of it.

When he arrived, John found that Bailey was ill at his home, The Knolls, in nearby Mount Vernon, but his representatives at Madison Square Garden said he was expected back in a couple of days.

While waiting for Bailey to recover, John called on several well-known newspapermen, including Arthur Brisbane, Morrell Goddard, and Charles Chapin, and dined with his good friend, Stanford White, America's foremost architect of the time.

White was a big, red-haired man with a sweeping mustache. A dozen years older than John, he bubbled with vitality and moved in the highest circles of society. Perhaps there was a bit of hero worship here, for the circus man admired White's achievements and his merry living.

John met the architect at the Hoffman House and later they dined at Moquin's, a popular French restaurant. As they left, John bought a copy of the early edition of the *New York Morning World*. In the glow of the streetlamp he saw the shocking headline, bold and black.

"Holy Christ!" he exclaimed. "It's Bailey. James A. Bailey is dead."

"No; you don't mean it!" said White, leaning closer to read the startling news.

"There it is," John replied. "It's a terrible loss."

"You know, I met him a couple of years ago when I went to the circus with Saint-Gaudens," White recalled. "Great man, that Bailey."

"Hell, yes. A real circus man; one of the best in the world. It's a terrible loss to everybody when a man like Bailey dies."

James Anthony Bailey—what a giant among men of his time! Somewhat overshadowed by the showmanship and promotions of Phineas T. Barnum, he was nevertheless the outstanding circus man of the age and a credit to mankind.

When he was born in Detroit in 1847 he was christened James Anthony McGinnis. He worked on a farm, then got a job as bellboy in a Pontiac, Michigan, hotel where he met Fred Bailey, a guest.

The latter gave him a job with the advance crew of a circus and McGinnis changed his name to Bailey. He rose rapidly to general agent, and, finally, became a proprietor in 1872 when he formed a partnership with James E. Cooper and organized the Cooper & Bailey Circus.

Bailey was slight and small in stature but every circus man knew him as one of the greatest figures in show business. His death, coming when it did, furnished John Ringling a powerful lesson in dealing with his fellow man and the public. John was impressed if not actually awed by the universal sorrow among circus people everywhere when Bailey passed away.

Many a trouper felt Bailey's influence and mourned his death for he was not only the most talented circus man of his time but the most human and the most admired. He was genuinely loved by those who worked for him and respected by his competitors, including the Ringlings.

His word was an absolute gold bond and hundreds who were with him in various capacities during his long and active life never troubled about a contract for they knew none was needed.

John went to Bailey's funeral in the Chester Hill Methodist Church in Mount Vernon on Saturday, April 14, 1906, and heard the Reverend H. H. Beatty say:

"Slight in stature but great in heart, James Anthony Bailey was ever mindful of the rights of others, and sorrow and helplessness always had his sympathy. I have seen this man, when engrossed in the trying details of mapping out intineraries of three great shows at the same time, stop and stoop to caress a frightened dog."

Flags on the Garden flew at half staff throughout the day as they did on all public buildings in Mount Vernon. Many who had known Bailey wept unashamed. Mourning for him was widespread.

After the funeral John Ringling returned to New York City but he didn't go to the Garden with Stanford White that night, for it was dark. Both afternoon and night programs were cancelled out of respect for Bailey. The show had been sold out for both performances and the management refunded all money for tickets bought, or exchanged them for future dates.

"Bailey's death was a tough break all around," John

reminded his friend, Charles R. Hutchinson, treasurer of the Barnum & Bailey Circus. "If he'd lived just two days more then the funeral would have been on a Monday. The show lost an awful lot of money by refunding all that Saturday cash in hand."

Hutchinson agreed. He knew that Monday was always the lightest day for business in New York City, and especially the last Monday of the engagement.

The show closed its Madison Square Garden stand a week after Bailey was buried, but even before it got out of town John was talking of buying it. His original idea of getting Bailey's share of Forepaugh-Sells had grown into a new project of enticing possibilities.

He cultivated Hutchinson's friendship and gathered all the information he could about the Barnum & Bailey enterprise, both physical and financial. He liked "Hutch" and concentrated on him rather than Bailey's widow, figuring the treasurer was the heart and soul of the organization.

"This is our big chance," John told his brothers by telephone to Chicago. "I've already seen 'Hutch' and I think he'll be favorable to us. By God, fate played right into our hands!"

Otto was quick to see his point and gave enthusiastic approval but Al, Alf T., and Charles held out. It was three to two with both sides standing firm. The way they operated, they would not attempt to buy until all agreed.

"Holy Jesus!" John whined. "Can't you see it? This is our big chance to get the 'Greatest Show on Earth' —the biggest circus in the world by name and reputation—dirt cheap. If we stall, the price will skyrocket and we'll have to pay plenty. Some other outfit might

grab it right from under us. What's to keep some fellow with a lot of cash from jumpin' in and outbiddin'
us?"

His brothers argued that, with Bailey gone, his circus
would be no match for theirs and the widow likely
would soon tire of the struggle and sell cheap.

"You're dead wrong," John insisted. " 'Hutch' is a
smart circus man and he's got plenty of help in the brains
department. Even without Bailey, they can make it
tough for us. We've never had a picnic when we ran
up against that outfit and you know it. I say, let's buy
now, while we can."

Charles, who often sided with John, was the first to
change but Al and Alf T. still refused to go along. The
score was still three to two.

"Just look at the prestige it'll give us," John pleaded.
"If we buy the whole thing at once, we'll control the
circus field. It'll be the biggest thing that ever hit the
amusement world. A deal like this will make headlines
in all the newspapers. It's a big opportunity for us; we
ought to grab it. This'll put us on top of the heap. By
God, can't you see it?"

Al and Alf T. couldn't, and said so. They reminded
him that they had plenty to do managing their own circuses and insisted the time was not ripe to plunge.

The Ringling show was scheduled to exhibit in Philadelphia during the week of May 21, 1906. The city
proper was billed heavily for it but the outside areas
were plastered with Barnum & Bailey posters and John
went there to check on business.

Barnum & Bailey didn't give the Ringlings opposition
in Philadelphia itself and didn't plan to, but played the
"feeder" towns and brought headaches to John, who

ROLAND BUTLER, HEAD OF THE RINGLING PRESS DEPARTMENT FOR THIRTY-THREE YEARS; NORMAN BEL GEDDES, ARTIST AND DESIGNER; AND MRS. ESTELLE BUTLER, WIFE OF ROLAND AND ALSO A MEMBER OF THE PRESS DEPARTMENT

WHERE THE WEALTH OF BIG SHOW ADVERTISING AND PUBLICITY IS CREATED

THE flood of advertising and publicity which sweeps through the territory played by the Ringling Bros and Barnum & Bailey Combined Circus each season—and that territory extends from coast to coast and from Canada to the Gulf of Mexico—is the result of months of planning and labor in the advertising and publicity office of The Greatest Show on Earth in its winter quarters at Sarasota, Florida.

There is conceived and executed the ideas for posters, stands of paper, banners, heralds, programs, rotogravure booklets, newspaper ads, stories and special features for each season's tour, under the direction of Sam W. Gumpertz, general manager of the Big Show. Mr. Gumpertz, who, as a youth was business manager and publicity representative of circus and theatrical enterprises, and who specialized in the publicity drives of his theatre and varied amusement projects in New York and over the country at large, has brought this specialized knowledge to the advertising problems of the world's largest circus. In the picture, he is conferring with Roland Butler, the show's general press representative, and other members of his staff.

Reading from right to left: Sam W. Gumpertz, sitting at the desk in the foreground; Roland Butler; Frank Braden, veteran story man; Pat Valdo, director of personnel; Col. Ralph C. Caples, advertising counsellor; Bill Cunningham, noted sports writer of the *Boston Post* and *Collier's Weekly*, a visitor; and Mrs. I. W. Robertson, executive secretary to Mr. Gumpertz.

PRESS DEPARTMENT OF THE RINGLING BROS. CIRCUS AT WINTER QUARTERS

Here all the big-show advertising and publicity material was created each winter for the coming summer season.

The Cocoon from which The Greatest Show on Earth Emerges in Its Might and Splendor Each Spring

WHEN the season of The Greatest Show on Earth closes, another season begins—off the road. Back to Sarasota, Florida, where the resort city's slogan is "Spend a summer this winter in Sarasota," steam the four long show trains. In the railroad, wardrobe, tentmaking, wagon building and other shops at the circus winterquarters, hundreds of men and women go into action, for railroad Pullmans, stock and flat cars must be overhauled, wagons must be rebuilt, new canvas must be made—each of the thirty-one great tents, as well as the smaller ones is new each spring—and seats, electric light plants, poles, harness, riggings, trucks, costumes, trappings

[Continued on page 29]

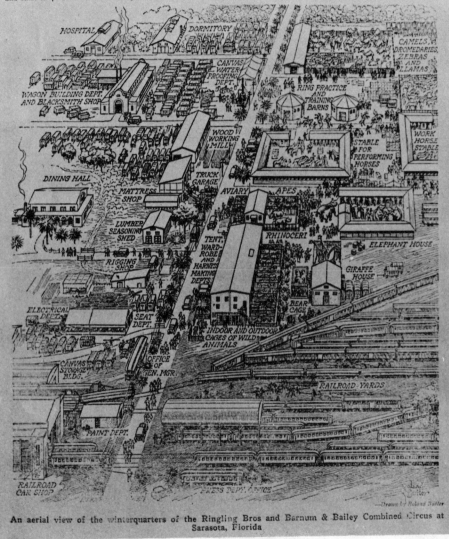

An aerial view of the winterquarters of the Ringling Bros and Barnum & Bailey Combined Circus at Sarasota, Florida

LAYOUT OF THE RINGLING WINTER QUARTERS AT SARASOTA, FLORIDA, AS DRAWN BY ROLAND BUTLER

The circus occupied these quarters for thirty-two years, from 1927 to 1959

ALL THAT
REMAINED
AFTER THE
CIRCUS
LEFT
WINTER
QUARTERS
AT
SARASOTA
AND
MOVED TO
VENICE IN
1959

Still intact
was this
huge sign on
the road east
of town.

could see business being drained off on all sides. He shook with disgust every time he looked at a Barnum & Bailey poster and realized that he and his brothers might have owned the show.

Barnum & Bailey played Atlantic City on May 7; Bridgeton, Camden, and Trenton on the following days, then moved into Chester. The Ringlings already had advertisements appearing in Camden, Trenton, and Chester newspapers for their Philadelphia date and posters were up, but Barnum & Bailey had come to the very doors before the Ringlings could play the City of Brotherly Love, and got the business.

John couldn't stand it. He visited the Barnum & Bailey show in Chester with Adam Forepaugh, Jr., on Friday, May 11. Forepaugh was a Philadelphia native and had been featured in his father's circus as the "World's foremost elephant trainer, who can no more have a peer than two suns can exist."

Studying the Philadelphia situation with his usual thoroughness and gathering all the facts he could from young Forepaugh and others, John returned to New York to see some shows and try to work out the Forepaugh-Sells deal with Bailey's widow and other heirs.

He promised his friend, Stanford White, that he'd attend the opening of the roof garden atop Madison Square Garden on the night of Monday, June 25. White was enthusiastic and said:

"I've been accused of being show crazy. When they see us together, they'll think I've gone into business—perhaps with you."

By this time John had come to be quite well known. The West regarded him as one of the brothers but in the East he was an individual, in theatrical circles as well as in the circus field.

For some time now he had given up traveling ahead of the circus on any sort of schedule, laying out routes and studying conditions as he had done in the early days. Now he was everywhere, meeting leading personages of the day, conferring with circus men, theatrical agents, politicians and promoters—anyone who would join him at dinner, for a drink or at a show, and perhaps pass along information he could use.

White, of course, was far better known. He was brilliant, witty, a member of the well-known firm of McKim, Mead and White; recognized as one of the foremost architects in the world. John valued his friendship and admired his architectural genius as much as he did his tastes in food and companions. They often dined together when John was in the city and occasionally attended the theater or made the rounds of night spots.

Once he visited White's country home on Long Island. This was a converted farmhouse and it gave John some ideas which he later was to incorporate in his own home. It was furnished with gilded Spanish columns, Renaissance fireplaces, Persian rugs, Roman fragments and Delft tile, much of which White had picked up on European junkets.

The architect had planned luxurious homes in New York and Newport. In his own Gramercy Park house he showed John some pedestals he had designed and brought out sketches of picture frames; magazine, book, and program covers; designs for jewelry and even gravestones.

"Now, here's a place I'm working on up in the Berkshires," he said. "Notice the rounded portico, like a Ringling haircut."

John blinked, chuckled, and the back of his neck turned red. He liked that, realized it was a trademark, and never changed the style of his haircut from that day, insisting on a rounded trim above the collar.

On the day that he was to attend the roof garden opening with White, John telephoned and promised to meet him that evening.

"I'm having dinner with my son," White reminded him. "He's down from Harvard, you know. I'll meet you at Martin's, or the Garden later."

John did not go to Martin's and didn't arrive at the Garden until almost eleven o'clock, which was a reasonable hour for him. As he entered, the first-night audience of stage celebrities, society figures, big business men, gamblers, and hangers-on was still excited.

Stanford White had just been shot dead at his table by Harry Kendall Thaw, the millionaire playboy from Pittsburgh, over a little showgirl named Evelyn Nesbit.

John had missed the shooting by minutes, because he was late. It was typical of his astounding good luck. He was shocked but glad that he had not been a witness, so he wouldn't have to spend long hours and days at Thaw's trial for murder.

To John time was too valuable to be frittered away in a stuffy courtroom while learned lawyers argued "unwritten law," "brainstorm" and other such words and phrases. He had other things to do, not the least important of which was to gain control of the Barnum & Bailey Circus.

CHAPTER ELEVEN

The Ringlings Become Kings

WITH BAILEY GONE, John Ringling closed the Fore-paugh-Sells deal and the brothers took over sole owner-ship of that good circus property on July 1, 1906. The show was in New Hampton, Iowa, the day it went completely under the Ringling banner.

Henry Ringling, who had managed the John Robin-son Circus when the brothers leased it in 1898, went out to represent them on the Forepaugh-Sells, which closed its season in the West.

Al and Alf T. still hadn't agreed to the Barnum & Bailey proposal but John kept hammering away. Their procrastination was to turn out to their advantage, so all the Ringling luck was not showered on John, though he had more than his share.

The 1906 season was disastrous for the Barnum & Bailey Circus, under the management of George O. Starr. First, there was confusion following Bailey's death, then rains, and finally one of the worst blow-downs a circus ever saw at Iowa City, Iowa, that left the great tented city in ruins.

W. W. Cole, perhaps no more capable but more experienced than Starr, became manager for the 1907 season and Barnum & Bailey stock went up a little. At John's urging, the Ringlings had bought shares of stock during the winter, and now they acquired some more.

John worked out a deal with Cole to divide the territory and keep down competition. He didn't want the Philadelphia situation to come up again and Cole was happy to go along.

The Barnum & Bailey Circus finished out the 1907 season and in October the Ringlings took over as sole owners. They paid $410,000—a virtual steal at the price, which would be returned twofold in a single good season. The Ringlings were the only experienced showmen in those tight financial times who had the cash to buy and successfully operate the big Barnum & Bailey holdings.

Under terms of the sale, Charlie Hutchinson remained as treasurer and Colonel William F. (Buffalo Bill) Cody regained control of his show. Cody was getting old and the Ringlings let him have it. There was considerable sentiment attached to the Buffalo Bill name and the brothers claimed they never wanted a Wild West outfit; the circus was their meat and potatoes.

Al Ringling went to have a look at the Barnum & Bailey property and dispatched his booking agent, Al Freeman, with orders to sign acts for the 1908 season. Freeman offered contracts at a flat 10 percent reduction. The Ringlings now had a monopoly and there was only one choice for performers and other leading circus personnel—sign if they wanted to work. Of course, nearly everyone wanted to stay with the leaders, even at a cut in pay.

John Ringling, now coming into the power and wealth he had so long worked to achieve, began to broaden the scope of his activities. He became a stockholder in Madison Square Garden, maintained an apartment on Fifth Avenue in New York City, and even dabbled in Wall Street.

He acquired property in many parts of the country and encouraged his brothers to invest, which occasionally they did on a limited scale. John became busier than ever, accumulating and living high.

He was often seen in the company of such public figures as John W. (Bet-You-a-Million) Gates, Diamond Jim Brady, Florenz Ziegfeld, George Ade, Frank Ward O'Malley, Frank Dallem, Charlie Still, Finley Peter Dunne, Richard Harding Davis, Alfred E. Smith, young Jimmy Walker, and Boss Frank Hague.

John went to the fights regularly in the Garden when he was in New York, having discovered Promoter George L. (Tex) Rickard and helped him move into the big time. He was seen often in Broadway night spots and liked it best where lights were bright, food tasty, and conversation easy.

He insisted that the Ringling Bros. Circus open its season in New York City instead of Chicago, where it had played opening dates for several years. He argued that the Ringlings now owned the two biggest circuses in the country and it was only proper for the one bearing their name to open in the nation's largest and richest city.

"Our show is the biggest and best, but it will never be a national institution until we get it out of the tall grass and into the big town," he said. "We ought to put our show where it belongs—we've swallowed Barnum & Bailey now, and the public knows it. There's more money in New York and the East, and you've got to go where the money is."

Al and Alf T. were against it, arguing that it would

cost more to haul their show all the way from Baraboo
to New York and that the circus had always enjoyed
good opening business in Chicago. Besides the brothers
now owned apartment houses in Chicago and they liked
the Windy City. It took some doing, but as usual John
talked faster and longer than the others and finally
had his way.

And so the Ringling Bros. Circus moved out of Baraboo winter quarters, went east, and opened the 1909
season in Madison Square Garden on March 25. At the
same time Barnum & Bailey went west from Bridgeport,
all the way to Chicago and opened in the Coliseum there
the first of April.

The Ringling show played the East, swung into Canada and went all the way to the Pacific Coast. Barnum
& Bailey toured the Midwest and South. Neither had a
very profitable season, with business just recovering
from the panic of 1907.

Besides the high cost of getting the two big circuses
ready and moving them to opening stands more than
eight hundred miles from their winter quarters, bad
weather struck at many locations and crowds seldom
reached expectations. When the tours of 1909 ended in
November, each circus was more than a thousand miles
from home.

The season taught John some forceful and valuable
lessons, brought home to him when the brothers gathered
at Al's house to divide the profits.

"You're not the only one in the family who knows
how to run a circus," they chided. "You might think
you're 'Mr. Big' but the rest of us know something
about operatin' the business, too. You and your high-
falutin' ideas gave us a lot of headaches and cost us

cash this time. You let us manage things, if that's the best you can do."

By this time more than thirty circuses were traveling by rail, headed by Ringling Bros. and Barnum & Bailey with eighty-four cars each. Others ranged from two cars to about fifty. At least as many more were on the road, touring by horse and wagon, and occasionally trying out the recently developed automobile.

Roads were few and hard to negotiate, so the automobile was used mostly for show. There was fierce competition, with every fellow for himself.

The Ringlings had the best reputation of any show on the road, because the brothers had constantly harped on a clean, dignified performance. It was Charles Ringling who suggested an organization of circus owners to curb unfair competition and eliminate unsavory dealings with the public.

Accordingly, representatives of more than a dozen circuses, including Ringling, Barnum & Bailey, Forepaugh-Sells, John Robinson, Hagenbeck-Wallace, Buffalo Bill, Sells-Floto, Miller Bros., Gollmar Bros. and Gentry Bros. met in White City, a Chicago suburb, late in December, 1910.

They adopted a constitution and by-laws, drew up rules of operation, and posted bonds totaling fifty thousand dollars to guarantee performance. They named H. H. Tammen as president; John M. Kelley, secretary, and R. M. Harvey, treasurer.

Membership was open to all circuses and Wild West shows. They agreed not to cover each other's posters and to remove advertising matter promptly after playing dates; to police each other and to give the public a square deal.

These were lofty ideals but the association had only a brief existence and within a year all agreements had been broken and competition was as fierce as ever.

John began to pay less and less attention to management and let his brothers run the circus. He continued to map tentative routes and make suggestions on the best stands when business would be at its peak, got all the concessions he could from his friends, and shared in the profits. But he was completely apart from the actual operation and had little or nothing to do with policies.

Even his brothers turned more and more of the countless details of running their three circuses over to capable and experienced assistants. All the Ringlings except Otto found time to relax and enjoy some of the luxuries they could well afford, like taking a weekend off to go fishing.

John concentrated on meeting business, civic, and political leaders, learning all he could about business in cities the circuses were to visit, and keeping a sensitive finger on the pulse of the nation.

Many considered him an authority on the circus but actually he had grown away from it, and vice versa. He knew little about its inner workings from the time it went on rails, and dropped in only occasionally.

One of his good friends was R. J. Reynolds, the North Carolina tobacco man who had started out peddling chewing tobacco and snuff from a wagon. When Reynolds entered the cigarette field about 1913 he chose the name "Camel" because it suggested association with the Orient and was appropriate to the new blend which contained Turkish tobaccos mixed with the native leaf.

"Camels" were the talk of the town when the Barnum

& Bailey Circus pulled into Reynolds' town of Winston-Salem for a fall stand. As was his custom, Reynolds closed down operations in his tobacco factory so his employees could go to the circus.

R. J. and John talked about business and the subject of the new cigarette naturally came into their conversation. John presented the tobacco man with a photo of an Arabian dromedary that was featured in the circus menagerie.

It was not actually a camel—the true camel has two humps, the dromedary one—but it became the world's most widely circulated picture of any animal in history, on billions of packages of Camel cigarettes.

John Ringling, smart operator that he was, knew little about such animals and never went to the bother even to read or ask about camels and dromedaries, although his circus publications constantly pointed out the differences in pictures and text.

Nearly everyone who went to the circus noticed the difference, but John wasn't interested in such trivia. Reynolds got a lot of mail calling attention to his dromedary, and came in for some good-natured kidding. He and John laughed over the incident in later years.

"The hell with them," John quoted R. J. as saying. "My friend Mr. Ringling ought to know more about animals than these people. All they know is what they read in books and encyclopedias. John's got practical knowledge. We'll keep using his camel, just as it is. Anyway, one hump's enough."

After the dromedary died, it was mounted and stood on display in a corner of the cigarette factory in the heart of Winston-Salem for many years.

CHAPTER TWELVE

The Ringlings—At Work and Play

ALL THE BROTHERS were big physically except Otto. John was the biggest of the five and towered over the others in aggressiveness and sharp dealings as well. The brothers were hardworking, practical circus men while John had verve and vision.

While the others concentrated on running their circuses to the best of their abilities and making money, John was busy everywhere, promoting and speculating. He was a mountain of a man, both in body and spirit. He thought not of ants but of elephants; not of one but an entire herd, and he operated on that basis.

Leading citizens often attempted to interest him in their communities and on such occasions he would extract from them every ounce of information that could be beneficial to him, and the circuses.

He often called on editors and publishers, who would welcome him and assign their star reporters and photographers. Often as not, this resulted in a story that dealt more with John Ringling than with the circuses he represented.

For he and the circus were synonymous, a fact that never failed to nettle his brothers. He stood head and shoulders above them in promotional ability, imagination, and aggressiveness, and was constantly in the limelight and outshone them all in the public's estimation.

Feature writers often sought him out and John never let them down. He was always good "copy" and, if he didn't produce a front-page story on the circus, his very presence in the city was reason for speculation.

He knew the country as well as any man of his time and could route the circuses as wisely as any experienced agent, but he gradually grew away from such details and, after the show achieved maturity, he was personally acquainted with few of the performers and none of the workingmen.

The friends he had were in high places, and he liked to associate with characters of every description. To outsmart even his best friends gave him tremendous satisfaction.

He was often called "colorful," and the very nature of his associations and his way of life gave wings to the thought, but it was a fallacy. He was unpredictable, crafty, and cunning, but never colorful in the sense of variety.

Rather, he was one of Dame Fortune's favorite sons. At the same time he was a conniver and a charmer; verily a triton among the minnows. When he was crossed he would spout vitriolic words that stung like hornets, and even his silence could be withering.

In his darkest moods he would whine and grumble among his oaths, but never did he shout or roar in the tradition of the old-time circus boss. He was more the cagey operator and the absentee landlord.

Though often misunderstood and mislabeled, he was never the circus man his brothers were, and he didn't claim to be. Al, Alf T., and even Henry and Gus had more actual experience with the show; Otto and Charles spent their lives with it and knew the operation from every viewpoint. None of those in personnel were strangers to them.

John was a trouper turned promoter, who blended his knowledge, resourcefulness, and astounding good luck into a fortune. After the circus was at its zenith, he seldom appeared on the lot. On those rare occasions when he did, it was to confer with his brothers, look over the operations while in a critical, fault-finding attitude, and dip into the till.

All the others despised the term "Mr. Ringling" for the simple reason that it meant John. It was a natural conclusion, for he was out ahead, meeting leading personages of the day, getting his name and often his picture in the papers, and representing the circus in the manner of envoy and flag bearer.

It infuriated the brothers to have some politician come on the lot and inquire for "Mr. Ringling." It was the image John had created, and he did nothing to change it, for he rather liked being called "Mr. Ringling."

The brothers, resenting it, insisted that the help call them by their given names, with the prefix "Mr." Thus it was "Mr. Al," "Mr. Alf T.," "Mr. Otto," and "Mr. Charlie."

They ran the circuses, by hard work and attention to details, while John went his merry way, enjoying life to the fullest and carving out a reputation as a man of wealth and distinction.

As the years wore on and the Ringling holdings grew and prospered, the brothers installed competent assistants so they could relax occasionally, going off to look over the opposition, such as it was, or enjoy a day or two of fishing in their favorite Minnesota lakes.

John liked stage shows and prizefights, but he was not the outdoors type. He traveled about the country aboard his private railroad car but if he planned to be in a city more than a few hours he would register at the leading hotel. He liked the comfort and convenience of the Jomar and used it for business reasons, too.

It pleased him to have leading citizens come aboard, be served their favorite beverage, including the best Scotch and imported German beer, and go on their way, impressed by his hospitality and his importance.

When he wished to score a ten-strike with a leading politician or businessman, he simply offered the use of his box at the circus. Nothing pleased a man more than to be able to say to his friend, "Mr. Ringling invited Martha and me to be his guests at the circus. Won't you and your wife join us in his box?"

Of course, by now John might be a hundred or three hundred miles away, ready to tackle new problems or embrace new opportunities, but the magic of his name was still working for him.

John could be a cold, phlegmatic man, as stubborn and unyielding as any of his Prussian forebears. He often acted frosty toward even his closest associates and most trusted employees. Consequently, few of those in his employ had any real affection for him, but they had to admire his audacity and admit his accomplishments.

If the circuses needed new acts, or he thought they did, he would take off for Europe and come home months later with the best he could find. Money meant little to him because he sealed a deal with a promise and he regarded the circus as a never-ending stream of cash.

"He could be a hard bargainer and a most exasperating man," said one longtime associate. "He was a very nervy old tyrant, who never missed a chance to make a profit. He was usually gruff, pleading poverty and putting off paying until next week or next month, if at all."

Once he owned a hotel in Los Angeles and, of course, circus personnel stayed there while in the city. John usually only glanced at expense sheets submitted to him, but occasionally, when an advance man turned in his detailed report, he would scrutinize it like a banker approving a mortgage, and would haggle over every line.

Once when he was in a cloudy mood he came across the item, "Hotel room, $4." He immediately called the hotel manager on the phone and delivered one of his typical outbursts.

"What the hell do you mean chargin' my men four dollars for a room in my hotel? That's too damn much money. I ought to get a concession."

The manager explained that all Ringling employees were given a special rate of two dollars.

"Well, that's not enough," John retorted. "They're chargin' me four dollars on these expense sheets. You make 'em pay the full price, so they won't be tempted to gyp me."

He hung up and said nothing to circus employees, but made certain one of the offenders overheard, and word went around.

The circuses grew in size and prestige, thanks to shrewd management and efficient operation. John added to his reputation, often by sheer luck. He liked to tell of his experience in Austin, Texas, embellishing the story as it unfolded.

He had arrived in the Texas capital a few days ahead of the show, to act as host to some of the state's leading politicians and businessmen. One night they were in a friendly poker game and John was in rare good humor. He liked to play poker—straight draw, nothing wild, with fifty cents or a dollar limit.

"We were playin' about two o'clock in the mornin' when a man rapped on the door and somebody let him in," John related. "This was in the governor's mansion. He was a big, angular fellow with an eager, honest look on his map. I could tell right away he amounted to something the way he talked and acted.

"After he was introduced all around, they started kidding him about his oil well.

" 'Still in a dry hole?' one man asked him.

" 'Yeah, still in a dry hole,' he admitted with a sort of disappointed grin. 'But there's oil under there and I aim to find it. One of these days I'm going to bring in a gusher.'

"Somebody asked how much he thought he'd need, and he said 'Oh, maybe fifty or sixty thousand.'

"Right then I knew he was a big operator, with a lot of guts. I started thinking about that oil and I said to myself, 'what if the damn fool does bring in a gusher? Maybe I ought to get in on it.' I'd always sort of liked Texas and its people, and made money there.

"We were feelin' pretty good, so we offered to back him. I believe we raised something like a hundred thousand dollars that night, in pledges and promises.

"Next time I was down there I checked up on him, and he still hadn't hit oil. He hit us for more money, and that went into dry holes, too.

"Well, the governor went out of office and it looked

ONE OF MANY FEATURED RIDING ACTS OF THE RINGLING CIRCUS

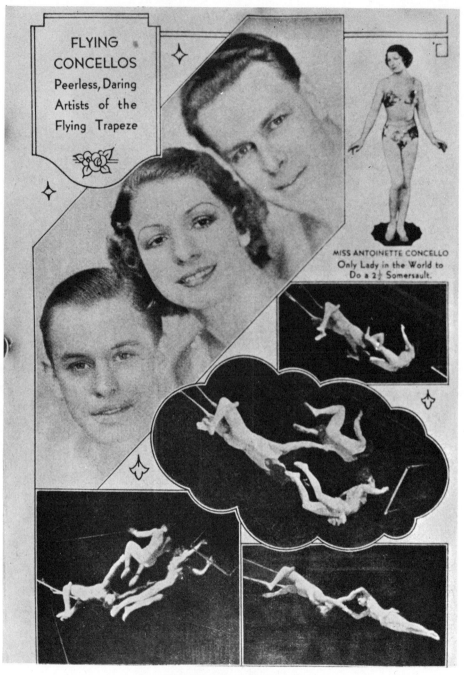

FLYING
CONCELLOS
Peerless, Daring
Artists of the
Flying Trapeze

MISS ANTOINETTE CONCELLO
Only Lady in the World to
Do a 2½ Somersault.

THE FLYING CONCELLOS

One of the feature attractions in the center ring for many years

RINGLING'S PYGMY ELEPHANTS WERE PRESENTED WITH TREMENDOUS FANFARE

A few years later the "pygmies" became a part of the regular Ringling herd, for they had grown up

IN 1953 THE CIRCUS FEATURED MASTER MISTIN, A CHILD PRODIGY,
ON THE XYLOPHONE

like the whole deal would peter out. I was busy and didn't get back down there for some time—just sort of kissed the whole thing good-bye.

"A year or two later when I went down, I looked into it. He still didn't have the oil but he thought he was getting pretty close. Most of his backers had given up and the poor fellow had his back to the wall—couldn't raise any more spondulix.

"I was tired of it myself, but something told me to stick it out. It was either go ahead or lose what I'd put in, so I told him to get releases from the others and I'd back him. And you know what happened?"

Here John would pause, look intently at his listeners, and shake his glass of Scotch and soda and draw every ounce of drama from his recitation, milking the moment like a great entertainer. Then he would go on.

"The very next week, I'll be damned if he didn't bring in a gusher—the biggest oil find in East Texas up to that time. It was one of the sweetest deals I ever made in my life."

John had time for fun, and he liked nothing better than a good belly laugh at the expense of his brothers, who were always absorbed in circus matters, had no sense of humor and no appetite for tomfoolery.

Once he dropped in on the circus in St. Louis, one of his favorite cities, where it was playing several days under canvas. He came on the lot just as the afternoon show was over, timing his visit perfectly.

Accompanying him was a distinguished-looking gentleman with flowing white hair—a pious-appearing individual who commanded the utmost respect. In the face he resembled Henry Wadsworth Longfellow, who had been dead for many years, but this man wore a clerical collar, black suit, and was "reverend" all over.

John called him "The Bishop" and they seemed to be warm friends, strolling on the midway and around the Big Top while the circus man pointed out various paraphernalia with his cane.

They came at last to the cookhouse, where the flag was up for dinner. Stopping at the staff table, John introduced "my friend the Bishop" to his brothers, who already had napkins tucked under their chins and were ready to tackle big bowls of steaming beef stew set before them.

They were there to eat, not for introductions to towners, and obviously wanted to make the repartee brief. The smell of nourishing food was penetrating their eager nostrils; they became bored and finally disgusted when John and his friend tarried overly long.

Finally, "The Bishop" said he felt he should say grace. The brothers bowed their heads in relief while "The Bishop" began to thank the Lord for just about everything. He prayed on and on, offering one of the most long-winded graces on record. The brothers kept getting madder and hungrier.

In the Big Top afterward, where John and "The Bishop" stood around watching the night crowds pour in, each brother in turn took John aside and gave him a dressing down. They told him they didn't like it at all and said there must be something wrong with his head to bring around "a man of the cloth" who would make such a nuisance of himself.

"We're not so wicked that we have to put up with that kind of an imposition," Al said. "And we won't stand for any more of it. Get him a seat to the show and then let him be gone. We've got work to do."

The four brothers had checked into a downtown hotel for the show's duration, renting one large room with two double beds. It afforded a welcome change from their somewhat cramped quarters on the train, and they could relax after the show without any interruptions.

They went to the hotel about midnight that night, tired and all in after a long, busy day. Half an hour later, when they had just turned out the light, John and "The Bishop" rapped on the door. Otto got up and let them in.

"The Bishop" explained that he had enjoyed their splendid performance, observed how clean and wholesome the show was, and wanted to thank each of them personally for giving him an opportunity to see it without cost.

"We have much to be thankful for," he said, rambling on about the liberal patronage the Ringlings were getting in his city and prospects for the season. Then he suggested, "Let us pray," and dropped to his knees.

The brothers crawled wearily out of bed to join him. "The Bishop" gave one of his best performances, praying earnestly for what seemed hours but probably wasn't more than ten or fifteen minutes.

When he finally said "Amen," Al had trouble getting up. He had such cramps in his legs the others had to help him to his feet and massage the legs to start the blood circulating again. "The Bishop" was full of sympathy.

After a lot more sweet talk and "good nights," John and his friend finally reached the door. As they crossed the threshold, "The Bishop" turned and said in the booming, dramatic voice of the Shakespearian actor that he was:

"Now, you ornery old bastards; you can all go to hell!"

CHAPTER THIRTEEN

Oil Wells and Bank Runs

IN THE SUMMER of 1910 the Jomar rolled into Ardmore, Oklahoma, with John and Mable Ringling aboard. It wasn't his first visit to the state—the circus had played Oklahoma Territory as early as 1898—but it was the first time he showed any particular interest in that area.

His recent success in Texas had given him a feeling of expansiveness, whetted his ambrosial appetite, and left him with a fancy for the land and whatever might be on or under it.

One of the first men he met in Ardmore was his friend, John F. Easley, publisher of the *Ardmoreite*, the town's leading newspaper. Ringling had met Easley earlier and was glad to see him again, not alone for the publicity the newspaperman would give the circus but for his knowledge of the country and business conditions.

Easley said he thought the circus would have a profitable stand and asked about friends on the show and its featured attractions, the kind of season it was having, and its Oklahoma tour.

Finally John began inquiring about a mineral called Grahamite, only recently discovered in the area. When or how the circus man had heard of Grahamite Easley did not know, but he soon realized that John Ringling was quite familiar with Oklahoma and its resources.

"Jake Hamon can tell you all about it," the editor said. "They say it shows some possibility as a building material—for roads, foundations, and walls. Some claim it can be used for making roofing and as a paint ingredient. Looks something like asphalt."

Easley told Ringling the man for him to see about building costs and labor conditions was Tide Cox, but if he wanted to know about the land he ought to talk to Jake Hamon.

Big Jake Hamon! What a working partner for John. Here was a man who had a flair for promotions and a thirst for money and power to match John Ringling's. He was a brisk, affable fellow who knew both law and the land; he had charge of most of the territory being opened for homesteading, and he had his finger in many pies—John Ringling's kind of a man.

Jake Hamon had come to Ardmore from Lawton a few years before and was just getting established when John dropped into his life. He gave the circus man a convincing sales talk about the area, its opportunities for profit, and painted a politician's gaudy picture of the state in the years to come.

John listened, nodding agreement and thinking right along with Jake, if not ahead of him. Jake offered to drive the circus man out to see the land, so he could view it firsthand, but John declined.

He was playing it cagey. He would be the rich man waiting to be taken, and he would plead not only lack of time but a sort of dumbness.

"I thought I might pick up some of this Grahamite," John said. "Anything to it?"

"Anything to it! Why, man, this is the biggest thing that ever hit the country," Jake shot back. "This'll dwarf anything that ever happened down in the Texas oil fields. We've really got something here.

"Tell you what—come up to my place tonight and I'll have all the information for you."

John paid a call at Easley's newspaper office before presenting himself at Jake Hamon's quarters in the Randol Hotel. The lawyer-promoter greeted him warmly and offered him a chair and then an after-dinner drink.

"This is Grahamite," Jake said, walking over to a table and picking up a lump of pitch-black mineral. "This is the thing that can make Oklahoma the richest state in the world. Not many people ever heard of it, but millions will."

John studied the lustrous, complex, bituminous substance for several minutes—looking, feeling and smelling it, blinking and hefting the hunk of matter like a man pondering a raw diamond.

John and Jake looked over some smaller samples of Grahamite, then moved over to face a map on the wall. John asked about land to the south, toward the Texas border. He thought he might link Ardmore with Dallas and Fort Worth by rail, and take an option on some land in between.

"You want to build more this way," Jake said, "west instead of south. In fact, I doubt if there's much Grahamite down that way. It's over this way, toward Lawton."

They studied the map, marked off in colors indicating what land had been claimed or sold and what was left. Jake traced roads and county lines, indicating streams and other landmarks.

John raised his cane and pointed, picking out a block

here and another there. Jake promised to help him build a railroad to the land, then on to Lawton and down to Wichita Falls. He said he could get the right-of-way and it would open up a lot of new territory.

With John's help, Jake dictated details of their plans to his pretty young secretary, Clara Hamon, a niece by marriage. He promised to see Tide Cox next day and get him to start work on the railroad immediately.

Tide Cox and his men pushed the railroad west from Ardmore as fast as possible, clearing and grading and filling; laying ties and swinging steel rails into place, tying them together for mile after mile. The railroad inched past the settlement of Lone Grove and as far as Healdton. There it stopped, for there was oil!

John and Jake, surprised and happy at the turn of fortune, found this more exciting than Grahamite or the circus at the moment, more profitable with less work and less chance to lose.

"By God, this is something," John exclaimed. "It'll match anything in Texas."

A few miles beyond Healdton, on land John had selected from the wall map with his cane, a gusher came in. Tide Cox and his workmen laid rails that far, but the railroad didn't get to Lawton, or even Waurika, for some time.

A settlement mushroomed at the end of the line—low, squatty clapboard houses among the pumps and derricks. People rushed in—rough, tough, and determined; some with sputtering, popping automobiles and trucks; some with tired mules and horses.

Soon there was a move to incorporate the community and establish some sort of law and order. Jake proposed it and the settlers were willing.

"Call it 'Ringling,' " Jake said, "after my good friend. After all, he's the man that built it. Might even get him to dedicate it. Have a picnic and invite him to come down and speak at the dedication."

John turned down the invitation, pleading the press of other business. Actually, he never relished such public appearances and spurned the idea of making a speech in front of a lot of workingmen and their families who had assembled to eat and enjoy themselves.

John sent as his emissary Charlie Wilson, head of transportation for the Ringlings. Charlie made a short speech and the dedication went off as planned. Thus was born the town of Ringling, Oklahoma.

Another oil well came into production a few miles up the road, a community sprouted around it and they named it Wilson, in honor of Charlie.

In those days railroads had a standing rule that an official of one line could ride free on any other. John was president of the new line from Ardmore to Ringling and thus he could go anywhere in the country aboard his Jomar, simply by having the private car hitched onto a train going his way.

This arrangement saved him many thousands of dollars in travel bills, at the same time providing rapid and comfortable transportation and adding to his prestige. When a man arrived in a town aboard his private railroad car, window shades drawn and gleaming brass rails enclosing the observation platform, he was truly a king.

John helped build and became an official in several other railroads, among them the St. Louis & Hannibal, White Sulphur Springs and Yellowstone Park, St. Louis & Troy, and Eastland, Wichita Falls and Gulf.

"I ought to get the oil royalties off your land," Jake

Hamon said jokingly to John one night. "After all, you bought Grahamite."

"It's not what I bought but what I got," John replied.

They sometimes wondered which might have been the more valuable, oil or Grahamite, but they never found out. The automobile became popular and the demand for oil and gasoline grew at an amazing rate. Grahamite was forgotten.

Jake did all right for himself without help from John, for he sold land, collected lawyer's fees, and dabbled in Republican politics. He became quite wealthy and his friendship for Ringling ripened with the passing months. Occasionally Jake was called to Washington on party business, and he even met John in New York once.

Clara Hamon had her heart set on one of these trips and thought until the very last minute that Jake would take her. Finally, Jake had to tell her that his wife was going along instead. A violent quarrel followed, climaxed by pistol shots.

Jake staggered out of the Randol Hotel, clutching his belly and streaming blood across the lobby floor. He collapsed in a taxicab after gasping out the address of a private sanitarium. Before he died there two days later, Jake told authorities the wound had been accidently self-inflicted.

His story didn't stand up in the light of official investigation, however, and Clara Hamon was brought to trial for murder. She testified she shot Jake when he swung at her with a chair.

"He wronged me and made me his slave," she told the jury, and it brought in a verdict of acquittal.

With his usual luck, John Ringling had missed that shooting, too.

While he was busy scouring the country for the best stands, meeting people and embracing opportunities for profit, his brothers were engrossed in making their outdoor amusement enterprises the biggest and best in the land.

Al continued to devote his full energies and talents to the Ringling show as equestrian director and general boss. He was an active, vital force on the lot and was familiar with every phase of the operation. Al knew all the performers and one of the first questions he asked any new employee was "What's your name, your first name?"

When storms came up, Al donned sou'wester and hip boots and pitched in with workingmen and performers to get the show out of the mud and keep it going.

"The circus is getting too big," he sometimes lamented. "I used to know everybody, but now, look at 'em. It's getting entirely too big."

Al wanted it kept down to three rings and two stages, but the brothers refused to go along, so the show went on with three rings and four stages, all presenting the best acts and attractions the Ringlings could find in this country and abroad. One of their features was fifty flyers in the ring at the same time, a spectacle never seen before or since on any circus in America.

Alf T. planned the great displays in every detail, even to costuming, lighting, and the music, which he wrote himself. One of the Ringling classics was "The Field of the Cloth of Gold," with a cast of 1,200.

When the Ringlings acquired the Barnum & Bailey show, Otto went there and for the rest of his life he gave his whole attention to building that circus, putting it on its feet and making it as big and profitable as it had been in the Barnum and Bailey heydays.

Otto looked at everyone with a critical eye and practiced the most rigid business and personal economy. He watched every facet of the complex operation, frowned upon the slightest display of extravagance or waste, and was always ready to save a dime if it could be done.

Charles, the friendly, even-tempered brother who always kept his word, stayed with the Ringling show after the Barnum & Bailey deal and kept the big family of nearly a thousand employees of many tongues and tastes happy and contented. He traveled with the show wherever it went, aboard his private railroad car, and was always concerned with the welfare of the backyard.

Al and Louise built a magnificent red stone mansion that became one of the showplaces of Baraboo when it opened in 1906. Alf T. and Charles had less pretentious homes but these, too, were quite large and in keeping with their social and financial status.

The Ringlings had always been well and favorably known in their hometown, and ever since the early days of the circus the names Ringling and Baraboo were synonymous.

George Merton was president of the Bank of Baraboo when a run was started on it. He got off a telegram to the Ringlings and, when the run was at its peak with angry depositors swarming up to tellers' windows demanding their money, Charles Ringling walked in with a handbag full of cash.

He elbowed his way through the crowd and quietly handed the satchel over to Jake Van Orden, the head teller. Van Orden opened it and began counting the bills slowly, in plain view of everybody.

The crowd watched in silence a moment, then began to whisper. Soon depositors stopped withdrawing their accounts and some even attempted to put the money back in.

But bank officials refused to accept deposits, claiming they had to get the books back in order and count the cash on hand, including the bundles of money Charles Ringling had put at their disposal.

Thus many depositors had to sit up all night and guard their cash with shotguns, until the bank opened next day and resumed normal operation.

The Ringlings and Van Orden were good friends and he handled most of their financial affairs. The brothers often sent money to him to be invested in city, county, state, and railroad bonds, or to be put in the bank.

When the brothers came home at the season's end, Van Orden would stack all the bonds in a suitcase and take them to Al Ringling's house. There the oldest brother, seated at the head of the table, would pass them out as though he were dealing cards in a poker game.

CHAPTER FOURTEEN

One by One, the Giants Fall

AUGUST RUNGELING, WHO had toiled with his hands for so many years in harness shops and carriage factories to feed and clothe his family, never quite comprehended their achievements.

But he was happy in their prosperity, as shown in a family photograph made in 1895. August now had snow-white hair, a bushy, graying beard and sparkly brown eyes. Across his vest stretched a massive watch chain with solid-gold links, a gift from the boys.

The picture showed all the brothers with round, full faces, high foreheads and canopy-type mustaches, sporting batwing collars and big cravats—images of affluence. Ida was in the picture, too, wearing a full skirt, fitted waist with shirred front and buttoned collar, in the style of the day for young ladies.

August Rüngeling now could bask in the sunlight of his sons' accomplishments, but he was not long to enjoy the luxury that had come from what he once called their "stupid undertaking." He passed away in 1898.

The first of the brothers to die was August, in 1907 at the age of fifty-three. Gus was never an active partner in the circus nor was he an important factor in its operation. He did quit his job in Minneapolis in 1889 to take charge of one of the advertising cars, and gave long and faithful service as an employee.

The family always had Christmas dinner at Mama Rüngeling's house in Baraboo but in 1906 this festive occasion was postponed because John was in Europe. Mama Rüngeling was ailing and she wondered if she would ever see her son again.

John and Mable Ringling finally came home to Baraboo and at last all the sons and their wives and Ida and her husband were gathered around the big dining table loaded with good things to eat. Mama Rüngeling sat at the head of the table, beaming her happiness. This was worth waiting for.

"Here are all my boys," she said. "I never was happier in my life."

Then she died January 12, 1907.

First of the five brothers who founded the circus to pass away was Otto. The "Little King" died in John's Fifth Avenue apartment in New York City on March 31, 1911, just when the circus was ready to open another season.

Otto left his share of the property to Al and Henry. The latter, who had joined as a ticket taker, was an elephantine man with massive shoulders, a round, full face, and bushy mustache. He managed some of the properties for his brothers and was a capable circus man, but he never was an owner until he came into the legacy from Otto.

Following the death of the "Little King," the brothers discontinued use of their famous trademark—mustachioed faces of the five slanted across programs and posters. It was not seen again until the circus celebrated its golden anniversary in 1933.

They also discontinued the Forepaugh-Sells Circus at the end of the 1911 season and concentrated on the big ones, Ringling Bros. and Barnum and Bailey.

Al Ringling built a fine theater in Baraboo which, according to members of the family, he planned to leave to his hometown when he died. But when his will was read, it was found to contain no such provision. Control remained in the family.

Al, one of the most respected and popular members of the circus fraternity and active on the show until the very end, died on January 1, 1916. During his last years Al had to give up his duties as ringmaster because of his health but running the big circus bearing his name was part of his life and he stuck with it to the very end.

He left his share of the circus to the four remaining brothers—Alf T., Charles, John, and Henry. To his widow he bequeathed life occupancy of their home in Baraboo; furnishings, personal property, automobile, and other items. Lou was to have the use of the home until her remarriage or death, after which it was to go to their only sister, Ida North, or to her heirs.

Louise Ringling soon found the cost of maintaining the big house prohibitive, so she moved out. Ida North and her family, which included her husband Henry W. North and their three children, moved in and made it their home for many years.

Finally, in 1935, the Al Ringling home was sold to the Baraboo Elks Lodge for $8,250, to be used as a clubhouse.

Louise Ringling, who made investments and prospered in Iowa, returned to Baraboo in 1933 for the circus reunion and was given a hearty welcome. She was approaching eighty years of age at the time but was still active, took a prominent part in the program, and said afterward she "thoroughly enjoyed every minute of it."

Meanwhile, by purchase and inheritance, the four remaining Ringling brothers controlled the major portion of America's outdoor entertainment business. They had attained great wealth and had kept the nation's two biggest circuses going through good seasons and bad.

But the circus had lost two of its most vital parts—Otto the treasurer and Al the leader. Also, World War I had broken out in Europe and all circuses faced serious problems.

Many leading performers had come from central Europe and the general public showed some reaction. But the Europeans who did not go home to fight gave their adopted land loyal support and many took up arms in the cause.

The supply of European acts dwindled after 1914 and when the United States declared war on Germany in April, 1917, it dried up because all countries on the continent were involved.

At that time the Ringling Bros. Circus alone had more than 1,000 personnel, 335 horses, 26 elephants, 16 camels, and an enormous collection of other animals, birds, and mammals, and traveled aboard ninety-two railroad cars. The Barnum & Bailey Circus was approximately the same size.

Transportation difficulties and wartime shortages seriously hampered them, but they continued to tour the country, promoting Liberty Bond drives and enlistment campaigns, entertaining soldiers and war workers, and sending many able-bodied men from their own ranks into service.

Adding to their troubles, an influenza epidemic swept the country, killing thousands of all ages and bedding down millions more.

Charles Ringling now was convinced that the time had come to combine, something his brother John had advocated for years. When Henry Ringling died unexpectedly in 1918 at the age of fifty and Alf T.'s health began to fail, the brothers agreed they must consolidate.

Henry Ringling left a son, Henry, Jr., who managed the Al Ringling Theater in Baraboo for a number of years but had no part in the circus operation. Young Henry was a giant of a man, too, and was active in Republican politics in Wisconsin until his death in 1956.

Meanwhile, the Forepaugh-Sells properties had been incorporated into the Ringling show after the Sells headquarters in Columbus, Ohio, closed in 1910 and the show made its last tour in 1911.

For years the Ringlings had protested high taxes in their hometown and had threatened many times to pull out. But the war actually provided the excuse they needed to leave Baraboo.

So, when their Ringling Bros. World's Greatest Shows and Spectacle ended its 1918 tour at Waycross, Georgia, on October 8, it headed north to Bridgeport, Connecticut, instead of going home to Baraboo as it had done every season since 1884.

The Barnum & Bailey Greatest Show on Earth closed its season, also on October 8, in Houston, Texas, and went home to Bridgeport.

There the two properties were merged into one mammoth organization that included more than fifteen hundred men and women in personnel, herds of show horses, work stock, animals, chariots, cages and wagons; lines, stakes and seats; scores of trucks, acres of canvas and nearly two hundred railroad cars.

The following spring it appeared as Ringling Bros. and Barnum & Bailey Combined Circus, "The Greatest Show on Earth," owned and operated solely by the Ringling brothers.

It opened the season in New York's Madison Square Garden on March 29, 1919, and played there four weeks, through April 26. Then it moved to Brooklyn for five days before going on to Philadelphia.

After playing the East, it went as far west as Denver, then headed south through Oklahoma, Texas, Louisiana, Arkansas, Tennessee, North Carolina, Virginia, South Carolina, Georgia, Alabama, Florida, then back to Savannah, Georgia, to end the tour on November 21.

Alf T. Ringling had long entertained the thought that all circuses would travel in motor trucks—as they were to do forty years after his time—and he spent a fortune on such an outfit for his only son, Richard T. Ringling. It turned out to be quite a lesson in financing for the father.

Alf T. named his son's circus the R. T. Richards "Supreme Show of the World," and put in Art Eldredge as manager. Richard, twenty-one-years old at the time, not only had something to keep him occupied but he could test his father's theory of traveling overland by automobile and truck.

None of the brothers gave Alf T. financial assistance nor did he ask it, and the R. T. Richards Circus was his alone. Young Richard was not a circus man and his show came up with some weird experiences, even for an outdoor amusement enterprise.

Once it engaged a desirable lot, went there and set

up for business along the highway just outside Marlboro, Massachusetts. The location was ideal but the show was advertised for another spot ten or fifteen miles away, and not a single paying customer came to see the circus that day.

The R. T. Richards Circus managed to struggle through two seasons, 1917 and 1918, but they were disastrous and it faded from the scene.

Alf T. maintained a country estate at Oak Ridge, in northeast New Jersey, and he died there on October 31, 1919, aged fifty-six. His one-third interest in the circus went to his son.

Dick Ringling's appetite for the circus had been thoroughly satisfied by his own show and he took no active part in Ringling Bros. and Barnum & Bailey. Instead, he had a fling at promoting indoor entertainment but this, too, proved unprofitable and he moved to the family ranch in Montana where he managed rodeos and other such attractions until his untimely death in an automobile crash, August 31, 1931.

Success of the Ringling Bros. circus inspired others to go into the business, including their cousins, the Gollmars—Charlie, Ben, Walter, and Fred. A fifth, Jacob, started with them in 1891 but he died the following year.

The Gollmars bought Ringling wagon equipment when the big show went on rails and started out with a dozen wheeled vehicles, a sixty-foot round top, two thirty-foot middle pieces and a "menagerie" that included a few monkeys, a black bear and a leopard.

They advertised as "Gollmar Brothers, Greatest of American Shows," beneath walrus-mustached portraits of themselves. It grew into a railroad show and operated until 1916, when it was sold to Jim Patterson, a carnival man from Paola, Kansas.

Henry C. and Corwin G. Moeller, also cousins of the Ringlings, operated the Moeller Carriage and Wagon Works in Baraboo for many years and these gifted craftsmen became famous for their circus wagons, built to withstand hard wear.

Most of the Ringling vehicles came from this shop and one of the most famous was a gigantic thing called the "Bell Wagon," now in the Ringling Circus Museum at Sarasota, Florida.

Henry Moeller, Jr., perhaps feeling the Ringling influence, went on the road as a bandsman with the Gollmar show in its 1891 season but returned to his father's wagon factory.

CHAPTER FIFTEEN

And Then There Were Two

AFTER ALF T.'s death, a substantial portion of the Ringling Circus empire passed from the founders to their wives and children, but actual management was in the hands of the two surviving brothers, Charles and John.

The combined circus had booming business in the postwar years and in 1920 it boasted ninety-two railroad cars. The brothers aimed for the century mark and made it in 1922, when the show traveled coast to coast and twice into Canada aboard one hundred double-length steel cars—the largest circus ever on rails in America.

Charles was in command on the lot and John went ahead as usual, supervising routing, meeting old friends and making new acquaintances; dabbling in numerous promotions. Charles was the heart of the operation, but it was John who represented and personified the circus.

What a study in contrasts they were! Two brothers near the same age who had grown up together but now were as different as a Shetland pony and a Thoroughbred.

Everyone on the lot called one "Mr. Charlie," and the name fit like the well-tailored suits he wore. A stocky, mild man, he was friendly and would take the trouble to get out of his limousine for a chat with the filling-station operator or mechanic; he was never too busy to exchange a few words with anyone.

"Mr. Charlie" was tenderhearted, understanding, and unusually generous with those on the show. He was extremely popular with most of those in personnel and enjoyed the respect of his employees.

He had one whim he practiced as long as he lived, and the circus folk indulged it. He liked music and once a season he appeared under the Big Top, horn under his arm, to tell Merle Evans, the bandleader, he was ready for his number.

After the solo, rendered with soft accompaniment from the fifty-piece band, "Mr. Charlie" would take a bow, tuck the horn under his arm and walk briskly away.

He did not wish to be called "Mr. Ringling" and bawled out those on the show who sometimes forgot and addressed him that way. It was like mistaking him for John, or comparing him with his younger and more flamboyant brother. There was never a basis for comparison.

Charles was sarcastic and touchy on occasion. He always wanted to be considered an important person rather than merely a likeable one, but somehow he couldn't quite escape the shadow of his larger, more impressive and conniving brother. He secretly admired John's method of operation and his accomplishments, and sometimes tried to imitate him in a timid sort of way.

When John was on the lot, Charles was content to play the role of milder brother and remain "Mr. Charlie." But when John took his leave, the older member would attempt to mount the pedestal of importance and sound off to his subordinates in what could only be a weak imitation of John.

"Then," said one who knew both men very well and worked for them for many years, "he'd play the part of 'Mr. Big' and toss bouquets to his flatterers."

There were times when Charles made decisions, only to have them reversed by the one he sarcastically referred to as "My big brother." This happened to both circus executives and leading performers, but Charles always tried to make amends.

It caused a sharp division in personnel, especially among those who applauded John's boldness and daring, his skill and imagination as a promoter and strategist. For there were many on the circus who had genuine admiration for "Mr. Ringling" because of his achievements and his very way of life.

Charles lived with and for the circus; it was part of his very existence. He stood by his promises and often complimented an executive or a performer for a job well done. It gave him satisfaction to be part of the great family for he had known the circus and grown with it.

John was seldom there. He was on the road, a hundred or five hundred miles away, in New York, Florida, Europe, or half a dozen other places. If he came on the lot he usually stopped at the main entrance, proudly showing leading citizens some of the outstanding attractions, or conferring with executives.

He might even stay for the performance, whining his criticism of this or that act or attraction, then make a quick call at the red (ticket) wagon, pick up some kush and be gone.

More often he was in the city, staying at the leading

hotel, mingling with friends in high places, consuming fine food, seeing a play or the prizefights, or working on a business proposition.

Since the early days, circus life had had no appeal for him; he was a front man all the way, who liked luxury and high living. Perhaps it was more than mere coincidence that he did not show up for business conferences until the fag end of the day. By that time most men had done a day's work and were tired, thinking of getting home to wives and children.

Not John. He had no children and his wife waited patiently at the hotel or aboard the Jomar, or was occupied with club meetings or other social interests.

John commenced his day in late afternoon, fresh and ready to match wits with the shrewdest traders. To him life was a game and he was the quarterback.

He'd had astounding good fortune in cities and towns across the land but Florida was to be the scene of his most spectacular promotions. His operations there proved even more exciting than those in other states and became monuments to his foresight and courage.

He first learned about Florida soon after the turn of the century through two other circus men—Charles H. Thompson and W. H. English. At one time Thompson managed the Forepaugh-Sells Circus and in 1895 he bought 154 acres of land on Sarasota Bay, on the Florida Gulf Coast fifty miles south of Tampa, for $1,650.

The next year he built a winter home on the property and sold a lot to English, who was advance agent for the Wallace shows. Later English built a home on his land.

Ralph C. Caples, general agent for the New York Central Railroad, bought the English home in 1909 after spending several winters in the fishing village of Sarasota, about a mile to the south. In 1911 he bought the Thompson place, together with considerable land in the area. Caples, who had been connected with several other railroads before taking the New York Central job, began to preach the gospel of Sarasota to John.

At the time "Mr. Ringling" was reaping big profits from his circuses, oil wells, and other interests and was busy at every stop on the line, but he managed to go and have a look. He routed the Forepaugh-Sells "Enormous United Shows" as far south as Tampa in the fall of 1911 and continued on to Sarasota.

John spent five days in the area, visiting Caples and, as was his custom, talking with all the leading men in the area, asking questions about such things as land, timber, climate, and taxes.

By the time he met the circus in Tampa on October 23 he was familiar with most of southwest Florida and had promised Caples he would be back that winter.

Soon after the New Year, John and Mable went to Florida from New York and spent a few days with Caples and others. At the time Sarasota was shivering in one of the coldest spells in years.

"You ought to buy yourself a home down here, Mr. Ringling," Caples suggested. "Then we'd be neighbors. This place is going to go places."

"If it's going to be this cold, I might as well hole up in Baraboo," John retorted.

"This won't last but a day or two," Caples assured him. "You know, land is mighty cheap now but every time somebody buys a lot, the price jumps."

John rattled the ice in his drink, thought a moment, and said:

"Tell you what, Ralph; if you'll sell me the Thompson place cheap, just like it stands, I'll buy it tonight."

"Mr. Ringling, you've bought yourself a home," Caples replied.

Next day they drove to the county seat at Bradenton and recorded the transaction, January 31, 1912. Most of the land Caples had bought from Thompson was included in the sale. It turned out to be one of the most stimulating moves in John Ringling's life.

He and Mable moved into the Thompson house and soon Charles, his wife and their two children came down. John bought more land and Charles invested. Caples remodeled the English house and John did the same to the Thompson house.

The town had a total population of 840 in 1910, but two years later it had grown to 1,276. By the time school opened in September, 1913, there were 353 pupils to enroll.

The Ringlings were enchanted with the area, bought more land and improved their property. Even Alf T. became interested in Florida.

It was his idea to establish a wildlife preserve, where animals from all over the world would be allowed to roam the swamps, providing an attraction for tourists and replacements for the circus menagerie. The land he bought was in west Florida, between Crestview and Milton. The settlement was called Floridale, but the project never got off the ground.

Henry Ringling also lived in the state for a short while, at a town called Eustis, in central Florida.

But it was John and Charles who fell in love with the state and helped it grow and prosper. They built hotels, developed property, and took an active interest in business and civic matters. Their activities rivaled and at times eclipsed those of busy land promoters and their very presence provided a tonic and inspiration to others.

Charles built a large pink tile and stucco house for his wife Edith and their children, Robert and Hester. It had teakwood and mahogany floors and paneling and was hidden from the road by bearded oaks, pines, palms, and tropical shrubbery.

John built a seawall for half a mile along the bay to protect his property and took over the Sarasota Yacht and Automobile Club holdings.

Charles played the violin very well and often entertained friends. John liked music, too, but the old French horn of trouping days had been forgotten. Now he attended concerts and the opera, and often went to New York to see glittering stage productions put on by his friend, Florenz Ziegfeld.

One night during a poker game in Montgomery, Alabama, John bought a block of land in what was to become the southern part of Sarasota County but was then a part of Manatee County.

Before going to bed, he telephoned Charles and insisted that they go in together on the deal and split the cost. Charles sleepily argued that he wasn't even at the poker game and knew nothing of the land, but John persisted and had his way.

A short time later John was in Sarasota and went to see his good friend, Arthur B. Edwards, a native and the town's first mayor.

"I've got 66,000 acres of land down there around the Myakka River," John said. "Bought it off a senator up in Alabama."

"That's fine, Mr. Ringling," Edwards replied. "I hope you didn't pay too much for it."

"Oh, I didn't pay much. How much you think it's worth, A. B.?"

"I'd say a dollar seventy-five, maybe two dollars an acre. If you paid more than that you got stuck. Mind telling me what you had to give for it, Mr. Ringling?"

"Two and a quarter."

"You did? Why, I had that land listed for a long time. I could have got it for you for a dollar seventy-five."

"You could?" John whined. "By God, A. B.; I've been clipped sure as hell. I thought I was getting a bargain, but he hooked me good and proper."

CHAPTER SIXTEEN

Florida Goes Boom, Boom!

IN SARASOTA JOHN RINGLING met a man who was a promoter and developer much like himself, with energy, imagination, and money. Balding, dynamic Owen Burns had reaped a fortune selling metal savings banks in the Midwest and discovered Sarasota about the time John became interested in the area.

Owen Burns and his wife Vernona soon occupied a prominent place in the community. He became a year-round resident, organized and was first president of the Citizens Bank, joined the golf club, was active in civic and fraternal circles, and turned into an enthusiastic yachtman, fisherman, and hunter.

Owen Burns and John Ringling liked each other from the first and were often seen together, exploring the bays and islands in the area and hatching plans for developments.

One afternoon they left the Burns launch at the bay side of St. Armand's Key and walked north to the point of the island. To their left lay the beach, a two-mile strip of powdery white sand sparkling in the semi-tropic sunlight.

To the east and north lay Sarasota Bay, an enchanting expanse of water half a mile wide in places and stretching a dozen miles up the coast, hemmed in by a great jade necklace of mangroves, palm trees, and bearded oaks.

Within a hundred yards of the spot where they stood was Longboat Key, and it stretched north to form the outer rim of the bay. Off to the west lay the Gulf of Mexico, shimmering in the descending sun like a vast prairie of gold, creamy waves rolling in like strips of old lace.

"This is one of the most beautiful bays in the world," Burns said, waving his hand to indicate the stretch of greenish-blue water.

John nodded, gnawed at his cigar and spat onto the sand.

"I agree with you a hundred percent, Burns," he said. "Reminds me a lot of the Mediterranean, only it's a damn sight better looking."

"With a causeway to the mainland, this would be one of the best residential sections in the state—ideal for waterfront homes," Burns went on. "All it needs is some streets and sewers, plus advertising. The causeway ought to run from Cedar Point, over where you see that clump of trees, to about here.

"Then a driveway ought to run over the hump of the key and out down there. The county might even build a bridge over to Longboat Key and get the state to run it up to Anna Maria Key and on into Bradenton. That'd give us a loop road, with a drive along the Gulf."

"By God, you're right, Burns," John agreed. "I can see the whole thing now. After we get to Anna Maria, build a bridge over to St. Petersburg; develop this whole area."

"And you could put a hotel over there, on the end of Longboat. It'd be ideal, with plenty of fine beaches."

"That's a hell of a dandy idea, Burns," John approved. "I can see all sorts of possibilities. Think you could get it for me at a decent price?"

"For practically nothing," Burns assured him. "It'll be so cheap you'll think you stole it."

"It's got to be reasonable, Burns. If I could get it at the right price. . . ."

Through Burns, John acquired St. Armand's Key and several acres on the south end of Longboat Key. He bought an old boat, the *Lotus,* that plied between Boca Grande and Useppa Island to use for hauling workmen and building materials to the island. He bought a dredge and put it to work beside one owned by Burns, called the *Sand Pecker.*

In the midst of his island fling, John bought Bird Key, a spit of sand and coral rock occupied for the most part by what the natives called "The Worcester House" and its grounds. This had been built by Thomas W. Worcester, of Cincinnati, and was the most imposing structure on any island in the area. Completed about 1914, it was painted a gleaming white and named "Ned Edzell Castle," after the ancestral home of Mrs. Worcester in Scotland.

John's good friend Ralph Caples had charge of Warren G. Harding's campaign train during his race for the presidency in 1920 and the circus man conceived the idea of a winter White House.

John had never been close to the scholarly Woodrow Wilson, although Charles Ringling once invited him to ride an elephant and Wilson was said to be agreeable, but his aides almost had apoplexy. Wilson did attend the circus several times, and thoroughly enjoyed it.

Now Harding was in the White House and John had

known him ever since he was United States Senator from Ohio and published a newspaper at Marion. John was certain that his acquaintance with Harding, and his friendship with some members of his cabinet, would pay off if he played it smart, as he told close friends.

His plans took shape in the winter of 1922-23 when Harding went to Miami Beach aboard the houseboat, *Pioneer*. Waiting there to greet the President were Attorney General Harry M. Daugherty, recuperating from a recent illness; David Mulvane of Kansas, Republican National Committeeman; Joseph Keating, of Indiana, and others.

John dropped in at the cottage occupied by Harding and his wife on the Flamingo Hotel grounds and invited them to be his guests. Harding said he couldn't make it this trip but hoped to do so at a later date. He said he wanted to see if what Daugherty said about Sarasota was true.

In late April, when the circus was concluding its month-long stand in Madison Square Garden, John went to Washington where he met his old friend, William J. Burns, the detective who had recently been appointed chief of the Division of Investigation, later to become the Federal Bureau of Investigation.

Billy Burns was, by his own opinion, the greatest detective this country ever produced. John thought so, too. Burns set up the national fingerprint identification system and was responsible for some other innovations in the struggling young department.

They were an odd pair, Burns and Ringling. Burns was small, neat, nervous and explosive; he was known all over the world as one of the most persistent and capable detectives of his time. Ringling was handsome and impressive, making money faster than ever and enjoying the limelight as "Mr. Ringling," the circus man.

Burns had never been close to Harding but the little sleuth played it smart by staying on the good side of Daugherty. The latter had visited Sarasota as Ringling's guest and was favorable to the Harding trip. Ringling knew this, and when he and Burns had set the stage, they called on the President, with Daugherty.

Harding was pleased to accept the specially-printed passes to the circus that was due in Washington two weeks later.

"I'd like for you to see the West Coast of Florida next time you're down there," John said. "I've got a nice layout where you could rest and do a little fishing and relax—away from all that Miami hullabaloo."

Harding looked at Burns, who nodded agreement, while Daugherty said he thought it was "a splendid idea."

"All right, gentlemen," Harding said. "I'll plan on it next winter. Better not say anything about it now or the Democrats will have something else to holler about. I'm going up to Alaska in July, you know, but the press doesn't even know about that yet.

"Sorry I can't get out to your circus this time, Mr. Ringling. I suppose it's the best you ever had."

"It certainly is, Mr. President." John beamed. "A great show. I wish you could see at least one performance."

That summer John Ringling followed his usual custom of traveling all over the country, occasionally dropping in on the circus. He told Owen Burns to get the place ready on Bird Key as they planned. Ralph Caples, of course, knew of the presidential plans.

"I want everything in shape," John said. "It'll mean a hell of a lot to have him down there and I don't want any slipups. I'll get some silver and art from Europe and we'll do the thing up right. By God, not every man can entertain the President of the United States."

In Europe he bought a Pierce-Arrow automobile, said to have been built especially for the late Czar of Russia. It had the driver's seat out front and the passenger compartment, richly finished in velvet and hand-tooled leather, was enclosed in thick, bullet-proof glass.

When it reached Sarasota by rail, it was put in the Ringling garage to await the arrival of Harding. John himself rode in his Rolls-Royce.

He bought a yacht, named the *Zalophus*, meaning "sea lion," which was a houseboat type craft 125 feet long with twin diesel engines and a high-speed cruiser called *Zalophus II*. As yet there was no causeway to Bird Key and the President and his party would have to be brought over to the island by boat.

"I want everything just right," Ringling insisted. "There'll be some writers and I want them to get a good impression. We'll give 'em the works. This'll be the biggest thing that ever hit this town. Ought to make the natives' eyes pop—and raise the price of land 50 percent."

"I wouldn't be surprised," Burns said.

But Harding never made the trip. He went to Alaska in July and was on his way back to Washington when he died in the Palace Hotel in San Francisco on August 2, 1923.

Thus ended John Ringling's dream of entertaining the President in Florida. For once, Luck had looked the other way.

The circus man estimated it had cost him fifty thousand dollars but that was a good round figure in the days when fifty or a hundred thousand was par for the course.

After Harding's death, the widowed Ida Ringling North and her three children—John, Henry, and Salome —set up winter residence in the Worcester House.

It was a happy household, where Mother North liked to help with preparation of the food. Dinner was served very late and everyone sat around telling stories until the wee hours.

CHAPTER SEVENTEEN

Every Man a Millionaire

THE REAL-ESTATE fever that had started in Miami in the early 1920's spread like an epidemic into every city, town, and village of the peninsula, in those days facetiously referred to as "Uncle Sam's Chin Whiskers."

It even extended into the Panhandle, or northwest Florida, and brushed Pensacola, but the real boom was a thunderous commotion that stretched from St. Augustine diagonally across the state to Tampa and St. Petersburg, and into the Keys, emanating from Miami like the rays of the rising sun.

The theme song, shouted from every stone, brick, wood, and canvas real-estate office within the state and beyond conveyed the idea:

"Find a buyer, get a binder; everybody's coming here.

"You can sell your lot tomorrow, and become a millionaire!"

The thrill, the excitement, the mad scramble of a million men and women trying to get rich quick, off land alone, sent prices sky-rocketing. Phenomenal profits were reported—even heralded in the newspapers, whose presses were busy around the clock grinding out fat special editions that ran to five hundred pages and more for a single issue, profusely illustrated and packed with pages and whole sections of gaudy advertising.

Lumber, cement, nails, wire, glass—all building materials were scarce and the price went up. A man could work as many hours as he could stay on his feet, and when he finished one job, another was waiting. Wages hit the ceiling, along with rents, groceries, and everything else. Nobody argued over price; credit was universal.

Cities and towns boasted that their populations had doubled or tripled between seasons, or would next year. Every village, and even developments far out in the woods, organized chambers of commerce and crowed about "unlimited opportunities for all."

Catchy slogans were everywhere and the mails were flooded with color postcards, booklets, and brochures; the nation's leading artists and writers prepared thick, leather-bound volumes, profusely illustrated.

Thousands of people poured in by train, automobile, bus, airplane and seagoing yacht, seeking riches. Knickered, white-shirted and straw-hatted promoters were everywhere. Dealers in such staples as clothing, furniture, and groceries quit their stores, filled briefcases or back pockets with maps and brochures, and started selling land.

In courthouses and in upstairs rooms along many a main street clerks worked far into the night preparing abstracts and deeds, but many couldn't wait for them— it might take three to six months. Anyone knew he could sell any piece of property for twice the asking price between morning and night, or at least by tomorrow; make a thousand or ten thousand dollars on a single deal!

Countless thousands swarmed to distant lot sites to buy raw patches of land covered with grass and sand-spurs. They'd have a chance to win a new automobile, sitting there gleaming in the sun, bogged to its running boards in sand or mud. And there would be free chicken dinners, served to the accompaniment of band or orchestra music.

Railroads crawled across the flatwoods and sawmills went into operation where half a century before only Seminole Indians and wildlife existed. Roads inched through the swamps and man conquered the Everglades, laying a strip of paving 144 miles from Fort Myers to Miami—the Tamiami Trail.

In Sarasota the boom became a John Ringling production and he led the grand march. He and his friends —Owen Burns, Ralph Caples, Sam Gumpertz, Joseph H. Lord, and Arthur B. Edwards—bought lots and acreage, and planned eye-popping projects.

Charles Ringling, also in love with the town, bought the old Gillespie golf course, dating back to 1886, and property adjacent. He opened a subdivision, paved streets, laid sidewalks and sewers, erected business buildings and a three-hundred-room hotel called the Sarasota Terrace.

Burns built a fine hotel and named it in honor of his wife, the El Vernona, a Spanish-style structure with tile on the roof.

Caples put up business buildings on Main Street; Edwards erected a magnificent theater, large enough to seat almost half the people in town, and called it the Edwards Theater.

Gumpertz built for himself a rambling, Spanish-type home; bought a big wooden hotel, cut it into five or six sections and floated them across the bay to Lido Beach, where they were put together again.

John Ringling and Gumpertz went into partnership to build a long wooden pier and a casino there.

The Burns and Ringling dredges dug a channel six feet deep across the shallow bay from the foot of Main Street to the open Gulf of Mexico, more than a mile away. Millions of yards of sand and mud were dug to fashion a harbor.

For months the town bragged about becoming a seaport, and one day a ship steamed down from Tampa amid tremendous fanfare. It brought in a few cartons of goods but there was nothing for it to take out and it never came back. They called it "The million dollar harbor party."

John invited Julius W. Boehler, whom he had met in New York some years before, to visit him in Sarasota. Boehler, a Swiss art dealer, brought along a mutual friend, Albert Keller, a New York hotel man.

They reached St. Armand's Key by boat, and John went into detail about his plans for developing that island.

"I want to put in a park here, with a bandstand and benches," he said. "I plan on cuttin' it up into lots and making a residential section—exclusive as hell, you see? What do you think of it?"

"I like it very much," Boehler answered. "Landscape it with some native palms and shrubbery, put in some fountains and arches, perhaps? You should have a double driveway, with the park in the center.

"The best way would be to go to Italy and Spain, where you can get good copies of old fountains and all kinds of decorative stone. I think it could be beautiful, like a plaza."

"I want you to go with me and help pick out what we'll need," John said. "I'm busy as hell right now, as you can see, but we'll go over in the fall."

They talked about a proposed hotel on Longboat Key, and John told Keller he'd pay five thousand a year for use of the name, Ritz-Carlton.

"It's got to sound big as hell and I think that's the ticket," John said. "We'll call it the 'Sarasota Ritz-Carlton' and get the New York crowd."

St. Armand's was one of John's favorite spots and he gave it the lion's share of his time and money. He wanted it to be the finest residential section in all Florida, for the yacht-owning segment.

Workmen laid miles of water and sewer mains, paved roads and streets, built parkways and poured concrete sidewalks, flanking them with royal palms and flowering shrubs. Streetlights were clusters of bulbs. Dredges cut a canal between St. Armand's and Lido keys, wide and deep enough to accommodate seagoing yachts twenty feet abeam.

A double driveway was spread across the hump of St. Armand's to form a park two hundred yards long by fifty wide, with walks, colored lights, stone cupids, and a cupola sitting atop the bandstand. There were rows of hedge plants, including poinsettias, hibiscus, and oleander interspersed with ixoria and flame vine. Orange, grapefruit, tangerine, and other tropical fruit trees were added to lend color and variety.

John brought in pieces of statuary from Italy and Spain—most of it pink and white marble—and set the figures along the walks and driveways.

The circus man and Sam Gumpertz met Boehler in Germany in September, 1925. John told friends he planned to book some new circus acts, but as usual he had other things in mind. He had been interested in art ever since his friendship with Stanford White; he had an inborn appreciation of fine paintings and cultivated the taste.

He studied architecture and art, becoming especially interested in that of the Renaissance period. He acquired, by gift and purchase, an extensive collection of books and catalogs on art, which he read with zest. By the end of World War I, John Ringling had become a connoisseur of art and owned a small collection.

In line with his other promotions, he made up his mind to go in for art and plunged with all his enthusiasm into rounding up the finest he could obtain, in both paintings and sculpture.

With hunger, uncertainty, and distress stalking through Europe in the postwar years, the German mark, Italian lira, and Austrian krone had depreciated in value and were worth very little compared with the American dollar. John realized that for an outlay of a million dollars he could buy art worth ten or twenty times that figure.

He led Boehler and Gumpertz to Venice, Rome, Naples, Florence, Madrid, Barcelona, and other cities of southern Europe where he bought tons of marble columns, polished stone, and terra cotta; hand-carved doorways and quantities of statuary. In Naples he bought half a dozen life-size figures and a copy of Michelangelo's statue of David, twenty feet high and cast in bronze.

On their last day in Naples, John astonished his traveling companions by announcing that he was going to build a museum in Florida. He said he and his wife wanted it to be the finest in the entire South.

Boehler, recalling the conversation years later, said he was thunderstruck, for it never occurred to him that John was buying with a museum in mind. He was even more astounded when John asked him to buy a couple of paintings for him, mentioning them by name rather casually.

"I couldn't possibly do that," Boehler protested. "You must first examine them, at least see photographs of them, Mr. Ringling."

"To hell with photographs," John retorted. "If you think they're good, I know they'll be all right. Buy both of them, and I'll meet you in New York. And, by the way, don't let on I'm buyin' for a museum. You and Gumpertz keep it under your hat until I'm ready."

John returned to New York late that fall, bringing with him contracts for some new circus acts and a Czecho-Slovakian band. The following February the causeway he had built across Sarasota Bay was finished. It connected St. Armand's and Lido with the mainland, and there was the Ringling Estates.

Crowds swarmed in by automobile, ferryboat, steam yacht, and canoe; some even arrived on foot, streaming over the causeway and bridge like pilgrims to Mecca, attracted by the name Ringling.

Here was activity on a mammoth scale, a whole residential island taking shape. Salesmen, natty in their freshly laundered knickers, aided by tipsters known as "bird dogs," herded prospective buyers into the park to listen to golden-voiced orators expound the gospel of Florida.

Waiters hurried among the crowd, bearing heaping trays of sandwiches, orange juice, coffee, candy, and cigars. Gleaming silver and glassware sparkled in the bright sunlight. The Czecho-Slovakian band played John's favorite selections, giving two concerts that day.

"Get a binder," salesmen advised. "A little down will hold any lot for you. By tomorrow all this may be gone. These lots can't last long, at this price."

Thousands bought, for a little down and a promise to pay, or simply said "put me down for two lots; I'll give you a check later."

When the day was done more than a million dollars' worth of lots had been sold on the sandy, shell-strewn island where not a single house had been built.

Over to the north, where Longboat Key ended in a wide, sandy beach, John's Sarasota Ritz-Carlton Hotel was taking shape. Beyond it a park had been laid out and a golf course was being built, by public subscription. To the north of it was Longboat Shores, where a thousand lots had been laid out, at two to ten thousand dollars each.

The Ritz-Carlton was the big attraction on Longboat. Foundations had been laid and massive concrete and steel pillars rose above the powdery white sand. Under John's constant prodding, the building went up rapidly that winter and spring.

Construction crawled past the first floor and the second; framework jutted into the sky like a giant centipede on its back. Window casings and door frames went in; tons of bronze and brass fittings, doorknobs and bathroom fixtures were brought to the site by barge to be dumped on the unfinished floors, piled in corners, or stacked outside.

There hadn't been timbers or time to bridge the channel between St. Armand's and Longboat, but work had started on that, too, and piling had been driven into the sandy bottom for forty yards or more.

"Push it," John commanded. "Keep things movin'. I want that hotel finished by October—Thanksgivin' at the latest. We'll count on opening then."

He turned to other matters—getting the circus ready for the road: mapping routes, conferring with his brother and top executives on the show; going to New York for the opening, then to Oklahoma, Texas, and Chicago, aboard the Jomar.

Then he hurried back to Florida, watching the real-estate boom like a ringmaster. This was a real, live, seething circus of humans and John had an intimate and vital part of it. He savored every moment.

He maintained an office upstairs over the Bank of Sarasota, in the peak end of a building that was squeezed between two streets at Five Points, in the heart of town. He became a director in the bank, and soon took over as president.

An officer in a New York City bank of which John also was a director came to town, ostensibly on vacation but actually, he confided, to check on John's financial condition. He made discreet inquiry about the circus man's cash.

"He keeps very little with us, and we were wondering," he said. "I was under the impression he kept it all down here."

He kept little money anywhere. He was always spending, expanding, promising; making deals as fantastic and exciting as any circus act he ever signed. Nobody knew when he might close a million-dollar deal, or play poker all night; when he'd show up for an appointment, or sail for Europe. John was an unpredictable man.

Even his brother couldn't keep up with him, though he gave it a gallant try. When John became a director in the bank, Charles opened one of his own, called the Ringling Trust and Savings Bank. Charles bought a yacht, larger than the *Zalophus,* a real seagoing vessel named the *Symphonic.* He also promoted real estate.

John's house was a gathering place for many whose names were known throughout the land, when he was at home. His guests included Will Rogers, Harry M. Daugherty, Mayor Jimmy Walker of New York, "Boss" Frank Hague of Jersey City, Florenz Ziegfeld, Tex Rickard, and such circus figures as Fred Bradna and Charlie Sparks.

Occasionally John would cruise with them up and down the bay or out into the Gulf, north toward Tampa or south to Fort Myers. If the trip ended at one of his island projects, the more agile members of the party would leap ashore and extend a helping hand to John, bulkier and slower than in his younger days. He would lumber up to the bow, in quick, short steps, cane tapping the deck or dangling from the crook of his arm.

"These old pins can still carry me," he would say, and break into a brittle, cackling laugh. Then he would extend his free hand with the command:

"All right, hands across the sea. Come on, everybody; hands across the sea!"

Friendly, helping hands would extend in a human chain while he made it ashore.

CHAPTER EIGHTEEN

The Party's Over

JOHN RINGLING WAS sixty now and passing years had commenced to pencil lines in his bronze face and sprinkle silver in his hair. His "old pins" were beginning to creak with gout and other ailments but his mind was still sharp. He continued to buy on a colossal scale, by the gross and the ton; planning, promoting, and projecting; spending as fast as he accumulated.

The real-estate boom was speeding toward its end. By the fall of 1926 land transactions in Sarasota had zoomed to a peak and were skidding toward the bottom. From a high of twelve million dollars a month they tumbled to six, four, two, and finally nothing.

The music had stopped, the party was over; it was time to clean up the debris. What a wild and wonderful party it had been, but now the cold, sobering light of dawn had come.

Within a few months this spectacle had grown into the biggest, most intoxicating real-estate boom the nation had ever known; the most buoyant, fascinating bubble in Florida history had burst. Nobody knew just when or how it happened for the end, like the beginning, was a gradual and indefinite thing.

The "binder boys" headed out, quietly and without fanfare. There were grumbling and some weeping be-

cause many had departed in the night, with promises un-
filled and bills left behind. But no one was to be chas-
tised, for no one dreamed the boom wouldn't last forever.

For the moment, nobody wanted real estate or could
afford it, and that had been the backbone of the boom.
You couldn't sell climate, or eat it. The whole populace
became discouraged, moaning their luck and their losses
in cries heard throughout the land.

During the height of the excitement, the town had
swollen to Greater Sarasota, surrounded by a county
bearing the name Sarasota, sliced from the southern end
of Manatee.

The county commission, school board, and drainage
districts, in the spirit of the times, floated bonds for
roads, bridges, canals, schools, streets, sidewalks, sewers,
lights, parks, and playgrounds, not to mention a court-
house, jail, and other facilities.

When the bubble burst the town and county lay blan-
keted with bonds—more than a thousand dollars worth
for every man, woman, and child, with nothing but
sand and sunshine as security, and the land was mulched
with mortgages.

John Ringling, able to keep going better than most
because the circus was still bringing in cash, hatched
new ideas. He told the mayor and town councilmen that
he had spent six hundred and fifty thousand dollars on
his Sarasota Ritz-Carlton Hotel alone and didn't intend
to put another dime into it or on St. Armand's Key as
long as the property stayed within the city limits.

"Ruinous taxes are killin' us," he moaned. "They've
choked off building and they're keeping people from
buyin' property anywhere in this part of the country."

City officials agreed and the citizenry as a whole applauded. "Let the big bondholders suffer; they can afford it," became the general attitude.

Council ordered an election and the area known as Greater Sarasota went out of existence by a margin of thirty votes to one. The town's land area shriveled overnight from sixty-nine square miles to seventeen.

John gave another dramatic performance. The causeway he had so hurriedly flung across the bay to St. Armand's Key was old and unsafe in spite of its few years of service. Engineers reported the pilings were weak and wobbly and the floorboards warped and rotten. They said the span must be repaired at once or closed.

John offered to turn it over to the city in exchange for his years of unpaid taxes, with the understanding that it would be put into first-class condition and kept that way. The city accepted.

The Sarasota Ritz-Carlton was still an unsightly skeleton and John wanted a hotel, so he acquired the El Vernona from Owen Burns.

It wasn't the biggest in town but it was gaudy, with polished terra cotta trimmings. The name was changed to the "John Ringling Hotel" and the new designation appeared on the silverware, dishes, linens, and books of matches.

It was whispered that John objected to this personal publicity but it wasn't true. He was determined to make the El Vernona better known than his brother Charlie's Sarasota Terrace.

In front of the El Vernona's terraced entrance he stationed a towering doorman—a giant from the circus who stood more than seven feet tall, decked out in glittering blue and gold uniform, with big brass buttons down the front of his cutaway coat, and wearing a shako that added at least eighteen inches to his already imposing stature.

Thus the brothers' rivalry continued on a friendly basis and provided a topic of lively conversation for the townsfolk until Charles fell ill at his home. He passed away on December 3, 1926, two weeks short of his sixty-third birthday.

John, weeping at the bedside, muttered, "I'm the only one left."

A throng of mourners bade Charles farewell when he was buried in Manasota Park, on the road to Bradenton.

More conservative than John, more democratic and far more human, Charles Ringling had been a powerful force behind Sarasota's growth and there was genuine sorrow when he died, especially among the big circus family.

Now John was ruler of the circus. He had lived to become, in reality, Mr. Ringling, the circus king—the only man left in the family to run the gigantic organization bearing his name.

Like many others, John had not received the cash he expected from his beach properties and other Florida projects. Many of the lots on St. Armand's Key that had been sold for promises came back, with clouded titles. Now everything lay still and deserted.

The Czecho-Slovakian band had quit playing in the park and grass grew there. Palm fronds became scraggly and died; each passing wind whipped them until they went crashing to the ground, to lie untouched or lean against rusting light standards whose bulbs had long since gone dark or been shattered by boys at play.

Sand drifted into channels now lined with unsightly weeds, and the opening mechanism on the drawbridge to Lido Beach had rusted away. It didn't matter, for all the yachts had gone to the north or to the bottom, or lay tied up in the mouth of sluggish Hog Creek on the mainland, rotting in the sun.

Flowers bloomed on among the tall grass and hedges, peeking out from behind shabby shrubbery that grew pale and spindly, like ragged, undernourished children.

The bridge that John had started across the channel to his hotel on Longboat Key hung at an awkward angle, half finished and slowly crumbling, its pilings standing in clear greenish water, gathering barnacles.

The hotel itself was naked and half completed, rough walls enclosing empty rooms. The skeletal framework had mellowed rapidly in the weather, cracking and gathering dust; a roosting place for bats and owls and a playground for sparrows.

A few adventurous souls picked their way across the island on Sundays and found excitement in exploring the ruins, tripping over the massive beams covered with rust, and climbing scaffolding thick with dust.

Others came by night or day to take brass and copper fittings, and haul away the stacks of sinks, bathtubs, faucets, doorknobs, and even locks and hinges to use in their own homes or to sell for scrap.

The grounds grew up in weeds and sandspurs, almost hidden by lush hibiscus and oleander bushes laced with briars. The tennis courts, laid out carefully but never used, were still outlined in greenery.

Stretching north from the hotel ruins, the once meticulously measured, planted, and tended golf course was isolated patches of green velvet among the palms and mangrove bushes. Cows wandered down from far up the island to graze there in solitude.

Through the long days and nights, Sarasota slept. John went to Europe.

CHAPTER NINETEEN

Here Come John and the Circus

ALL FLORIDA WENT into a paralyzing depression. Scores of banks closed, their vaults filled with worthless paper. Businesses by the hundreds and thousands went bankrupt, and people left the state in droves.

The hangover from the great party lingered and everywhere lay ghastly reminders of what a wonderfully intoxicating binge it had been.

Buildings started with tremendous fanfare stood like gaunt, bony skeletons or squat upon their foundations with not even crumbling walls to hide their nakedness.

Streets and sidewalks that rambled far out among the pines and palmettoes warped and cracked in the idleness. Weeds and sandspurs covered parkways and vacant lots while scraggly grass spewed up through cracks in the pavement.

The whole community lay gripped in lethargy and appeared ready to give up when, unannounced as usual, John Ringling rolled in aboard the Jomar.

The circus king was a big, inspiring man, with tremendous energy and fists full of luck. His very presence gave courage and confidence to others and when he returned from Europe in that dreary winter of 1927, the natives began to stir.

Soon there was speculation that John had great plans

for the area—that he would finish the Ritz-Carlton Hotel and turn it into a mecca for tourists; that he would build on the mainland and even spread his activities and influence into adjacent towns and counties.

Communities up and down the coast were saying, hopefully, that John was interested and would invest. He wasn't one to discourage optimism and while he seldom divulged his plans and often did not follow them, he would neither confirm nor deny the rumors and his silence gave them wings.

About this time a geologist named B. F. Alley was telling everybody he knew where oil could be found. He said he had positive knowledge of not one but four such locations! He claimed to be something of an expert, having learned the oil business while working for a young operator named Harry F. Sinclair.

Newspapers gave generous space to Alley and the oil, usually mentioning John Ringling as an interested party or urging him to take the lead in making Sarasota County an oil center. Editorial writers pulled out all stops.

Nobody knew if John Ringling inspired the oil talk, but it was intriguing speculation. The circus king was well acquainted with Sinclair, and owned a lot of land in the county. Conclusions were obvious.

Five hundred hopeful souls assembled for a mass meeting in the Mira Mar Auditorium to hear Alley describe the great new oil empire in the making. He told them what most had come to hear, and spoke convincingly.

"You people down here haven't seen anything yet," he was quoted in the Sarasota *Herald* next day. "Why, the real-estate boom was a mere shower compared with the cloudburst that will come with oil. And it is coming as sure as I'm standing here tonight. I know most of you will want to get in on the ground floor, and that's where you'll be.

"I know the oil business and I know there's oil in Florida. Before you realize what's going on, we'll bring it in. I can see it now—oil wells up and down the whole coast. It'll be the biggest thing that ever hit this state. It'll make Florida the richest state in the world!"

John didn't make a speech that night, but he was there and his very presence spurred speculation. Harry Sinclair wasn't in the state at the time but the very mention of his name and the hint that he was interested was added assurance that it couldn't miss. The picture was complete, and a very pretty picture it was.

With a fellow like John Ringling in front and an oil man like Sinclair behind it, how could it fail? Why, this would be the most stupendous development that Florida ever experienced—far more prosperous and permanent than any real-estate promotion.

Everyone who could scrape together a little cash joined in the new oil boom aborning, giving it all the support and enthusiasm of a county fair.

The Associated Gas & Oil Co. was organized and drilling operations commenced on John Ringling's acres in the southern end of the county, conveniently close to the highway that led to Punta Gorda and Fort Myers.

In the latter town Thomas A. Edison spent the winter and was visited by his close friend, Henry Ford. Together they roamed South Florida, looking for plants to produce rubber, and even paid a brief visit to the drill site.

With his usual boldness and flair for the dramatic, John arranged to "spud in" the first well. It was widely advertised in the newspapers and announcements were made over the radio. John aimed at boosting the natives' morale and proving to them that he hadn't given up on Florida.

Automobiles and buses streamed to the site thirty miles south of Sarasota. John was there, shuffling among the crowd, chewing his cigar and blinking in the bright sunlight, cane swinging on his arm and a straw skimmer atop his head.

Ringling had persuaded his very good friend, John J. McGraw, to bring the New York Giants baseball team to Sarasota for spring training. The circus man had even made arrangements for the team to be quartered at a boardinghouse where the woman who managed it thought a baseball team was made up of nine men.

Hurried accommodations had to be found for thirty athletes and a retinue of coaches and sports writers, among them Westbrook Pegler, Hype Igoe, and others of that era.

The Giants went to the spudding in, led by their captain, Rogers Hornsby, recently bought from the St. Louis Cardinals. McGraw was on hand, of course. He became so enamored of the Florida doings that he promoted a subdivision near town called "Pennant Park."

Hornsby smashed a bottle of champagne over the drilling rig while Ringling's Czecho-Slovakian band tootled lively tunes. More than five thousand persons were at the scene that day, according to newspaper reports, and there were cigars for the men and boxes of candy for the ladies.

Drilling operations lasted only a few weeks and nothing more valuable than dribbles of salt water came from the hole. Enthusiasm soon subsided and in no time at all the great oil boom expired with a feeble "poop."

Some fifteen years later oil was found in Florida, in the Everglades a hundred miles south of the Ringling project, and by 1966 production had become sufficient to justify a pipeline to Port Everglades.

John gave little thought to the oil well. He was busy conferring with executives in Bridgeport and New York City on advertising and routes for the new circus season and giving his other interests such attention as was necessary.

Meanwhile, he had built a radio station and opened a studio in the John Ringling Hotel. He liked to drop in there and listen to programs going out over the air waves. This new medium fascinated him and he soon cashed in on it, in a small way. He encouraged delegations from surrounding towns—chambers of commerce, clubs, lodges, and school groups—to appear for a fee and give out with vocal and instrumental music, interspersed with blurbs about the community.

Sometimes he would sit through an entire evening, chewing on his cigar and listening, blinking, and occasionally offering suggestions for improving the programs.

Or he would greet delegations in the lobby or in the hallway outside the studio, shake hands, appear deeply interested and ask questions about roads, crops and business conditions.

A few days before he was to leave for the North and another circus season, John was approached by a group of friends who presented a new and appealing proposition. For years Caples, Owen Burns, Edwards, and Gumpertz had urged the Ringlings to move their circus winter quarters to Sarasota. Now that Charles was gone, they concentrated on John.

Caples, Edwards, and A. E. Cummer had sold 160 acres of land to the county for fifty thousand dollars with no cash involved. They took a mortgage and helped promote some buildings for a county fair.

When the bubble burst the fair was discontinued and the land and buildings lay empty and deserted.

Gumpertz went before the county commissioners, with John's approval, and told the board the circus man might be interested. The next afternoon a committee called upon John in his office.

Caples was spokesman and he reminded Ringling that the circus could end the season in Jacksonville, Tampa, or Miami and move right into winter quarters rather than go all the way back to Connecticut.

"And think how much you'd save in hauling costs and fuel bills," Caples added.

"I know, Ralph," John agreed, "but you'd have to go North to open the season. A lot of towns want us but they don't have much to offer. You gentlemen know how I feel about Sarasota, but I've lost a hell of a lot of money down here and it would cost a pile to make the switch from Bridgeport. What sort of proposition do you have in mind?"

John knew about the county property but he was driving a hard bargain, as usual, and making the best deal he could.

They suggested several possibilities—the Ringling acres north of town, over on St. Armand's or Longboat, or in the southern end of the county.

"We can't put the circus out in the woods," John reminded them. "We've got to stay near the city, where

we can get supplies, and living quarters for the help.
We'll need a lot of things, you know."

John, actor that he was, milked the moment of all its
drama, looking from one to another of his visitors, im-
pressing upon them that moving the circus quarters
was a giant undertaking that would be a tremendous
thing for any city in the country.

"If you'll give me the old fairgrounds, I might consider it," he said at last. "That's petered out now and
you won't be using the property, the way things look.
There's some stuff out there we might be able to use,
but it'll take a lot of cash to fix it up."

That did it, and three days later the commission
agreed to give the fairgrounds to Ringling if he would
establish permanent circus winter quarters there. With
the property would go adjacent land being used for
the county mosquito control project and a nursery.

Caples, Edwards, and Cummer agreed to waive their
mortgage, with the stipulation that the circus would
maintain permanent headquarters on the property, and
advertise Sarasota.

"All right, gentlemen," said John Ringling. "You've
made a deal. I'll move the show down here this fall.
Ralph, you get after the Seaboard [railroad] to build a
spur track out there. I'll handle the Atlantic Coast
Line."

The circus was to publicize the city and county
through its programs and advertising, and this would
cancel out its taxes.

The next day, March 23, 1927, newspapers printed
the story under banner headlines: "Circus Moving to
Sarasota."

John Ringling marked the occasion with one of the

most sumptuous dinners the town ever saw. The finest and most exotic foods obtainable, including such delicacies as green turtle soup, pheasant under glass, and wild rice were served to sixty invited guests who sat down to feast at John's table and drink toasts to him and to the coming of the circus.

CHAPTER TWENTY

Peanuts, Politicians, and Prohibition

THE NEW WINTER quarters became one of John Ringling's pet projects and he gave it his usual enthusiasm,
personally supervising all the details of layout and construction.

He spent hours walking over every foot of the property with his longtime friend, Fred Bradna, equestrian
director, who had married pretty, petite Ella Bradna
and took her name when the couple signed with Barnum
& Bailey in London in 1902.

Fred and Ella remained with that show until the
merger in 1919, when he became equestrian director or
stage manager, responsible for keeping performers on
their toes and packing the program into a solid two hours
and twenty minutes, but no more.

They discussed car sheds, horse barns, and animal
dens; training pens, roads and walkways; even spots for
the cookhouse and first-aid room.

"A concession ought to be over here, near the elephant kraal," John said, "where a working man could
get a cup of coffee or a bottle of pop—don't you think,
Freddie?"

Bradna agreed, for he was Alsatian, too, and had
genuine admiration for the circus king.

"Use that house for a paint shack, and swing the railroad over this way, so the cars will be near the paint. Put the elephant house out beyond that clump of pines, well out back.

"We'll put the cats and monkeys in the big house; build cages along the side. We can store wagons there, too, and put tents and props on the second and third floor. Make a tent loft up top. This arrangement is ideal, don't you think, Freddie? Ought to draw a lot of tourists when rehearsals start."

When Bradna nodded agreement, John continued:

"I want to build an open-air arena exactly the size of the one we use in the Garden. We've got an ideal spot for rehearsals, out in the fresh air, and folks can watch the performers work—they'll think they're gettin' in on something special."

He smiled approval of the thought, nibbled at the end of a fresh cigar, and went on outlining his dreams and ambitions for the new and finer quarters.

"We ought to make money out of that concession stand, Freddie; carry a line of soda pop, picture postcards, pennants—that sort of thing. Stock up on peanuts, and let 'em buy them to feed the elephants. See what I mean? They'll get a big kick out of that, and we can buy peanuts cheap by the ton, right up here in North Florida."

"Mr. Ringling, you're a genius," Bradna said.

John was building his equestrian director up for a disagreeable task that must be done, and soon. It was time to spring it.

"Now, here's what I want you to do for me, Freddie," he said. "Go up to Bridgeport and break the news to everybody. A lot of 'em were born around there and the kids are in school; they ain't goin' to like this. It'll be a sort of ticklish proposition.

"You've got to get 'em excited over the new location; how much better it'll be for all concerned, and the possibilities down here. Make their mouths water to come to Florida; sell 'em on the idea, don't you see?"

Bradna went to Bridgeport with misgivings, to deliver John's message to the circus executives—Charlie Hutchinson, the treasurer; Carl Hathaway, his assistant; Fred de Wolf, accountant; John McLaughlin, head of transportation; Mickey Graves, property man; Tom Lynch, boss hostler; Mrs. Irving Nelson, wardrobe mistress; Dr. William Shields, circus doctor, and others.

John had stopped off in New York, to see some shows and get ready for the circus' opening in the Garden, leaving the distasteful task of breaking the news about leaving Bridgeport to poor Bradna.

Naturally, it was a shock to many to have to pull up their roots in Bridgeport and move 1,200 miles to a strange community most of them had never seen. But, accustomed to the hard facts of life as all circus folk must be, they took it in stride.

Instead of whining and crying, they looked forward to winter homes in the Florida sunshine, especially after the sales talk Fred Bradna gave them.

The only real sour note came from "Good Luck" Lombard, half owner of the Lombard & Hathaway Circus in the early 1920's, and proprietor of a saloon across the street from the Armory that catered to show people. "Good Luck" Lombard was still moaning the blues when the last circus car pulled out.

John Ringling returned to Sarasota earlier than usual that fall to get ready for winter quarters opening. It nettled him to see that work had not been completed, as expected, and he sputtered and swore at subordinates.

John was disappointed at the changes that had come over the townspeople. The oil fever had subsided almost as quickly as it had come; promises and prospects had vanished. Once the people had been busy and expectant but being caught in the collapse of real-estate and oil booms in the same decade had almost knocked them out. Even John's enthusiasm and his grandiose plans and promises could not change their outlook in general. They'd had it.

Nobody extended or expected credit any more, and the more cautious began to curtail dealings with "Mr. Ringling," and cut off his credit.

The day after he came home, the circus king rode down to the south end of the county to look at his oil operations. He was amazed to find the place deserted and growing up in weeds. There was no sign of oil.

The old wooden tower still stood, leaning against the semitropic sky; a rusting gasoline engine sat in a puddle of dirty oil and rainwater on a slab of concrete, and a few odd lengths of pipe were scattered about in the scrubby grass and sandspurs.

They drove to St. Armand's Key but the pink field office, set among the palms, was closed and deserted. It had been opened only occasionally since the boom collapsed, and not at all that summer.

"Wonder why they quit so early?" John whined. "They could be choppin' weeds and cuttin' the damn grass around here if they didn't have anything else to do. How can a man buy land over here, even if he wanted to, with nobody around? It's a terrible way to run a business."

EMMETT KELLY
The clown who later performed with the Brooklyn Dodgers baseball team

JOHN RINGLING NORTH
For many years he was head of the circus founded by his uncles

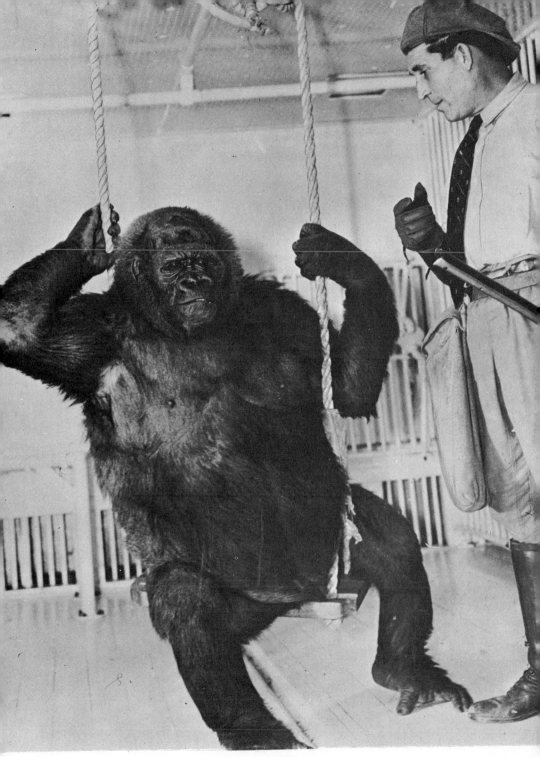

MRS. GARGANTUA

With her keeper, José Tomás. She came to this country as Mlle Toto

SCHOOLING HORSES

He grumbled on while the chauffeur drove to the north side of the island, facing Longboat Key. This was one of John's favorite spots and from his vantage point in the old Rolls-Royce he could look out across the channel to the skeleton of his Ritz-Carlton Hotel.

"By God, Al, I wonder if they'll ever get that thing finished," he said. "I'll make money with it if they ever do. Ought to fill it with tourists every night."

The circus ended its 1927 tour in Tampa on the third of November and soon after midnight the trains began rolling into Sarasota and on out to winter quarters. Townspeople were there in droves to welcome performers and workingmen, and offer their goods and services.

Quickly the canvas was spread out to dry, animals transferred from cages to pens in the big house, and the camels, giraffes, zebras and such moved into open pens. The herd of elephants lumbered one by one into a kraal, and the hundreds of horses were stabled out back.

Pens and cages were provided for the vast collection of monkeys, birds, and other animals which went to make up the biggest menagerie on the road.

Florida took the circus to its heart. Sarasota became "home" to trapeze artists and clowns, bareback riders and grinders, midgets, the fat girl, and the giant; strange people and skilled performers, executives and workingmen. The townspeople came to know them as neighbors and friends.

Because John Ringling was still circus king by reputation, he maintained his community standing as a man of vision and achievement despite some sour remembrances of his promises and promotions.

For John was an impressive and important man, a

most convincing fellow who had a dozen things going at once and was always planning more. Many still admired him for what he had attempted to do and looked upon him as the boss elephant of the herd.

The Florida boom had knocked out countless men of lesser boldness and daring; it had even dealt him some heavy blows but had not stopped him. He continued to carry on boldly, to plan bigger things, and he inspired others to have faith and hope.

He was willing to share his vast store of practical knowledge and those who took his advice usually found it helpful, for he was one who knew his fellow man's foibles and failings better than even his own.

John maintained a box at the American Legion Coliseum, where young huskies from the circus often appeared on the Monday night boxing programs. The circus man always attended when he was in the city and his box was a magnet for politicians, businessmen, and fighters, who always stopped for a word of greeting.

One of these was Carpet Murphy, who had the concession to sell soft drinks and peanuts and to rent seat cushions to the crowds.

"How are things goin', Murph?" John asked one night.

"Not so good, Mr. Ringling. It's too cold for cold drinks and these people ain't hungry; even the hot dog business is bad. I've rented a few cushions but the loss on them is terrific. I'll rent maybe a hundred and lose thirty. I can't figure it."

"I can," John shot back. "The stingy bastards take 'em home. Figure they've paid for 'em and sneak 'em out under their coats. I'll give you a little tip, Murph;

don't rent cushions when it's cold like tonight. The people have on coats and sweaters; that gives 'em a place to hide your seat cushions on the way out. Don't you see?"

John knew all the curves and corners on life's twisting highway.

During the protracted Democratic National Convention in New York City in 1924, John had several delegates as guests at his summer home near Alpine, New Jersey.

At other times he entertained politicians and business leaders, actors and writers, and a wide assortment of friends and acquaintances, overnight or for a weekend, in an atmosphere of gaiety.

Although the country was still in the throes of prohibition, that didn't hamper John to any great extent. He had friends, and connections. He converted a large barn on the premises into a barracks to house New Jersey state police and turned it over to them without charge.

In return, Boss Frank Hague and others saw to it that agents of the prohibition department never bellied up to John's bar or visited his well-stocked cellar—on official business, that is.

CHAPTER TWENTY-ONE

The House of John

JOHN RINGLING LIKED to entertain, and to be invited to his house was a rare treat. Among his guests was Will Rogers, the noted humorist whose witty comments on everything from the President and Congress to the local baseball team made him known throughout the world.

Will could hold an audience of a thousand spellbound in a steaming hot auditorium for an hour or more, and send every one away limp with laughter. His observations appeared in newspapers all over the country.

The night Will headlined the opening of the new Edwards Theater in Sarasota he was a guest in the Ringling home, but he had to hurry from the dinner table to keep his engagement downtown.

John and his other guests went in later and as they moved down the aisle, Will Rogers halted his gum-chewing, rope-spinning act until all were seated, then said:

"Well, I see the folks from the country just got in. What's the matter, Mr. Ringling; you late with the milking again?"

The audience howled with laughter.

At that time John Ringling was rated the tenth, eighteenth, or twentieth richest man in the world—depending upon who estimated his wealth. Some put his fortune at 180 million dollars.

John didn't know. He had few confidants and kept his own counsel. To him nobody could do a thing the way he wanted, and while he liked to delegate a task, he was never satisfied unless he was meddling in it.

Those who worked for him always knew that "Mr. Ringling" was boss—when he was at his office or on the lot.

After the circus went into winter quarters, the holidays passed and time came to plan for the next circus season, his favorite spot was the old Thompson house. Built of heart pine and cypress, with gingerbread above the doors and windows and a wide, rambling porch, it was comfortable and with every convenience of the era when houses were designed for full and gracious living.

It commanded an excellent view of Sarasota Bay and the islands beyond. Native pines and giant live oaks sheltered it and nearby was a fine stand of stately royal palms.

Mable liked the place, too, but as their fortune grew and social prominence demanded more of their time, she wanted a more pretentious winter home, to match their reputations as leading citizens.

Once during a visit in Madrid the Ringlings saw a place that caught their eye. It was "Ca d' Zan" and the phrase intrigued them, especially after the guide explained that it was the home of a famous clown who had shortened the words "casa" and "zany" to "Ca d' Zan."

Venice was one of Mable's favorite cities and she particularly liked the Doges' Palace, so she made up her mind to build a house like the famous Venetian landmark and call it "Ca d' Zan."

They discussed it while they traveled about Europe

in the winter of 1923 and the year following. John appeared only mildly interested while giving most of his attention to booking new circus acts and buying paintings.

Mable made drawings of what she wanted and when she showed her outlines to John, he made his usual comment.

"Holy Jesus!" he whimpered. "A thing like that'll cost an awful lot of dough. We don't need a big mansion, do we?"

"This is what I want," she replied. "We need a place where we can entertain friends; this will be it."

John never wished to deny Mable any pleasure she desired. It was second nature with him to gripe about the cost of anything, from a mansion to a month's supply of milk.

"All right; have it your way," he apologized. "If that's what you want, we'll build it."

Back in Sarasota, Mable went to see Thomas Reed Martin, who had designed many homes in the area, including one called "The Oaks" for Mrs. Potter Palmer, of Chicago.

In Martin's office, Mable opened a briefcase stuffed with sketches and photographs she had brought from Europe. She outlined what she had in mind, showing the material and then shoving it back into the briefcase and taking it home.

Each time she returned to Martin's studio, she brought the sketches and pictures, but guarded them carefully. Martin and his son, Frank, transferred her suggestions to drafting paper, bringing to life her plans for a Venetian palace on the Florida shore. When word reached John, he put on his usual pauper act.

"Why, I never heard of such a thing," he whined. "That's too damn much money. You're 'way too high, Mr. Martin. Get your figures in line, then let me know."

Months later the Ringlings commissioned Dwight James Baum, a New York architect, to modify Martin's plans and start construction.

Thus was created the Ringling mansion—a great mottled brown house two hundred feet long with a tower rising more than sixty feet above the ground, ending in a balcony overlooking the bay, the whole in complex Venetian Gothic style.

Along the landside of the seventeen-acre tract John built a great rosy cream stucco fence that hid the house from public view. There was an imposing gateway house of pink stucco and brown masonry, framed by glazed tile colonnettes. Above the entrance was an apartment for the caretaker. The words "Ca d' Zan" were etched in pillars beside the driveway, in Prussian blue.

A lane two hundred yards long, lined with flowering plants and interspersed with palms and pines, led to the house. Stone cupids aimed their arrows toward the mansion at the end of the road.

Approaching the house the driveway parted to form an oval filled with grass, manicured like a putting green and bisected by a broad walk of polished terra cotta, with a sundial and signs of the zodiac.

Off to the right was a swimming pool, sixty-five feet long by twenty-six wide, of white, red, blue, and brown tile that added a colorful motif.

There was a wading area at one end and at the other it dropped to nine feet deep beneath a diving platform made with Persian and Italian tiles. And there was a curving marble seat, in the center of which stood a copy of the Medici Venus.

Out among the live oaks and banyan trees were several stone lions brought from Europe. John liked to escort guests about the grounds—especially members of Mable's garden club—and bring them unsuspecting face to face with the lifelike beasts. The women would scream and run for shelter, or cling to John while he cackled with delight.

Word went around that the lions had been brought over from the circus quarters and turned loose for the entertainment of John and his friends, but this was another of the Ringling legends. John liked pets and often played with a monkey or a parrot perched on his shoulder, but he never chummed with a live lion.

Another rumor was that there were gold-plated chamber pots under the Ringling beds, but nobody reported seeing them and the servants wouldn't tell. Bathrooms were conveniently placed throughout the house, including a powder room for the ladies and a rest room for men on the ground floor.

The house was built largely of polychrome terra cotta, polished brick, veined marble, pecky cypress, and mahogany. Massive doors with handwrought hinges and great brass knobs led into the foyer and the cavernous main room called the "great hall." The reception room was on the right and the dining room on the left.

The main hall measured fifty by sixty-five feet, with an Aeolian organ at one end and a grand piano at the other. The organ pipes were hidden behind rich tapestries hung on balcony walls and the deep, heavy tones of the organ made the whole mansion ring.

The organ could be played manually or electrically,

and it was a source of considerable pleasure to music-loving John Ringling and his wife.

The hall was filled with inlaid tables, deep-cushioned chairs, thick velvet-like rugs, hand-hammered table and floor lamps, and rich Flemish tapestries dating from the seventeenth century. On either side of the marble fire-place was a painting by the Russian-American artist, Savley Sorine.

The life-size picture of John showed him in rich brown suit, tan shirt and shoes, and dark necktie. A big brown overcoat was flung over his arm. The smaller water color of Mable showed her in opera gown, with a lace mantilla over her shoulder.

Once Will Rogers was asked how he liked the painting of his friend, John.

"That's a mighty fine painting, Mr. Ringling, but it's not a bit like you; it's not characteristic."

"Why not?" John demanded.

"Because you've got your hand in your own pocket!"

The hall had a coffered ceiling of Florida pecky cypress framing inner skylights of colored glass. It extended the entire three stories and had a balcony with painted ceilings surrounding it on three sides at the second-floor level.

The ballroom was large enough to accommodate thirty couples. It also had coffered ceiling, painted by Willy Pogany to represent dancers of many nations. Adjoining the reception room was the solarium with lounging chairs, a hammock and enormous pillows in light tan with the letter "R" in gold.

The dining room was paneled in black walnut with inlaid ceiling. There was a painting by Paris Bordone and a glazed terra cotta tondo of the Virgin adoring the child, by Andrea della Robbia. Cabinets along the walls held rows of exquisite china and silverware. In the center was a mahogany table large enough for thirty diners.

The breakfast room, with floor of black and white checked marble, was furnished in dark walnut and had a green crystal chandelier. There was a Luca Giordano painting over the open fireplace. A dozen persons could eat here at a sitting.

There were roomy pantries and a kitchen with huge ranges, refrigerators, sinks, and cupboards. Over the kitchen wing were an apartment and rooms for servants.

The bar lounge was just off the main dining room and was complete with mahogany rail and brass foot rest from a famous old drinking place in St. Louis. It was stocked with domestic and imported spirits and mixings to suit every palate. Over the leaded mirror behind the bar was a set of Texas steer horns six feet across, a gift from Amon G. Carter, the Fort Worth newspaper publisher.

The bar was lined with glasses of all shapes and sizes, cigarettes and big, black cigars imported from Havana, with John's name embossed on the wrappers.

A winding marble stairway led around the automatic elevator from the foyer to the upper floors and the tower. John's office was an alcove off the bedroom and it was furnished with a flat-top desk, two chairs and a bookcase. He kept a Manhattan telephone book and a railroad guide on hand, and referred to them often.

Adjoining the office was the master bedroom, thirty-five by fifty feet. It had two double beds with mammoth head- and footboards of hand-carved mahogany, and a chaise lounge. A thick, red carpet was on the floor and rich, heavy drapes shut out most of the light from French windows facing the east.

There was a large dresser and a mahogany chest with drawers six feet wide and deep in proportion, where his shirts and underthings could be laid out flat without creasing. His closet was stocked with suits, straw and felt hats, overcoats and shoes.

"Mr. John" slept here, on one of the king-size beds beneath a painting of Napoleon's first wife, the bosomy Josephine.

A dozen walking sticks rested in a stand near the door. Ironwood was his favorite—light and strong—and he seldom was seen in public without a cane. In the early days it lent dignity and distinction but in the final years he needed it for support.

John had a barber chair that could be wheeled into his room and tilted beside his bed, but it usually stayed in the bathroom, which was a dozen feet square with walls veneered in yellow sienna marble and a burnt sienna marble tub large enough for a hippopotamus, cut from a solid block of stone and equipped with gold-plated faucets.

On occasion John liked to shave himself with straight razors kept in a tiny drawer on a heavy, three-legged stand. He'd picked up this bit of furniture in France and it was one of his favorites, with three double-sided mirrors that would swing into any position and stay there. It also had a marble shelf waist high and drawers for shaving equipment.

Mable's bedroom was only a few steps down the hall, finished in soft blue and gray, with thick drapes that swished down to the polished floor. It had a double bed, several chairs, and a dresser of inlaid sandalwood.

Mable made her bedspreads and pillow tops out of fine linens and laces collected in her travels. She liked to do needlework and had ample time for it while waiting for John.

Mable's bathroom and dressing room adjoining had full-length mirrors, delicately tinted wall decorations, and a large marble-topped chest filled with monogrammed towels and linens, initialed blankets and a wide variety of toilet articles.

The house had several guest rooms and baths but no showers, and at the end of the balcony overlooking the great hall from the third floor was a playroom with ceiling by Willy Pogany. It depicted a gay dancing party, with John and Mable entering the room, wearing Spanish costumes, as if they'd just come from the Pageant of Sara de Sota, an annual celebration they sponsored for several years.

From the third floor terra cotta stairs led to the tower, a modification of the room atop old Madison Square Garden, surmounted by an open kiosk. When the Ringlings were in residence, a light shone from this tower and could be seen for miles.

In the basement was an auxiliary power plant, storage space, and a mammoth icebox to hold John's favorite brand of beer, brought from Bremen. John and his cronies liked to slip into the basement at night, drink a few beers, and admire the large painting of a recumbent nude which he kept concealed behind a square of canvas.

There were two formal gardens, one with shrubs and flowering plants and the other a rose garden. This was Mable's pet, and it contained a circular temple surrounded by a wrought iron latticed dome.

And so this was "Ca d' Zan"—House of John. Some said it cost one million dollars to build and another to furnish. Others estimated it at two and one-half million. All were pure guesses.

John himself didn't know. He had bought tons of polychrome terra cotta and carrara marble, stacks of polished brick and miles of iron grillwork; quantities of statuary, hand-carved walnut and mahogany furniture; inlaid tables, rich tapesteries, cut glass, china, and silver. In Barcelona, where rows of houses were being wrecked in a street-widening project, John bought carloads of red barrel tile.

He was certain Ca d' Zan was as big and ornate as anything in Florida outside Henry M. Flagler's Whitehall at Palm Beach, including James Deering's Vizcaya at Miami, and it was.

CHAPTER TWENTY-TWO

Art and Circus Animals

CA D' ZAN was nearing completion when John undertook another and even more spectacular project. He and Sam W. Gumpertz conferred at the Ritz-Carlton Hotel in New York City on plans for the new circus season and naturally their discussion got around to business conditions in Florida.

Sam, who was well acquainted with the state after several years residence there, reported that Sarasota was having a disappointing tourist season and needed a lift. Ringling was the man who could give it.

"Now's the time to spring the museum," he told Gumpertz. "Go down there and tell 'em I'm going to build the finest art museum in the South. That ought to show 'em we mean business. I intend to put in a college, too, to teach art and things like that. You know what I've got in mind, Sam. Go down there and give 'em a bellyful!"

Sam went to Sarasota and told a hastily called meeting of the merchants association:

"I'm here to announce that John Ringling is going to build a great museum and educational center in Sarasota. This will be the largest and finest in the country devoted entirely to paintings, statuary, and the study of art.

"I don't need to tell you John Ringling has a natural gift for art appreciation and owns some of the finest paintings in the world. An art museum has been in his mind for years and it will be a tremendous asset to Sarasota and an appropriate and lasting memorial to John and Mable Ringling."

This was exciting news although it came from a bronzed little showman with a high-pitched voice, myopic eyes, and jug-handle ears, and it was all the more thrilling because it was the first time Gumpertz had spoken for Ringling in Sarasota.

At the time, John and Mable were in New York City to attend the theater and opera. They also discussed available paintings with Julius Boehler and looked around for a qualified architect.

They decided on John Hyde Phillips, who helped design the Metropolitan Museum of Art. Phillips met the Ringlings later in Sarasota and they walked over the spot John had chosen—twelve acres lying south of Ca d' Zan. It was an ideal location between the highway and the bay, dotted with pines, palmettoes, and wiry native grasses.

"Have it face the road so people can get in and out," John suggested, waving his cane. "But you'll have to leave the west end open so they'll get a good look at the bay. We'll want a big archway in front and a fence along that side, to match the one around the house."

John thought eighteen or twenty rooms would be sufficient, and said he had enough art and sculpture to fill them, or knew where he could get it.

"Florentine design, built around a courtyard like Mr. Boehler suggested, terraced toward the bay," Phillips offered. "Is that what you had in mind?"

"Exactly; leave that end open, with a walk connecting the two wings. We can put David's statue on that end."

Phillips noted trees and soil, distances and directions, lights and shadows. He looked over some of the paintings and observed the mounds of polished terra cotta, marble statuary, and building stone on the premises.

John never knew how much material he had piled out among the oaks and palmettoes but he often had the chauffeur drive past the spot so he could see that it was all still there. "Mr. John" was like that.

The museum was chartered by the state of Florida as a nonprofit institution on August 7, 1927, with John Ringling as president and treasurer; Mable as vice-president and secretary, and William J. Burns, Richard Fuchs, and J. M. Wadsworth, other incorporators.

That winter John found time to fiddle with the circus program and make his usual suggestions for acts and attractions, but most of his energy was spent on the museum and supervising finishing the home.

Back in New York, he bought some interesting canvases, among them works of Titian and Tintoretto. He attended several house sales and bid in cut glass, china, and paneling from old Fifth Avenue mansions being razed.

He attended the circus opening in Madison Square Garden, then sailed for Europe. Boehler met him in Hamburg and they toured northern Germany, visiting practically all the art galleries and museums of note.

In Berlin John bought Granacci's "Cardinal Albrecht

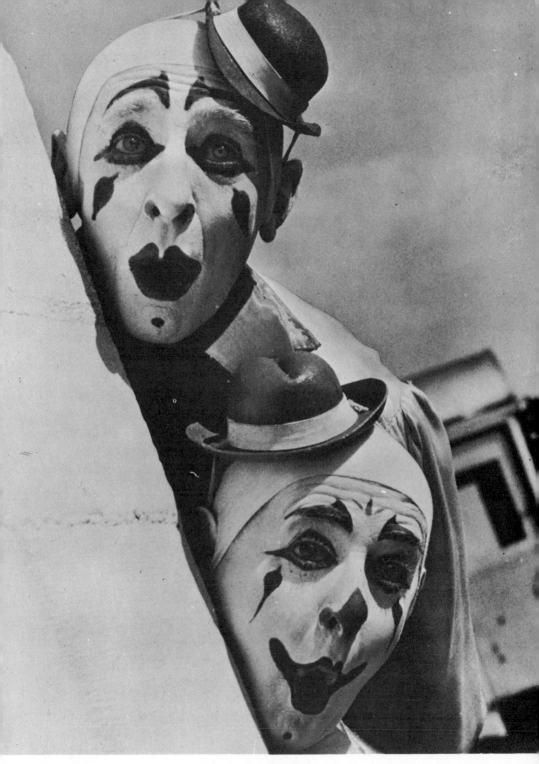

A PAIR OF CLOWNS

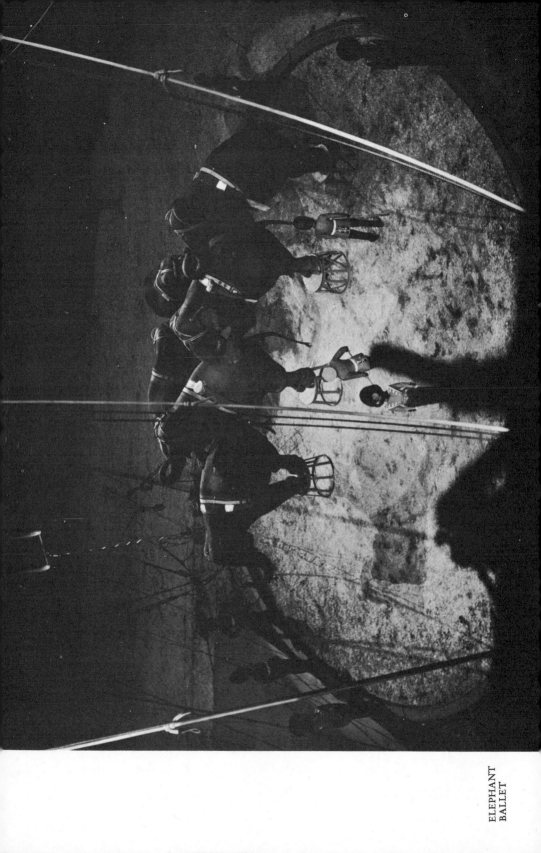

ELEPHANT
BALLET

GOING UP!

HIGH ABOVE THE CROWD

St. Jerome." He also acquired three portraits of An-
toine Pesne from the Imperial family—"Philippine Car-
lottee, Princess of Prussia," "Sophia Dorothea, Princess
of Great Britain," and "Portrait of a Queen."

He heard the Duke of Westminster was trying to sell
his four Rubens but they were so large no one wanted
them. John became enthusiastic and insisted that Boehler buy them at once, or at least go to London and see
what the Duke wanted for them.

Boehler reported that the price was five thousand
pounds apiece—slightly less than one hundred thousand
dollars for the four. He advised John not to buy, but
the circus king wouldn't hear of it.

A day or two later, at John's insistence, they went to
Grosvenor House where they inspected the paintings.
John was ready to close the deal immediately.

"Look here," he told Boehler in his soft, persuasive
voice. "We want those pictures; they're just what I
want for the museum."

"No, you don't want them, they're too large," Boehler protested. "That Rubens must be twelve feet high."

"Hell, yes; I want them," John insisted. "I've got no
use for midgets—they belong in the sideshow. Paintings ought to be big enough to be seen from the back
of the room. Everybody can't get up close, you know.

"These four Rubens will add a lot to the museum.
There's nothing in the United States to compare with
them. I'll have a bigger room built; they'll look wonderful in our museum, and create a lot of good comment.

"Go ahead and talk to the Duke's solicitors. Make 'em
an offer. Get hold of the old boy himself; tell him we
might be able to use his four pictures, but hold him to

twenty thousand pounds, no more. They're worth all of that, don't you think?"

Boehler agreed, and so John Ringling became owner of the Rubens "Abraham and Melchizedak," "The Four Evangelists," "The Fathers of the Church," and "Israelites Gathering Manna in the Desert."

He arranged to buy Murillo's "Immaculate Conception" and several other good works. He never tired of visiting dealers' offices and showrooms and talking about art. He learned all he could about a picture and knew what he was buying.

In the city of Genoa he bought Rubens' "Portrait of a Monk," and Fra Bartolommeo's "The Holy Family and the Infant St. John."

Back in New York he attended the Huntington and Astor sales where he bought several paintings. At the Stillman sale he got the Coypel "Portrait of Madame de Bourbon Conti," and Rembrandt's "St. John the Evangelist." That one cost him eighty thousand dollars and was probably the most valuable single painting he owned.

The John and Mable Ringling School of Art and Junior College opened on October 1, 1931, in what had been an apartment house and a commercial building about a mile from the museum. Students from all parts of the country enrolled.

That same afternoon some 350 leading citizens assembled in the museum's courtyard for formal dedication of the John and Mable Ringling Museum of Art.

"I hope this museum and the art school will promote education and art appreciation, especially among our young people," John said in one of his rare public speeches. "It is my earnest hope and desire that these works of art may be a lasting inspiration to all the people of Florida and to our visitors, and that they may come and enjoy them.

"And it is my wish that the young people of America come here to study and gain knowledge and benefit from the masters represented in this museum.

"I want to keep the museum open to all the people, for their enjoyment. I want it to be open one day a week free of charge, so all may come in. I want them to see the treasures we have here."

Senator Duncan U. Fletcher, a ruddy-faced, white-mustachioed old man who had represented Florida in Washington for many years, was principal speaker. He paid tribute to the circus king and called the museum "the finest south of Washington and in many respects the best in the entire world."

John then announced that he would give the museum with its priceless collection, and the art school, to Southern College, a struggling Methodist institution located some sixty miles away, in Lakeland. It was the plan, John said, for the museum and school to become the art branch of the college.

The Board of Deacons, through its chairman J. Edgar Wall, of Tampa, expressed deep gratitude and each of the eighteen members pressed forward to shake John Ringling's hand and thank him for his generosity.

Wall told the crowd that the college would be "highly honored and pleased to accept Mr. Ringling's great and generous gift."

Then the crowd trooped over to the Ringling home next door where refreshments were served, and those who wished were taken on a tour of the house and grounds.

Some said the museum building alone cost two million dollars but this was only a good guess. Nothing of the total cost was ever made public and most of the records were lost or destroyed. John once said he figured he spent more than eleven million dollars for art, and well he might.

The museum had thirty-two rooms built around a courtyard a hundred and fifty by three hundred and fifty feet. At the end of this terraced and landscaped courtyard stood the statue of David, a copy of the original by Michelangelo. It overlooked a pool where Australian black swans floated lazily among the lily pads.

The building itself had vast corridors supported by Italian marble pillars and the roof was of pink tile, surmounted by ninety-six life-size statues brought from Europe. There were hundreds of antique marble statues, arches, and doorways, and in one part of the building was the Asolo Theater.

From the outset, some did not like the idea of giving the museum to anyone but the city of Sarasota, and especially to a college in a rival community. Others strongly opposed using circus money to assist a Christian school, saying it was "tainted."

"Sure is," others chided them. "You just think 'tain't enough!"

The Florida Legislature had only recently passed a bill permitting pari-mutuel wagering with local approval, provided each of the state's sixty-seven counties shared equally in the revenue, to go toward education and projects in the public interest.

The law was passed over the governor's veto, and some religious groups vigorously opposed using racetrack money for schools. In some instances foes of circus money for a religious school and gambling cash for public education joined hands.

Members of the Board of Deacons were well aware of the grumblings but preferred to ignore them, which they did for several months, until it was mouthed about that live models were being used in the art classes. That blew the lid off the pot.

"Some of us wanted to keep the museum and give the art school back to Mr. Ringling," the chairman explained later, "but we couldn't do that. The two of them went together.

"Public attitude changed rapidly after that, especially when World War II came along, but in those days we wouldn't dare let 'nekkid' women run around in the school, art or no art. So we gave the whole thing back to Mr. Ringling."

The John and Mable Ringling School of Art and Junior College became a private institution, with enrollment limited to 250 students. The art museum reverted to John, who permitted the school free use of its facilities.

Ugly rumors circulated about John and his museum, even that he went there after dark to raid the till. These stories were far off base. Actually, John seldom got around to visit until after dark, what with all his other projects demanding his attention.

It cost only thirty cents to get in and less than fifty thousand people came to the museum in all of 1935. At the same time there were such expenses as the superintendent's salary, plus maintenance and repair. John spent money on his museum rather than made it.

He was disappointed when more residents and visitors did not come to see his paintings, even on Mondays when admission was free. It was a matter of deep disappointment to him that the general public showed so little art appreciation.

He planned to leave the museum to the state of Florida when he died, or to the city of Sarasota, but until that time he was forced to maintain it with cash from his own pocket.

And so it galled him when visitors who linked the name "Ringling" only with the circus wandered through the great rooms and corridors, surrounded by priceless works of art, and inquired in all sincerity and seriousness, "Where are the animals?"

"By God, you must be gettin' a lot of ignorant folks in here," he said to the superintendent one night. "Imagine expectin' to find circus animals in an art museum, just because it bears the name 'Ringling.'"

CHAPTER TWENTY-THREE

Ringling and Rickard

DURING THE 1920's, when all America was wallowing in the postwar boom, John Ringling was making money faster than he could keep track of it. In New York he was frequently seen in the company of his longtime friend, George L. (Tex) Rickard, who through John got a toehold in Madison Square Garden as a promoter.

John had a personal interest because he liked prize-fights and wanted to keep competing circuses out. And so Tex, with John as his sponsor and financier, took a lease on the Garden and promoted his first fight there on September 17, 1920, between Johnny Dundee and Joe Welling.

He followed that with a bout between Jack Dempsey and K. O. (Bill) Brennan that drew 16,000 and a $208,000 house. Rickard was on his way and his promotional genius reached a pinnacle at three o'clock on the afternoon of July 2, 1921, when, in a giant wooden saucer known as Boyle's Thirty Acres near Jersey City, Jack Dempsey fought a French dandy named Georges Carpentier.

John Ringling was at ringside, of course, along with 77,327 others, including most of the biggest figures in politics, commerce, the theater, motion pictures, sports, and other lines of human activity. They had gathered from everywhere, aboard private yacht and railroad car, chauffeured limousines, streetcars, taxicabs and every other available means of transportation.

The press section was jammed with more than seven hundred working newsmen and the fight brought in more than a million and a half dollars—the first such "gate" in fistic history.

The Garden made money, too, for Rickard and his backers, on boxing and wrestling matches, six-day bicycle races, basketball, hockey, the circus, and even Sunday-night dances.

While all this was going on, Rickard was riding in a chauffeured limousine, as were most of his friends. All of them were stunned when he was indicted for rape. Rickard promptly turned over control of the Garden to John Ringling, who already had more fish on the string than he could handle.

A jury cleared Rickard and John insisted that he take over the Garden promotions at once. Rickard was in no hurry, and insisted on first taking a short vacation trip with his wife. After a few days in Bermuda, Rickard resumed management of the Garden without any interruption in the flow of profits.

Rickard and Ringling talked about building a new Madison Square Garden, on Eighth Avenue between Forty-ninth and Fiftieth streets, to cost around $5,650,-000. When someone asked Rickard how he would finance the project, he answered: "My six hundred millionaires will help me."

The new Garden opened in late November, 1925, and made money from the start. Rickard was president of the corporation and Ringling was chairman of the board—two master promoters in a single enterprise in free-spending days when money was plentiful and people wanted to play.

It seemed, however, that the more money Ringling made the more he would haggle over inconsequentials and pinch pennies, especially around the circus operation.

For longer than the oldest trouper could recall, it had been customary for the circus to contract performers and department staffs in August for the following season. This made everybody happy and let them know where they stood. It helped create a smoother, more efficient and more satisfactory operation all around.

To the end of Mr. Charlie's days the Ringlings kept this arrangement, and everybody was satisfied. Often what other circuses did depended upon the Ringlings. John had repeatedly argued against such an arrangement and suggested that they delay contracts until late in the fall or even after Christmas, but his brothers voted him down.

After Charles died, John announced that there would be no more contract signing in August—it would be done after the circus finished the tour and went into winter quarters.

"Then we can tell just what the season amounted to," he said, "and know just where we stand. We can make contracts accordingly, and save money. From now on, we'll wait 'til after Christmas to sign 'em up."

Circus executives were strongly opposed, pointing out that waiting to make plans for the following season was unwise for many reasons. Many performers had winter engagements, too, but still they needed to know what their prospects were in the spring.

Experienced staff men pleaded that they must know

before time for the show to go out just what was
planned, and insisted it would be difficult to lay out programs and provide all the art necessary if plans were not
made long in advance for the following season.

"Hell, there might not be a next season," John snorted,
knowing full well there'd always be a circus; at least as
long as he lived. "The way things are goin', there might
not be. There's no tellin' what will happen. The country's in one hell of a fix right now. We'll just have to
wait and see."

Thus every department of the great and complex old
circus became disturbed, with employees and performers living day to day in an atmosphere of uncertainty
and suspense. Rumors added to the general confusion.

Executives did all the maneuvering they could and
made promises much more liberal than John would
have approved to keep their staffs intact. Usually, by
the time he got around to signing contracts and approving agreements, other circuses were completing
their programs, having their printing done, and were
almost ready for the road.

The mere fact that John Ringling had the biggest
and best circus in the country was often the principal
reason he was able to keep experienced executives and
the world's best performers.

Most of them stuck because they were real troupers
and liked the prestige of working for the "big one,"
even though smaller outfits might offer them a better
deal.

Thus John Ringling, giant operator and manipulator
that he was, caused more unrest and dissatisfaction
among circus folk than any other man of his time.
Through his procrastination he created confusion and

ill will among some of his oldest and most valuable employees.

He liked to cut corners wherever possible and nothing
escaped his critical eye. Many times he devoted attention to inconsequential things that shouldn't have
drawn even a second glance, while ignoring essentials;
grasping at picayunish items and finding fault in his
jaundiced, disparaging manner.

In the hall outside his office over the bank were three
sagging old settees where circus folk often waited
through the long afternoon and evening hours to see
him and inquire about work for the coming season.

If he showed up at all it might not be until after dinner or the prizefights. As he labored up the stairs and
thumped his way to the office, he would give his callers
a quick, appraising eye.

Then he'd walk hurriedly past in short, shuffling
steps and disappear in the office while leaving them with
no more than a nod or a brief word of recognition. This
happened even to faithful and loyal men and women
who had worked for the Ringlings for nearly half a
century.

Usually he knew at first glance who was there and
what his mission might be, or he could gather the information from Charlie Kannelly, the circus secretary.

"Who's that old buzzard on the end?" he might ask.
"What does Mickey Miller want? What's the matter
with that clown acrobat? How much does he expect?"

He might send word out to them that he'd see them
in a few minutes, or tomorrow, but more often he'd let
them wait. "Let him sweat it out" was one of his favorite expressions—until he was ready to bargain.

He usually lay abed until noon, then got up for a leisurely bath and breakfast. He liked to relax in the tub or in his barber's chair while the valet, Frank Tomlinson, gave him the full tonsorial treatment and helped him get dressed for the day.

Breakfast over, he might stop in at his office downtown, ride out to winter quarters or over to St. Armand's Key for a look around. Occasionally he would call on sister Ida at her home on Bird Key, but as time went on these visits became less frequent and friendly.

In New York he would emerge from his Park Avenue apartment or his suite in the Waldorf Astoria or Ritz-Carlton in late afternoon or early evening, impressive in brown braided suit, custom-built alligator shoes, and silk shirt, with his overcoat flung over his arm. He would go to dinner and perhaps the theater, more than likely meeting friends and making a night of it.

In Sarasota to attend the annual Pageant of Sara de Sota, a Spanish fiesta he and Mable had sponsored for several years, John was party to an incident that provided a good illustration to his way of thinking.

He planned to meet his friend Burns, the detective, at the office and go with him to the parade and coronation ball. Mable wasn't feeling well and stayed home.

Burns had rented a Spanish costume and donned it at the office. He had considerable difficulty squeezing his short, paunchy middle into the tight pants and buttoning the waistcoat, but he finally made it.

While pacing the floor waiting for John to arrive, Burns sat on a lighted cigarette on the edge of a table and burned a hole in the seat of his rented trousers. The little detective was more annoyed at having to peel off the tight pants, have them mended and put them on again than he was at the slight blister on his backside.

While the office boy took the damaged pants down-
stairs and around the corner to Bill Gold's tailor shop,
John came in, blinking and puffing. When Burns explained what had happened, the circus man cackled
with laughter. The office boy returned to report Gold's
price would be seventy-five cents.

"Why, that's highway robbery!" whined the notor-
iously tight-fisted Burns, although he knew the price
was most reasonable.

"Seventy-five cents for doin' a simple little mendin'
job like that?" John joined in. "Why, he's money mad."

"Certainly," Burns agreed. "It wouldn't take more
than ten or fifteen minutes to do the job."

"Tell you what," John advised, "stay away from
him for a few days and sweat him out, Burns. After this
pageant thing is over, he'll come down to earth and do
the job for thirty or forty cents."

Burns tossed the damaged trousers onto a table in the
corner and there they stayed for years. He didn't go
entirely Spanish that year, but wore his own conservative blue trousers, the tight-fitting jacket and black
sailor hat with red pompons dangling from the brim.

"Your pants don't look too bad, with the rest of that
getup," John chided him. "A nearsighted judge might
take you for a Spaniard, but I doubt it."

At the time Tex Rickard's services were much in demand and late in 1928 Tex went to Miami to lend his
promotional skill to the Young Stribling-Jack Sharkey
fight. Stribling was a promising young boxer from
Macon, Georgia, and Sharkey was a veteran from New
York. The fight was a "natural."

Rickard became ill during the holidays and put off
going to the hospital until it was too late. He died of

a gangrenous infection of the appendix on January 6, 1929, just four days after his fifty-ninth birthday.

Rickard's death was a tremendous shock to John Ringling and to the boxing world. It very likely changed circus history.

John had already made up his mind to play two indoor spring dates in New York in 1929 instead of the usual one. So he opened a ten-day engagement in the Bronx Coliseum on March 21.

The Coliseum was packed and every person in the crowd had come to see the circus instead of an opera, and didn't appear as stilted and uncomfortable as a smartly-dressed first-night audience in the Garden.

Alfred E. Smith, the popular ex-governor of New York who only the year before had run for President on the Democratic ticket, was there and made a short speech. He told a few stories about his friend, John Ringling, and drew thunderous applause.

Al Smith wore his familiar brown Derby and John had on a black one that night. They swapped headpieces while the crowd roared. Then the band struck up "The Sidewalks of New York" and everybody had a good time.

The circus did a tremendous business in the Bronx that spring, including two sellouts on Good Friday, a most unusual thing in show business. Amusement circles were impressed and John was happy for he saw in it a personal triumph.

From the Coliseum the show moved into Madison Square Garden on April 1, stayed there for three weeks, and then went to Boston.

The shock of Rickard's death had barely worn off when John experienced another even more severe and stunning blow. Mable Ringling, who had suffered from Addison's disease for several years, entered a sanitorium in New Jersey the first of June and passed away a week later, at the age of fifty-four.

John was overcome with grief and despair. Something inside him seemed to flicker and go out the day Mable died. He followed the remains to a mausoleum in Brookside Cemetery at Englewood, New Jersey, then returned to their New York apartment.

For days he was cloaked in sadness. He had several of his fine braided suits and silk shirts packed up and sent away; he wore only black.

"The party is over," he said. "I never want to be gay again."

CHAPTER TWENTY-FOUR

John Ringling's Garden

LET US LOOK backward briefly to bring the circus picture of the late 1920's into proper focus. Jerry Mugivan and Bert Bowers, who had gone into the business in 1904 with a few rented cars and little equipment, continued to grow and expand through the years and by 1920 they owned the John Robinson, Howes' Great London, Hagenbeck-Wallace, Dode Fisk, and Gollmar Bros. circuses.

That fall they bought the Yankee Robinson and Sells-Floto circuses and acquired title to the Buffalo Bill Wild West Show. Ed Ballard joined as the third member of the triumvirate and in 1921 they organized the American Circus Corporation.

By this time tensions of World War I had eased and America entered an era of prosperity that was to continue until late 1929. The nation's economy boomed and wages went up so that people had money to spend not only for automobiles, furniture, and phonographs, but for recreation.

Bidding for the entertainment dollar were such circuses as Ringling Bros. and Barnum & Bailey, Sells-Floto, Hagenbeck-Wallace, John Robinson, Walter L. Main, Al G. Barnes, and many smaller ones, including the brothers Campbell, Christy, Cole, Kay, and Wheeler.

Competition was so fierce that there was talk of agreements and mergers. Many of the big ones played competing dates and suffered the consequences.

In the fall of 1922, Charles Ringling and his right-hand man, George W. Smith, went to White City, near Chicago, where they met with Mugivan, Bowers and Ballard in what had been rumored as a "buy or sell showdown."

Such a deal never was consummated because, according to reliable sources, Charles Ringling insisted on a clause in the contract whereby when the last of the Ringling brothers passed on, the Ringling title would die.

And so the situation continued through the "Roaring 20's" with expansions and general prosperity. By 1929 the American Circus Corporation had acquired the Al G. Barnes Wild Animal Show and the Sparks 20th Century Wonder Circus, both well-known properties.

The Ringling Bros. and Barnum & Bailey Combined Circus had opened the season for years in Madison Square Garden under normal business contracts. But with Charles Ringling and Tex Rickard gone, John Ringling had no written agreement and didn't ask for one. The Garden directors decided to make a change.

They told John that the corporation had lost sixty thousand dollars that spring because the circus interfered with Friday night boxing programs and they insisted the circus give up these nights so the fights could go on.

"I'll do no such God-damn thing," John exploded. "Why, I helped put up this joint and my friend Tex Rickard filled it for you. All of you know Friday night is always a sellout for me—the only night in the week when those who are circus-hungry can come and bring the family; when the kids don't have to get up early to go to school or Sunday school.

"I'll fight this thing to a finish, and the public will back me up a hundred percent. I'll tell you one thing: You'll never give the kids in this civilized community a wallop like that and get away with it. The people won't stand for their favorite entertainment being frozen out by a lousy boxing show."

The circus king was certain he was bigger than the Garden and he saw this as a showdown between lovers of the circus and Madison Square Garden management. He was confident that public sentiment would be with him all the way.

"I'll show 'em," he told several of his top executives. "We'll take the show to the Armory on Twenty-second Street. I can get that place pretty cheap.

"Bear down hard on that kid angle—we'll give it to all the papers. Tell 'em we're determined to bring good, clean entertainment to all the people in New York as we've always done.

"That'll fix the bastards up in the Garden. They can't tell me where to put the show, nor when to exhibit. Let 'em have boxing. I'll run the circus the way I want, and open their eyes once and for all. We'll have the people on our side."

The Garden directors stood their ground. They leased the Garden to the American Circus Corporation, which in turn combined the Sells-Floto and Hagenbeck-Wallace shows for the 1930 season's opening in New York. The combine would play the Ringling dates in the Garden, and close on Friday nights for boxing.

Sells-Floto was a ghost come alive to haunt the Ringling show. It was first organized by Harry Tammen, co-owner of the Denver *Post* with Fred Bonfils. It was called the Floto Dog and Pony Show, named after Otto Floto, the *Post's* sporting editor who had no interest in the enterprise but whose euphonious name struck Tammen's fancy.

As it grew, Tammen and Bonfils needed another name to go with Floto, so they chose one well-known in the amusement field. They hired a man named William Sells and called their circus the Sells-Floto.

Brazenly they used pictures of the four Sells brothers of circus fame—Ephraim, Lewis, Peter and Allen—in their advertising and billing matter.

Naturally the Ringlings didn't take kindly to this bit of chicanery, and opened fire on Sells-Floto. They brought suit asking damages and a restraining order against Tammen and Bonfils using the Sells name, claiming infringement of rights.

The Ringlings claimed that for years they owned the Sells Bros. title because they'd bought into Forepaugh-Sells Circus in 1903 and acquired the remainder of that valuable property from James A. Bailey's widow in 1906.

The court ruled that Tammen and Bonfils could not use pictures of the Sells brothers, dead these many years, but it permitted the Denver operators to keep the Sells name in their title, on grounds they bought that privilege when they employed William Sells, even if he had no connection with the four brothers of the same name.

That took care of the Sells-Floto Show until the Garden matter came up. Now, John Ringling must talk turkey with Mugivan, Bowers and Ballard.

There were two avenues open to him—let the Sells-

Floto and Hagenbeck-Wallace circuses open in the Garden in the spring of 1930 and play his dates, or buy the American Circus Corporation for its asking price of two million dollars.

"God-damn it, I'll buy," he sputtered on September 6, 1929.

He paid $450,000 cash and signed two notes with New York banks for the balance. One was for $800,000 and the other $750,000. The larger carried 72 percent of the value of the collateral and the other 28 percent.

For his cash and two notes, John Ringling became owner of all the American Circus Corporation's property and titles, and the right to open in the Garden, which was what he really wanted most.

He also acquired John Robinson, Al G. Barnes, and Sparks circuses, along with titles to Buffalo Bill, Howes' Great London, Yankee Robinson, and Gollmar Bros. These included some railroad cars, hundreds of wagons and cages, animals and canvas, performers and working-men scattered all over the country.

John Ringling already owned the biggest circus in the land. It traveled aboard one hundred railroad cars, exhibited hundreds of wild animals under acres of canvas; moved on scores of wagons, tractors, and other rolling stock; boasted forty elephants, nearly four hundred horses, and half a hundred clowns. Ringling employed nearly twelve hundred persons on his circus alone.

The merger gave him a virtual lock on the outdoor amusement business in America. He was king of the circus in truth now, and ruled his vast domain of sawdust and spangles like an Indian potentate.

Within six weeks after John ascended the circus throne, America slid into a paralyzing depression that was worldwide. The stock market collapsed, mortgages and notes went unpaid, and creditors began to close in on John like hounds after a fox.

"The crash cleaned me out," he would whine, and beg for time.

Just how much he lost on that bleak Friday in October, 1929, cannot be counted in dollars for it affected every line of activity. He had no large investment in stocks, for his money was in circuses, railroads, oil wells, land, and valuable paintings. But everything went down in actual worth.

The crash had repercussions in every line of industry and commerce. The entertainment business was jolted severely. Many circuses were stranded on the road or never left winter quarters.

John became more griping and penny-pinching. Now and then old cronies would call, when he was at home, to gripe about business conditions and the administration over Scotch and soda, or while quaffing his favorite imported beer.

To shed his grief over Mable's passing and get away from his horde of creditors, John went to Europe. He planned to see the Circus Medrano and have a look around the Mediterranean, perhaps book some new circus acts and pick up some bargains in art.

After stopping off in Paris, he went on to Monte Carlo. The season was in full swing and there he met the charming Widow Buck.

It is said she lost thirty-two thousand dollars the night they met and perhaps she did, for she was wealthy, as later events were to prove. John saw in her many things to arouse his interest, and not the least was her financial status.

Emily Haag Buck was lively, vivacious, witty, and almost twenty years younger than John. She had a home in Orange, New Jersey, and they had a kindred spirit since he, too, owned property in the state.

It didn't take John and Emily long to decide they were for each other, but he had to cut short his stay in Europe and return to Sarasota, where Owen Burns had ordered him into court to answer charges of fraud and such in connection with bay and beach property transactions and the El Vernona Hotel.

The legal hassle involved two of the most prominent families in the community and interest in the proceedings was widespread. After lengthy hearings, the court sided with John.

It was one of the sweetest, most satisfying triumphs of his life, coming at a time when he needed a mental uplift. The thought of beating Burns in court and having clear title to the land stimulated and pleased him no end.

As soon as the court ruling was made, John boarded the train for New York, to meet Emily coming home from Europe.

"We ought to get married at once," he suggested. "It's no use waitin' and wastin' a lot of time. Why don't we just have it over with?"

"Who will perform the ceremony?"

"There's only one man in this country to tie this knot," John replied. "That's my friend, Frank Hague."

John had known "Boss" Frank Hague, the mayor of Jersey City, for years and had admired the old political figure not alone for his power in high places but for his ability to rule his city like an absolute monarch.

Tall, slender, with keen eyes and the suave air of a

master politician, Hague always found time to relax each winter with other well-heeled tourists in the very exclusive turf club at Hialeah Race Course.

Before John and Emily exchanged marriage vows, they took care of some minor business, in the presence of Boss Hague. One thing was to draw up and sign a prenuptial agreement recognizing that John had established his museum and converted a sizable portion of his estate to it. The other was an open note which John signed promising to repay Emily the fifty thousand dollars she loaned him on their wedding day. John needed the cash and Emily had an eye for business.

Mayor Frank Hague then performed the ceremony that united the pair in Jersey City on December 19, 1930. Best man at the brief and simple service was Thomas N. McCarter, chairman of the New Jersey Public Service Commission.

John and Emily went immediately to New York and then to Florida. They settled in his mansion but the honeymoon was brief.

CHAPTER TWENTY-FIVE

The Yacht Struck a Jellyfish

JOHN'S FINANCIAL BURDENS grew, taxes piled up, and claims against him multiplied. Sometimes he hollered that he was being robbed or he begged for time, but more often he refused to show his face and instructed his secretary or butler to "let 'em sweat it out."

He often neglected to pay current bills and allowed them to pile up so long that even his telephone was disconnected for nonpayment.

"Money ain't as plentiful as it used to be," he whimpered to his cronies. "It's a mighty scarce article—a hell of a lot harder to get hold of than it used to be, with all these taxes eatin' it up."

Sometimes the servants had to go without their pay and they once threatened to walk out with dinner half prepared and guests arriving. They claimed they hadn't been paid in two months.

"Holy God!" he whined. "It wasn't that long ago. I know I owe you a little but it wasn't more than five or six weeks since I paid you. You've made a mistake in your figurin'."

They settled for seven weeks' pay, but the next time it happened they claimed nine week's back salary.

"You're robbin' me!" John said. "I paid you not over

six weeks ago, before I went to New York. You ought
to keep track of these things."

"That's what we'd done," one of the servants explained later. "The way we figured, he owed us for
seven weeks and paid for nine. That way we got even
and went one up on him. Of course the old bugger
never knew it or he'd be hollerin' yet."

John was always the comedian and liked his little joke.
Any buffoonery seemed to act like a tonic to his cantankerous old body. Mummery was part of his makeup
and he was more the Merry-Andrew than many who
wore the motley.

One afternoon, while he was confined to his New
York apartment with gout, John called one of his executives to come up at once so they could talk over some
features to stress in the circus' billing. While they
talked, the telephone rang and John answered it. The
caller asked to speak to Mr. Ringling, not recognizing
his voice.

John, without knowing who was calling, said Mr.
Ringling was not in at the moment but this was his
secretary and he could speak in his absence. The party
quoted prices on some equipment the circus man wanted
to buy.

"How much did you say?" John asked in apparent
astonishment. He listened a moment, then said:

"Well, I know Mr. Ringling wouldn't be interested
at that price. Holy God! That's too much money.
You're 'way out of line on it. I don't mind telling you
that you're asking too much. Better get a pencil and
paper and do some figurin'."

There was another long pause, then:

"Yes, I'll tell Mr. Ringling you called but you'd

better get your price in line. You're 'way too high for him and I know it."

John replaced the receiver, then laughed heartily.

"That guy was wise," he said. "He told me 'You may not be Mr. Ringling, but you've got a line of bellyachin' just like the old sharper himself.' "

When the depression spread like a fog throughout the land, men of lesser strength shot themselves or leaped from tall buildings, went into bankruptcy or fled the country, but John never weakened. He was certain good times would come back to America and that the circus would share in this prosperity.

With all his other troubles, life was anything but serene in the mottled brown mansion behind the pink stone fence. Emily nettled him from the beginning by changing the decorations and moving the furniture around. She also gave frequent parties.

John later told the court he didn't like these social gatherings because "the guests would get high and come in and annoy me." He testified this way: "I objected to an army drinking in my apartment every day."

Emily once hid out for four days and John said he didn't know where she had gone or what might have happened to her. Emily denied this, saying she was holed up in a hotel at John's insistence. She claimed he had sent her there because he was in the midst of a big lawsuit and the opposing lawyers were anxious to get her testimony.

While this was going on, Richard Ringling died, in 1931, at the age of thirty-five, of injuries received in an automobile accident. He left his portion of the circus, inherited from his father, to his widow. Aubrey Black Ringling, and their daughter, Mable.

Thus a controlling interest passed into the hands of two women—the widow of Charles and the widow of Richard. John owned the rest and he was still in the driver's seat. The change did not immediately affect management. The two women got along well and John had his way.

It was the only arrangement he would have accepted. He was still "Mr. Ringling" to the employees, most of whom had a sympathetic understanding of his problems and tremendous respect for his ability as a circus man and promoter. They gave him loyal support and worked harder than ever to keep the big show going through those depression years.

John Ringling stayed abreast of all that was going on in the circus world, and especially was he aware of leading acts and attractions. Since 1925, when Clyde Beatty moved to the Hagenbeck-Wallace Circus, Ringling had kept his eye on this young man with the great cat act.

In 1928 Beatty set a record for a mixed cat act with twenty-eight lions and tigers. He was billed as "America's youngest and most fearless wild animal trainer," and the following year he was "Captain Clyde Beatty, presenting the world's greatest collection of African and Nubian lions and Royal Bengal and Siberian tigers." He now had thirty of these beasts in the arena at the same time.

By 1930, still on the Hagenbeck-Wallace show, Beatty had forty jungle-bred lions and tigers in the arena at once, and his act was a sensation everywhere.

John Ringling put Beatty on the big show for the first

time in 1931, the first time the Ringling-Barnum show had presented a cat act since Mabel Stark left the show in 1924. Beatty was billed as "the sensation of the century, greatest and most daring wild animal act ever presented."

In each of the years 1932, 1933 and 1934, Beatty was on the Ringling show for its Garden dates, then returned to the Hagenbeck-Wallace show for the road tour.

After that Beatty toured with the Cole Bros. show, made movies, played at Hamid's Steel Pier in Atlantic City, framed his own wild animal circus, joined Wallace Bros., operated jungle zoos in Ohio and Florida, was featured at many of the outstanding winter Shrine circuses, and toured with the Clyde Beatty-Cole Bros. Circus before his death of cancer on July 19, 1965, aged sixty-two.

John brought other outstanding attractions to the Ringling-Barnum circus, and his press department lost no time in making the public aware of them through newspapers, the radio, and billboards.

In February, 1932, John suffered a coronary thrombosis and was confined to bed for several weeks. Fortunately it was not severe but while he was thus incapacitated he could feel the circus slipping from his hands and there wasn't a thing he could do about it.

Much as he wanted to be in the thick of things, there was nothing to do but nurse his ailments and hope.

Often the nurse and butler would lift him into his wheelchair, roll it across the terrace, and, with the help of Captain Al Roan, put him aboard the *Zalophus II* for a cruise down the bay. He liked to sit on deck and watch the fish play in the clear water, or anchor and count the big green turtles in the pens near his house.

The old *Zalophus I* had been put out of commission. It was wrecked one night while on a pleasure cruise to Boca Grande, fifty miles to the south. John wasn't aboard that night and fortunately so, for in his condition he might have drowned.

The *Zalophus I* left Sarasota with a group of golfers —thirty or forty. The party was quite gay and there were dancing and partying amid the music and mirth. Roan was in command, with thirteen of his normal complement of fifteen crewmen aboard.

It was three o'clock in the morning and very dark. Heavy black clouds boiled up over the Gulf of Mexico and the wind kicked up whitecaps. Suddenly, it happened, although no one aboard seemed to know what caused the big, white-hulled old yacht to shudder and shake as with a chill and then go down on its side.

Some thought it struck a log and went scudding through the breakers, far off course. Others said it struck a piling or rammed buried wreckage. A standing joke for years was that it hit what was left of the Florida boom.

All aboard managed to reach safety with little more than a thorough wetting and the inconvenience of having to wade ashore and find transportation back to town.

For months the old vessel lay on the sand, battered by waves and warped and cracked by the sun and water. A diver working with a salvage crew drowned when his lines fouled, but at last the derelict was towed into the bay and up to Hog Creek, where it was anchored.

Several years later when Al Roan was asked to confirm

newspaper reports of the time and add additional details, he would have nothing to say.

"Well, Captain Roan, just what actually happened on that final voyage of the *Zalophus I*?" he was asked.

"I'll tell you," he snapped. "It hit a jellyfish!"

CHAPTER TWENTY-SIX

John Becomes a Loser

JOHN RINGLING HAD many things to worry about in that fateful summer of 1932, when the business depression was at its worst. Banks everywhere were closing and money was hard to come by, even for the circus king. He defaulted on the notes he had signed to buy the American Circus Corporation.

During the three years since he had signed these papers, John had reduced the larger one to $316,000 but had paid only $50,000 on the other, which made them total $1,016,000.

A number of New York financers known as Allied Owners, Inc., held the note for $316,000 and they were anxious to assume control, which they did, incorporating the circus—John Ringling's circus—in Delaware as "Ringling Bros. and Barnum & Bailey Combined Shows, Inc."

The new owners put Sam W. Gumpertz in charge as senior vice-president and general manager. John still held the title of president but was on fixed salary—reported to be $25,000 a year—with absolutely no authority on or off the lot.

It was the first time a Ringling had not been in command since their first tent was raised on a vacant lot in

Baraboo nearly fifty years before, and it rankled his soul.

For years John Ringling and Sam Gumpertz had been companions and friends. Sam had started with an acrobatic troupe, managed a theater circuit, and was agent for Eugene Sandow, the strong man. He managed Harry Houdini, the magician, and gave Florenz Ziegfeld his start in the theatrical field.

He had helped build Coney Island's Dreamland and Brighton Beach in Brooklyn. He had known John Ringling for many years, visited him in Florida starting in the winter of 1919, and finally built his own home there.

To John Ringling, losing control of the circus was the most humbling, humiliating experience of his life. It had been a vital part of him for half a century; he had helped originate it and had nursed it and watched it grow from an idea into a vast tented city of more than 1,200 people with the largest single spread of canvas in the world.

Now it was in the hands of financiers new and strange to the Big Top, who had never been in the "backyard," and knew nothing of circus acts, attractions, and operations. And it was being run by a little man with a leathery face, big ears, and a whiny voice who was not a Ringling by blood or marriage.

It was Sam Gumpertz' job to keep the circus going and to see that Allied Owners, Inc., made money, which was no easy task in those days of depression. John's friendship for Gumpertz turned to bitter hatred.

"I had to borrow two hundred thousand dollars from Mrs. Edith Ringling to put the show in winter quarters at the end of the season and try to rehabilitate it," Gumpertz reported. "It was run down frightfully; was in terrible shape."

John was in bad shape, too. His Bank of Sarasota closed August 29, 1932. The Ringling Trust & Savings Bank, headed by Charles and later by his widow, also shut its doors that summer but it paid all depositors in full.

John's bank never did, but this wasn't entirely his fault. Others had managed it and while he held the title of president he was seldom there and most of its business was carried on without his consent or approval.

When the bank closed, the circus had $203,111.75 on deposit but it took a lawsuit and a Federal court order to make the liquidator pay a ratable portion of the assets to the circus. He contended it shouldn't have to pay because John Ringling owned the bank and owed it money.

Actually John was in debt to his bank for $40,621.90, and another director, Dr. Fred H. Albee, owed it $39,-868.51, principally because he was John's partner in the bank and other enterprises.

Albee was a well-known bone surgeon who had opened and operated the Florida Medical Center at Venice, the town built by the Brotherhood of Locomotive Engineers. For a time Albee did a brisk business as patients came from all parts of the country. Among them was James J. Braddock, the heavyweight boxing champion of the world, who was treated for broken bones in his hand.

The suit against Ringling and Albee named two other directors, but the court found that one of them was insolvent and the other was "out of the jurisdiction of this court," having hightailed it to Mexico.

By this time John was well on the road to recovery from his coronary but he still could do little more than sit in his big living room, blinking and scowling at Emily and her merrymakers, with now and then a cackle of laughter.

All this time Emily would flit amongst the guests with all the verve and enthusiasm of a ballet dancer, once prompting John to admonish her:

"For God's sake, woman; light somewhere!"

Emily told the court later that this remark caused her "terrible embarrassment." Their marital climate deteriorated rapidly thereafter and when Emily pressed for payment of the fifty thousand dollars, John retaliated with a suit for divorce.

Emily said she knew nothing about a divorce suit until one day in July, 1933, while she was shopping in the five-and-ten-cent store. She said she was surprised when a deputy sheriff found her there and was humiliated when he served the papers on the spot.

She agreed to extend the note but took a mortgage on three of her husband's more valuable paintings as security. Two of these were in a New York warehouse and the third, Rembrandt's "St. John the Evangelist," was in the museum next door to their home.

Emily also relinquished her dower rights and promised she would thereafter treat John with "love and affection." Whereupon he withdrew the divorce suit.

"If Emily hadn't put her name on that paper," John said, "I wouldn't have taken her back for ten million dollars."

The Florida Supreme Court took a look at the document and made this appraisal:

"It is somewhat ambiguous but reaffirms the ante nuptial agreement in every particular and then announces the release of dower was intended to apply only to the John and Mable Ringling Museum of Art.

"It then restores Mrs. Ringling's rights to dower in all the estate of John Ringling except the museum and the properties thereto."

Of course, no amount of legal phraseology could end their bickering and seven months later John filed another suit for divorce. He followed this with a will in which he stipulated that Emily Haag Buck Ringling was to receive the sum of one dollar, and nothing more, from his estate.

When life did not run smoothly in Ca d' Zan, John would lose himself in the sprawling museum, spending hours studying a Rubens or a Van Dyck. On occasion he tarried there until the first blush of dawn for there he found peace and quiet.

It was far more restful in the museum than in his own home, even after Emily moved out. He retained a nurse, butler, and other household help and brought in Willy Susa from the circus to prepare the exotic Oriental dishes he liked.

Willy was a Japanese chef who had been with the show for many years and was something of a culinary artist—just the sort of quiet, efficient workman John wanted in his kitchens. Willy hadn't been long on the job at Ca d' Zan when he began bickering with the nurse. Their quarrel became a running feud and Willy especially resented taking orders from her.

Once a noisy argument in English and Oriental dialect ended with Willy screeching, "You go hell! You not Missy Lingling yet." And he left the premises.

John didn't lose his foot in that summer of 1933 but he certainly lost his temper. It happened while he was laid up with gout and other ailments in Sam Gumpertz' suite in the Half Moon Hotel at Coney Island.

A reporter sent to check on the story that John's foot had been amputated could get no farther than the door, which was barred by the butler. Inside, he could see the circus man sitting in an easy chair by the window, his lower leg swathed in bandages. The reporter leaned close to the butler and whispered: "Is his foot amputated?"

The butler look at him blankly for a moment, then answered: "Yes, suh; hit's amputated all right."

The story was widely circulated and John was furious, but all he could do was resent it and simmer through the summer while his gout hung on.

He didn't see the show that season until early in October when he met it at Birmingham, coming on the lot whining and fussing about everything from location to billing matter, and even the program. One of the first men he saw was Roland Butler, head of the press department. John immediately launched into a tirade which was not unusual at that period of his life.

"What the hell do you mean, puttin' out that stuff about Mrs. Charlie being the 'mother of the circus!'" he snorted. "You know better than to spread any such reports, Roland. 'Circus mother' my eye! You know damned well there are plenty of bastards already full of that propaganda without the circus feedin' them any more. You cut out that stuff once and for all, Roland. I won't tolerate it."

Butler, who knew John as well as any man on the circus payroll, was well aware that Mrs. Edith Ringling had traveled with the show for years and was highly respected by everyone in personnel. Furthermore, Butler did not have to bow to John, now that Sam Gumpertz was running the show.

"We didn't put that out," Butler bristled. "The newspapers broke that story in Chicago; they got it from outside sources, without our knowledge. We had nothing whatsoever to do with it. It was their baby from start to finish, and I can prove it!"

"Well, it's a lie," John replied, cooling off rather quickly for him. "All that bilge water about her carryin' on the circus tradition while I'm ill has got to stop. Like hell! Remember, Roland, I'm still runnin' the show and while I'm on deck we'll have no more of this 'mother of the circus' crap put out by anyone. That's final."

Edith Ringling owned a third of the circus and was known for her honesty, sincerity, and fine character, but that made no difference to John—a sick, frustrated old man who snapped at those about him like a grouchy lion; straining and chafing at his disabilities and growing more suspicious and distrustful all the time.

For years actual management of the circus had been left to a group of capable executives who had trouped with Barnum & Bailey or the Ringlings for as long as anyone could recall and knew the operation from every angle. All had been thoroughly schooled, either by the working Ringling brothers or some other practical circus men, and had come up through the ranks.

They included George F. Meighan, director of railroad transportation after Charlie Wilson's day; William L. Horton, in charge of billing forces; Carl Hathaway and George W. Smith, who got the show on and off the lot; Curly Stewart, a twenty-four-hour man; Roland Butler, head of the press department, and Pat Valdo, director of performing personnel.

Charles R. Hutchinson, nephew to James A. Bailey, was watchdog of the treasury; John M. Kelley, shrewd lawyer from Baraboo, was general counsel; and Frank A. Cook held the title of legal adjuster, whose duties made him known on the lot as "the fixer."

There were countless others all down the line—superintendents of the many departments of the big show and even a "registered sanitarian," whose principal duty was disposing of sewage.

Each fit into the pattern like pieces of a jigsaw puzzle, to maintain a rigid schedule so the circus could complete its fifteen to twenty thousand mile tour each season, keep the 1,500 in personnel healthy and happy, and please and protect four million patrons.

One of the things that kept the Ringling Circus great was its press department. From the day John hired Willard Coxey, the brothers had skilled and experienced press agents to herald the coming of their shows.

When the circus was in its glory the publicity department was under the direction of Roland Butler, who for more than thirty years directed a staff that from time to time included Dexter Fellows, Frank Braden, Allen Lester, William Fields, Gardner Wilson, Eddie Johnson, and many more.

Butler, who was Boston-born and had served as art and amusements editor of several papers in that area before joining the circus, looked like a football fullback and was one of the few employees John Ringling respected and trusted, although at times they had violent arguments.

Perhaps this was because Butler was favorably known in every important newspaper and magazine office in the country. He insisted he was a circus press agent and snorted his disgust every time the title of public relations director was tossed his way.

He liked all reporters and photographers, got along well with editors and publishers, but he looked with a jaundiced eye upon anyone calling himself a journalist. He had a remarkable memory for names and places and once when a friend asked how many newspapermen he knew personally, he said:

"I don't know exactly, but I send out 2,800 Christmas cards every year, to people I can call by their first name."

Butler's job was to glorify circus attractions and he was a master with pen and brush. For more than thirty years he publicized such personalities as Lillian Leitzel, Vera Bruce, Alfredo Codona, Arthur and Antoinette Concello, the Cristianis, the Loyal-Repenskis, Mabel Stark, Alfred Court, Clyde Beatty, the Wallendas, the Zacchinis, the Alzanas, Mister Mistin, and many more.

Dexter Fellows became perhaps as widely known as any circus press agent of the century, not only because he was capable but because of his flamboyant attire. Decked out in gray fedora or straw skimmer, checkered vest with heavy gold watch chain stretched across the middle, white or gray spats, and twirling his gold-headed cane, Fellows invaded newsrooms in New York and other cities throughout the country like a breath of fresh air.

When he blew in, everyone knew the circus was not far behind and likely as not the editor called for a story on Dexter, for he was as much a sign of spring as the first robin.

Perhaps he would be invited to sit in on the copy desk, or even in the slot, and act as city or telegraph editor. He would accept, of course, and deal out "takes" of stories to copy editors. He might even write the headlines, pausing to inquire, "You want this twenty-four point boldface indent or shall I make it thirty?"

Frank Braden was a former officer in the United States Cavalry and he always stood ramrod straight with a military bearing. He was warmly greeted in newsrooms everywhere, for editors knew he would provide interesting stories about the circus and its operation.

Frank always dressed like a banker, with Homburg set at a rakish angle and white shirt whose stiff cuffs protruded from the sleeves of his well-tailored jacket. Braden was the man who once seated a midget on the lap of J. Pierpont Morgan, the financier, and saw the picture circulated throughout the world.

Lester, Fields, Wilson, Johnson, and all the others were skilled press agents who knew how to put their message across, and were accepted as professionals in every newsroom in America.

One other member of the Ringling Bros. and Barnum & Bailey Circus press department deserves mention. She was Estelle Mary Butler, the wife of Roland, who was officially listed as a member of the staff, and she was.

Estelle Butler, fat and friendly, drove Roland on his rounds and helped him in his work, crisscrossing the country to spread word of the circus. She was a lively, lovable person who survived all the other members of her husband's "press corps," and passed away February 13, 1966.

It was Butler and his crew who ballyhooed such attractions as the giraffe-necked women, the saucer-lipped Ubangis, Gargantua the Great, riders, flyers, and clowns. They put the faces of snarling beasts on front pages of newspapers and magazines everywhere, often in color and always in classic poses.

When John Ringling acquired an enormous sea elephant—actually it was a dugong or sea cow—he gave Butler orders to "build him up; make him bigger than hell."

The sluggish, herbivorous mammal was christened "Goliath" and shunted from winter quarters to St. Armand's Key, where a specially-constructed pen permitted him to wallow in the sea or waddle out on the white sandy beach and lie in the sun, collecting blisters on his hide.

John hoped Goliath would attract customers for his lots, and that when parents brought their children to see the critter they'd stop and buy. However, few came after the boom and the bulky old Goliath spent days and weeks in solitude.

Shortly before the circus was to go out, Goliath was moved back to winter quarters to be loaded on the train for New York and the season's opening. While John had given a lot of attention to Goliath's billing, he'd neglected the physical welfare of the animal. If anyone was in charge of caring for the beast, he didn't do his job.

Butler's clever billing met John's approval; advertising copy was being turned out in bales. Posters were completed, in color, and a season's ad cuts were in the making. The copy read:

"Goliath, the mammoth sea elephant. The only one of its kind ever captured and exhibited alive. Now one-third larger than last season and still growing at the rate of a ton a year! This monster of the deep weighs five tons and eats 490 pounds of fish every meal!"

Truly, Goliath was going to be the biggest animal the Ringlings ever exhibited, if he kept growing, but when he arrived at winter quarters panic set in. He seemed much thinner and smaller than anyone expected.

He was nothing like the animal whose pictures were about to burst forth in flaming color on virtually every billboard and barnside and in thousands of store windows from coast to coast.

Butler looked at the animal, now covered with great white splotches and rotting away in chunks. The bewildered press agent was sick but John Ringling, standing beside him, was sicker.

"My God, Roland," the circus magnate whined. "What the hell happened to him? He's a sorry lookin' critter—stinks to high heaven, too."

"Looks to me like he's lost a lot of weight, Mr. Ringling."

"Christ, yes; he's lost weight. I think he's sick— looks terrible to me. What do you think happened?"

Investigation revealed that some form of marine life —some authorities believed it was an octopus—had attacked Goliath, causing a deep infection in neck and shoulder. His blisters detracted from his general appearance, too.

The ailing animal was taken to New York with the show but died soon after arriving there, without drawing a single cash customer that season. The circus featured other attractions.

Butler had better luck with five baby elephants, temporarily. He put them among the forty pachyderms the show always carried and gave them this billing:

"Ringling Bros. and Barnum & Bailey's largest and greatest importation, direct from central Africa's darkest depths—The only family of African pygmy elephants that ever set foot on this continent. Not babies, but full-grown middle-sized tuskers, the most curious proboscidean creatures ever captured."

The program went on to explain that "This rare group of diminutive elephants was brought to America this spring after three years of intensive jungle exploration in the heart of Africa, conducted by Ringling Bros. and Barnum & Bailey Circus scouts under the leadership of Chief Explorer Howard V. Bary, at the cost of innumerable discomforts, difficulties, hardships and a staggering financial outlay."

The pgymy elephants were pictured with giant ears that almost reached the ground but bodies no larger than Shetland ponies. Their contrast with normal-size elephants, picture-wise, was stunning.

Within a few years the "pygmy elephants" disappeared from the circus. For those who wonder what happened, the veteran press agent once explained with a sheepish grin:

"Why, the damn things grew up!"

CHAPTER TWENTY-SEVEN

Learning About the Circus

JOHN SPENT MANY months recuperating at his home, usually with a few servants and caretakers. Sometimes, in the quiet of a tropic evening, he would ride into town in the old Rolls-Royce with the high wire wheels and faded green paint.

The car would roll to a stop in front of a restaurant and John would go in for a steak dinner, fillet of beef Wellington, sauerbraten, sweet-and-sour red cabbage and all the trimmings, or one of his favorites, pompano en papillote.

The meal over, he would shuffle out, nurse and chauffeur steadying and supporting him until he reached the car and climbed in. The engine would throb into life and the vehicle would rumble off down the street. Bystanders would notice and remark, "There goes old John."

His mind never was affected and somehow it seemed to grow keener as he became more determined to recover. His inactivity appeared to temper and hone his brain as the days dragged on.

He wanted very badly to regain control of the circus and he complained to close friends that not enough cash was being channeled into paying off Allied Owners. He claimed gross mismanagement but, of course, he couldn't prove anything, and he asserted that the show bearing his name had always made money when he was at the helm, which was true.

He nursed the notion that Gumpertz and his associates were trying to keep it from him when actually all they could do in those days of depression was to keep it going.

John's prime source of information was his fellow Alsatian, Bradna, who slipped into Ca d' Zan often when he was in Sarasota. John and Bradna were more cronies than employer-employee, and they drank beer and talked far into the night.

Word got around, and Bradna was fired, temporarily, because he was suspected of spilling circus secrets.

The bitterness John had for his New York creditors spread over onto his sister Ida and her two sons, John and Henry. It nettled the old fellow that his nephew used the full name of John Ringling North, and when young Johnny tried to follow in his uncle's footsteps he touched a sore spot.

The circus king regarded Henry as much more human and individualistic, and he always called him "Buddy" as a mark of affection, although he had no love for either of the boys.

Johnny North recommended a young attorney to his uncle but he soon disliked the lawyer and became suspicious of his nephew's motives and intentions. He accused the barrister and young Johnny of trying to get their hands on his property and when Ida defended her son, John turned on her and gave her a verbal spanking.

"You two are in cahoots," he growled, "an' I ain't dyin' fast enough to suit you. Well, I'll tell you, I don't intend to hurry. And when I do go, I don't intend to leave either one of you a God-damn nickel!"

It was in May, 1935, when he was preparing to leave New York for Sarasota that he telephoned an attorney to come at once to his suite in the Ritz-Carlton Hotel. When the lawyer arrived at a trot, John's bags were packed and in the corridor, the chauffeur standing by with cap in hand.

"I want you to change my will," John said bitterly. "Fix it so Johnny North won't get a thing. Make it airtight; I intend to cut him off without a cent."

The attorney hesitated, explaining that it was an unusual request and he should first see a copy of the will.

"I don't have one with me, but I want this thing fixed up right away, before I leave the city. I want him cut out entirely; get busy and draw up a codicil for me."

The lawyer said he could draw up a codicil, but it would become part of the will and he should know what was in the original instrument.

"I can tell you what's in it, but that shouldn't make any difference. The codicil will take care of that. Fix this thing up and make it so it'll stick, you understand?

"I want Johnny North cut out entirely; do the same thing to my other nephew, Henry North," the circus man said, wheeling on his cane and thumping the floor in consuming impatience.

"I want the will changed so my sister Ida won't get but five thousand dollars a year. By God, that's plenty for her."

The lawyer walked over to a desk, took out a sheet of hotel stationery, and wrote as John directed. The circus man signed with a shaky but determined hand, stuck the paper into his pocket and left for Florida.

His records were a mixture of papers, promises, and recollections, so he hired a young accountant named James A. Haley to straighten out the mess. Haley was a tall, personable fellow who had come to Florida from his native Alabama during the land boom and soon got to know the Ringlings as did everyone else in town.

Through his knowledge of the community, Haley soon was able to assemble a good general picture of John's affairs. When he had all parts of the jigsaw puzzle in hand, he began putting them together.

Haley soon realized that John Ringling was a smart man, indeed. While his affairs were complicated and in generally loose condition, the circus man had gone a long way toward protecting himself financially.

"We ought to have everything straightened out in a few months, don't you think?" he said to Haley. "The country's comin' back; money is loosenin' up a little. I ought to get off my behind and be back on my feet in a year at the most.

"By then I'll have the circus back under my wing and can kick those thievin' rascals out. By God, they've been milkin' it long enough!"

But about this time a storm that had been years in the making struck the circus. Uncle Sam wanted to have a close look at the whole operation, and he turned the job over to a young lawyer named Charles W. Clarke in Miami.

Clarke had come home from World War I in 1919 with the rank of lieutenant colonel and a beautiful French girl as his bride. He went to work for the Internal Revenue Service and among his achievements was helping send Al Capone to prison.

In his latest assignment as a special agent for the IRS, Clarke needed to know how much cash passed through the ticket wagons each season and how it was distributed. It was a monumental task.

His first move was to get acquainted with all the circus executives who, annoyed and suspicious but fully aware of how troublesome income taxes could be, promised cooperation, in a frigid sort of way. Then Clarke called on John, now lonely and ailing, bitter against those in command and grasping at any straw that might help or comfort him.

Clarke soon realized that he would have to deal with smart men, wise in the ways of finagling if not finance. Circus operators had to be smart, and cagey, to survive.

So Clarke moved his family to Sarasota, where he figured he'd be right in the middle of things. The family now included four boys, so they rented a large apartment and Clarke went to work. First they reported to the circus office for introductions, and when one of the boys saw a man busy at a desk in the corner, he piped up:

"Daddy, is that man working on the Ringling case, too?"

It embarrassed Clarke and his wife, Gabrielle, but John laughed, patted the youngster on the shoulder, and said, "Son, you're a smart boy."

Clarke visited John many times, and they talked until long past midnight, discussing painting and sculpture, comparing works of the old masters and recalling places both had visited in Europe. The two men became friends.

Each night when Clarke went home he made notes of what John had told him, and kept them. He read books and magazines, learning all he could about art and animals—two of the biggest things in John's life.

If Clarke didn't find out what he wanted to know in his small home library, he went to the public library and searched there. He made trips to Miami and Tampa to check with other agents and to gather information on such things as elephants, lions, monkeys, zebras, camels, polar bears, and such lesser-known creatures as gnus and sea elephants.

He talked with circus men, collectors, and zoo keepers, gathering all the information he could on the cost and care of animals, their life span and drawing power.

One night Clarke and John were discussing Flemish masters when the circus man reached into a magazine rack and brought out a pamphlet entitled, "Notable Paintings Collected by the Late Stanford White."

Clarke showed interest, and John told him, "Take that along; have it if you will. White was a great fellow; a very good friend of mine, too."

The time was ripe for conversation and Clarke switched talk to the circus.

"What do you pay top performers, Mr. Ringling?" he asked. "How much a week, or a season? Most work on seasonal contracts, do they?"

"Five hundred or even a thousand a week, if they're worth it, and we might go a lot higher to get good drawing cards. It all depends, of course, but the good ones come mighty high. This circus is a big operation, Mr. Clarke."

"How much did you pay Tom Mix, the movie star? He was one of your highest paid, wasn't he?"

"Three hundred thousand dollars in 1929; as high as ten thousand a week. Business was pretty good then, you understand."

"Wasn't there a lawsuit over that?"

"Yes, old Zach Miller tried to sue us for grabbin' Mix; he claimed restraint of trade, but he never got anywhere with it. We've been sued many times, Mr. Clarke, and had to pay out a lot of money for damage claims."

Thus John Ringling revealed many circus secrets as they talked; the cost of elephants, monkeys, horses; their cost and life span; their value as attractions and to help move the show. There were countless angles Clarke must explore; things he'd have to learn about the complex outdoor entertainment business.

"You can help us clear up this thing, Mr. Ringling," the agent reminded him several times. "There are a lot of things we need to know about the case; a lot that perhaps you can tell us or help us find out.

"There must be a great deal more taxes that have been paid since the law went into effect in 1913 than we have records on, or more losses than we know about. We need to get the overall picture of the entire operation."

They went upstairs to the office where John took out a sheet of circus stationery and wrote a short letter. It was one of the most important documents he ever signed.

The note authorized Ringling executives to turn over to the IRS agents all records pertaining to the circuses and their operation as far back as they were available, and any help they could give.

Armed with this authority, Clarke and the other agents working on the circus case—J. L. Oren, Hugh Ducker, John Williams, and J. J. Brown—assembled evidence from all over the country and sent it to New York for presentation before a grand jury.

The Internal Revenue Service reported that the circus had paid taxes on four million dollars profits after it became Ringling Bros. and Barnum & Bailey in 1919 and until 1932. At the same time the Ringlings and their heirs had withdrawn more than ten million.

Clarke and John discussed real-estate promotions, oil wells, railroads, and finally the agent asked, "What about this Floridale deal in northwest Florida? How'd you come out on that?"

"Oh, that never amounted to anything," John answered, astonished at the thoroughness of Clarke's investigation. "Dick Ringling was a vice-president of the townsite corporation after his daddy died but I think they just used him because he was a Ringling. I put a little in it myself, but it never got off the ground."

Clarke reminded Ringling that the American Circus Corporation represented a two-million-dollar investment in 1929, but five depression years later it had a book value of more than six times that.

"What do you mean?" John asked.

The agent called them off—Sells-Floto, three million; John Robinson, three; Hagenbeck-Wallace, two and a half; Sparks, a million; Al G. Barnes, two; and Howes' Great London, another million.

"That makes six circuses at twelve and one-half million dollars, and you got them all for two back in 1929, when things were considerably higher than they are to-day," Clarke reminded him.

John blinked and a wry smile crept over his ruddy countenance.

"I can see you don't know much about the circus business, Mr. Clarke," he said, "but you're learnin' fast."

CHAPTER TWENTY-EIGHT

Ordered from the Garden

FROM THE VERY beginning, John insisted he knew nothing of the financial skullduggery that had been going on for so many years and whimpered that he, too, had been taken. He did all in his power to help the IRS, whose agents reported that his attitude was one of complete and helpful cooperation.

The letter he had written, they found, was most helpful in ferreting out what records were available, and getting witnesses to testify.

"What a shame," Clarke would say as they talked into the night. "A great and respected name like yours being sullied by these characters, who were duty bound to keep your interest and protection at heart."

Next day Clarke would visit John M. Kelley, who had been the circus' general counsel for nearly thirty years.

"What a shame, Mr. Kelley," he would sympathize. "An honest man like you being used by a lot of ungrateful employers."

To the Federal grand jury, sitting in New York, it appeared that the Ringling brothers and their heirs were unconscious beneficiaries of the gerrymanderings, if they profited at all.

The government figured the Ringling partnership

had taken in $53,400,000 from 1918 through 1932, an average of $3,500,000 a season for fifteen years. At the same time it paid out about $42,000,000, leaving net profits of $11,400,000.

In only four years, the government claimed, were earnings less than $500,000 and in each of two seasons they exceeded a million. The Ringling's owed, the IRS reported, $2,826,000, with penalties and interest pushing it up to $3,600,000.

The grand jury indicted six men but not a single member of the Ringling clan. Agents said there never was a shred of evidence to indicate they were involved.

The government's attorneys, headed by Joseph W. Burns and his assistant, James Randall Creel, outlined some intriguing manipulations they said helped account for the staggering tax figure, and cited a clause in the law providing for losses by "abandonment."

There were instances where railroads cars and other rolling stock had been worn out and abandoned; canvas had been torn by high winds or rotted and must be replaced; sets and props had outlived their usefulness.

To claim these as losses under the abandonment clause was perfectly legitimate, but there were other instances where circus property could not be crossed off the books and forgotten.

For example, the agents produced evidence that in 1911 the circus built and featured an opening spectacle called "Joan of Arc," which it estimated cost $200,000. This was a lot to spend on such a production but it was a good round figure and might have been accurate.

The hitch was that, although "Joan of Arc" was used only one season, it was not abandoned on the books until a dozen years later, as a total loss. Agents said that other "specs" that had been used as far back as the 1890's were not "abandoned" until years after the income tax law went into effect.

Under this same convenient clause of "abandonment," the government charged, were forty-six elephants, twenty-three camels, eighteen bears, eight hundred horses and scores of monkeys, lions, tigers, giraffes, and other animals.

A rhinoceros which died a year after it was brought to this country was a legitimate loss, except that the beast cost $3,500 and was "abandoned" for three consecutive years at a book value of $35,000.

In a single season, the government said, the circus claimed it bought forty-five stallions for a staggering sum. A witness who had worked on the show testified there never were more than ten stallions in the barns.

"The show had a lot of mares," he said, "and if there'd been forty-five stallions there wouldn't of been no circus."

The jury also was told that the circus had "abandoned" many acres of land, several buildings and other such property when it moved out of Bridgeport, but it never actually owned these and merely rented.

Several witnesses who lived in the vicinity said they'd never heard of any animals being "abandoned," and if this were true, the whole state of Connecticut would be a jungle.

Of the six men indicted, three were found guilty of having had a hand in making out or passing the income tax returns and were sent to jail, the most severe penalty being two years in prison and a ten thousand dollar fine.

Ironically, the driving force behind the investigation, Clarke, never lived to see the end of his most important case. Pushing himself night and day to wind it up, he suffered a fatal heart attack before the jury's verdict was brought in.

"If I could just get my old mitts on a little cash," John said to a few old cronies like Caples and Edwards, "I could pay off that note and get the whole thing straightened out. The way the show's bein' run, it'll never get out of the red; the thievin' bastards don't want it to get away from them. They're milkin' it!"

He didn't blame Gumpertz alone but Sam was the main target for his wrath because he had the title of executive vice-president and general manager, and as such controlled the purse strings. His word was law, on and off the lot.

John went to New York for the opening of the 1936 season on Wednesday, the eighth of April. He had no particular reason to be there but he just had to meddle in everything.

"The show's horribly handled and going to hell fast," he told some of his old employees who would ignore his tirades, knowing he was a touchy, cantankerous old man anxious to ridicule the present management and criticize the program.

With his nurse at his side, he went to the Garden every night and never missed an opportunity to express his contempt. He was more bitter and acrimonious than ever and disliked everything about the new show, searching for something to criticize and carp at on or off the premises.

One night he started villifying the minute he set foot in the Garden. The posters flanking the inner lobby were the first things he saw and he pounced on them like a hungry bear. Pointing to one, he addressed his nephew, who was with him.

"Look down in the corner of that piece of crap and see who printed it, Johnny; it looks like hell. See what outfit turned out that lousy six-sheet bill and—holy God! Check that abortion next to it, the one of the sickly-lookin' tiger with the 'come to Jesus' expression on his map."

He cackled, signifying he'd found something he was looking for, something he could depreciate. The crowd was pouring in for the show and it was no time for a scene but he ranted on, spitting on the floor and sputtering his displeasure while he wheeled on his cane.

Not all the posters had been put out by the current management; some had been used for years, designed under John's direction and used during his regime. He knew this, but he was here to tear the show's billing apart and he found it easier to be critical than correct.

"It all stinks!" he sneered. "It's the stinkingest line of paper that ever carried the Ringling name. I'm absolutely ashamed of it. I want to find out about this, and do it damned quick. It's an insult to all of us."

The nurse helped him cross the lobby to the Forty-ninth Street side and down the corridor to the private office of Sam Gumpertz. John shuffled in, puffing and fuming. Gumpertz, watery brown eyes blinking behind the thick-lensed glasses with the big black frames, got to his feet and clashed with the old circus king.

"Get the hell out of here," Sam ordered in his sharp, clangorous voice. "You ain't got a damned thing to say around here now, so get out!"

"Why, you, you—" John stammered, searching for a retort. This had shocked him so he couldn't find words to express his anger and disbelief. "God-damn you, Gumpertz. You can't talk like that to me."

"I am talkin' to you. Now, get out!"

John was crushed and dumbfounded. He was ordered out of his own circus, in Madison Square Garden; told to get off the premises where he had been king; expelled from the very spot he had helped build and make famous, where his name had always been honored and his word the law.

He stood in stunned disbelief and foaming anger for a long interlude. Finally, he turned and headed for the exit, thumping the floor with his cane—a fuming old limper; a beaten, disheartened and frustrated old man.

John returned to Ca d' Zan, but he found no merriment or even wifely comfort there, for Emily had moved out months ago. Their divorce case was being bounced between the circuit and state supreme courts by some of the sharpest legalistic minds in Sarasota, Jacksonville, Tallahassee, Cincinnati, and New York City.

They used subpoenas, depositions, warrants, and other legal weapons as well as oral testimony to lay the whole story on the record. John resented such personal publicity and had no desire to give Sarasotans more grist for their gossip mill, but he had no choice.

Several attorneys who worked on the case were political leaders and their long court fight over the divorce and Ringling property caused bitter political and personal differences. Close friends became bitter enemies and never were on speaking terms again. These cleavages affected not only their fortunes but brought on a complete realignment in Florida politics that reached to Congress.

The Florida Supreme Court made this observation and report:

"We pass sub silentio the charges of bad faith and the verbal assaults of counsel on both sides, including aspersions they cast on litigants. If we did not know counsel to be such, the arguments and briefs in this case reveal a high degree of ability and industry and would drive us to the conclusion that they were very able lawyers."

Then, discussing John and Emily, their background and reasons for marital discord, the court said:

"To clarify the atmosphere and place the parties in their appropriate setting, it is not out of place to say that this is not the usual controversy that reaches this court. Neither is it the case in which a strong, overbearing complainant is pursuing a friendless and helpless defendant.

"Both parties to this cause 'knew their way around.' If we may give faith and credit to the record, they were both wealthy in their own right, at the time of the marriage he was 62 (actually he was 64) and she was 45; both had been married before, both had traveled extensively, were seasoned in experience.

"Both knew English in all its inflections, could call each other any kind of a name that the state of their temper prompted and whether called in the lingo of the drawing room, the boudoir or the sawdust trail, the other was ready and did respond in kind.

"Some of the elements that induce marriage were totally lacking. It was treated as any other civil contract would be and has little on which the equities of domestic relations are usually invoked.

"The settlement of divorce controversies, separation agreements and property controversies have gone hand in hand ever since the Good Master drew a rib from Adam's flank and created the first entrepreneur. When bounded by legal proprieties, such contracts have been approved by the courts of every civilized land."

John won his divorce in July, 1936, but it cost him $201,211.95—the largest amount of attorneys' fees ever paid out in a Florida divorce suit up to that time. He also regained possession of the painting, "St. John the Evangelist," which later was sold to the Museum of Fine Arts in Boston for a reported $85,000.

Soon after John received his final decree, one of the attorneys who worked on the case died and his partner married the widow, adding still another strange twist to the Ringling story.

CHAPTER TWENTY-NINE

A Lousy Hundred Dollars

JOHN RINGLING FELT more than ever the urge to visit the circus bearing his name. Well-dressed as always, with a fresh cigar between his fingers, he limped along the midway that Monday, the twelfth of October, 1936, in Mobile, Alabama.

The sun was bright and warm and the air was thick with dust and the aroma of popcorn, peanuts, hamburgers, onions, candy apples, pink lemonade, and clean sawdust, flavored with the smells of sweating animals and humans.

Canvas walls swelled in the soft breeze and pennants waved atop the ridge poles. Grinders were chanting their spiels and money was pouring in at ticket windows; food and souvenir counters were jammed; people surged like a great tide toward the main entrance to the Big Top.

John paused to squint at faded canvas paintings of Stella Card, the tattooed lady; Kay Haller, the snake handler, and Koo Koo, the bird girl. On a platform standing beside Jack Earl, the giant, was Harry Doll, the Ringlings' perennial midget, immaculate in white shirt with cuffs, black trousers, glossy shoes and tiny bow tie. Harry was the senior and only male member of

"Tiny Town Midgets," featuring Harry, Daisy, Tiny, and Grace Doll.

Through John's memory passed a long procession of great acts and attractions he had brought to this country and to the American public—Charlie Siegrist, Lillian Leitzel, the Wallendas, Canastrellis, Con and Winnie Colleano, the Ubangis and many, many more.

He walked on, past a rickety platform where half a dozen girls in grass skirts swayed and swished to the twanging of a steel guitar, billed as the "South Sea Islanders," guaranteed to raise the temperature of every young buck who saw them.

At the main entrance, ticket takers and ushers recognized the old circus king, of course, and one showed him to a seat in front of where Fred Bradna stood looking over the audience and twirling his silver whistle on a string.

Bradna came over, shook hands warmly, chatted for a minute, then walked briskly to the edge of the center ring and let go with a mighty blast of his whistle to bring the crowd to attention.

Into the ring moved the opening spec, "The Durbar of Delhi," while Merle Evans led his fifty-piece band into "The Queen of Sheba."

The program in three rings and on four intervening stages moved with military precision, opening with bareback riding and daring feats of horsemanship featuring The Imperial Viennese, Justin and Bruce Brothers; the Walter Guice troupe of gymnasts.

Then came the elephants, billed as "ponderous performers with trunks full of new tricks, exhibiting unexpected prowess as baseball players, and introducing Modoc, the four-ton piccolino dancer on the hippodrome track," with Captain Lawrence Davis, Ericka Loyal, and Gloria and Bonnie Hunt.

There were the aerialists on swinging ladders—the Belmont Girls, Fioretta Troupe, Mlle Jennee, Palmero Troupe and the Five Melbournes; the Pygmy Elephants and Military Riding Maids Dorothy Herbert, Ella Bradna, and Erna Rudynoff.

More aerialists came on—the Willos, Buemrang Troupe, Mlle Gillette, the Walkmir Trio, Edward and Jennie Rooney, Miss Amerika and Torrence and Victoria; Captain John W. Tiebor presented his "four troupes of marvelous, educated sea lions," followed by balancing and juggling with both hands and feet, wire walking and high perch acts.

Sixty performing horses and ponies came into the rings, then living art creations from Vienna, in gold and silver, contrasted by groupings of the Sandoval troupes and marblesque horses.

A brief introduction of Colonel Tim McCoy, "the screen's foremost western star with his congress of Rough Riders of the World and council of Plains Indians who will be seen in a thrilling exhibition immediately after the circus performance," was followed by high wire acts by the Wallendas and the Grotofents, then equestrians and comedians in contrast, and an acrobatic assemblage.

In the center ring were the flying Concellos—Arthur and Antoinette—generally regarded as the greatest man-woman team of modern times, with the Flying Comets on one side and the Otari Troupe on the other.

Jumping horses followed by a display of horses leaping over flaming high hurdles set the stage for the grand finale, billed as "Circusdom's outstanding super-finale—

in astonishment as the full impact hit him like the kick of a camel.

"You mean that?" he demanded in a voice that seemed plaintive, almost like an echo. "Who said so?"

"Mr. Gumpertz."

"I'll be damned," John sputtered. "Why that dirty son of a bitch."

He turned, spat in disgust, rammed his cane angrily into the dust, and started to walk away, confused and boiling mad. Then he wheeled like an angry bull and almost bumped into his longtime friend, Carl Hathaway, now the general superintendent.

"Damn it, Carl," he whimpered, "can you imagine anything as crackbrained and underhanded as that? Did you ever expect to see the day when I couldn't give my show the touch for a few dollars? That's all I asked, a lousy hundred dollars—and they turned me down!"

Hathaway shook his head in painful agreement. For many years Carl had been friendly with the old nabob and had always given him loyal support when others turned against him. Now he stood in perplexed silence, wondering what to do and what to say. John spoke at last.

"Carl," he said, "you know I put those half-baked bastards on their feet and greased their stinkin' guts when they came to me with wrinkles in their bellies, beggin' for work—actually beggin' me to give 'em a lift. You know how it was, Carl.

"Now the shylockin' sons-a-bitches have shut me off at the wagon and put the screws on me good and proper. And guys on the show that owe me better than an even break helped them do it.

two living persons actually shot through space
same instant from the mouth of a monster re
cannon. A thrilling presentation by Hugo and
Zacchini."

John Ringling had to like the performance, dee
in his heart, but he would never admit it. He
although he would never say so, that the cir
fighting back from the great depression with
mendous display of courage and plain guts, gi
people a thrilling performance that ran for a s
hours and twenty minutes.

The show had been put together and was bei
by Sam Gumpertz, now John's enemy, who
folding chair in front of his tent in the backy
vously moving his hands and talking with ever
came within his myopic eyesight.

John knew Gumpertz was there and he h
sire to visit the backyard. Sam waited, but he
tain his former friend would never come, a
not relish a meeting. Gumpertz wished no
not been on the lot that day.

John avoided the backyard and after a
with Fred and Ella Bradna just inside the B
shuffled along to the silver wagon, where he l
bling hand on the window sill and peered tl
thick glass at a clerk inside. John's real mis
hand.

"Let me have a hundred dollars," he said c
asking a waiter for a check.

"Can't do it, Mr. Ringling," the clerk rep
"We got orders not to let you have any mc

At first John was so shocked and bewilder
n't believe it. Then his leathery old countena

LILLIAN LEITZEL
Star woman flyer with the Ringlings

A TUMBLER AND CATCHER

THE CLOWN AND THE LADY
"Shall we dance?"

"Now the sharks are fillin' up the dirty, double-crossin' pimps—fillin' 'em up with that 'king is dead' malarky and tryin' to make a bum out of me. You know what they're doin', Carl? The dirty bastards claim the show ain't makin' any money.

"Look at this crowd; you know it's always made money, always will. They're gettin' the dough, all right. They're puttin' it in their hellish sticky fingers instead of where it ought to go. They want to keep the show out of my hands.

"I know everything that's goin' on. They can't fool me one minute. But I'll tell you one thing: The way they're operatin', I'll never get it back under my wing —not in a hundred years."

"You don't think so, Mr. Ringling?" Carl interrupted.

"Not on your life, Carl. Why, they could pay off the whole thing in a couple of seasons like this if they tried. But, do you think they intend to do such a thing? Intend to give me a chance? Certainly not. They want to keep the squeeze on me—that's what they're after.

"Imagine, my name's on every cage and wagon on the lot, on the railroad cars, and I can't touch the show for a lousy hundred dollars. I tell you, Carl, this is a God-damn outrage. That's what it is!"

He paused, looked around as if attempting to scatter his disappointment and anger, then said softly:

"Can you let me have a hundred, Carl?"

Hathaway reached into his pocket, drew out a roll of bills and counted out the money. He did not know when John would pay it back, or how. He didn't inquire.

"Thank you, Carl," John said, stuffing the money into his pocket. "By God, you and Bradna are about the only gentlemen left on the lot."

Then he turned and minced his way down the midway —a bent, craggy old man, sweating in his bitterness and frustration, angrily stabbing the dust with his cane. He moved slowly, each dragging, painful step churning the bile in his heart, chilling and hardening his hatred for the circus owners.

The sun was etching long shadows about him now, painting the acres of canvas and hundreds of wagons and trappings with gold, like lights coming on at the climax of a glittering stage production.

He had been the star, had played his part to the hilt, and now he was moving into the wings. It had been a a magnificent performance on his part, but there was no one to cheer, no one to send flowers; no one to pay tribute to this exceptional and unconformable man, this Bohemian character who had brought sunshine and laughter into the lives and hearts of millions.

John walked alone.

CHAPTER THIRTY

The Finale

THE CIRCUS KING returned to Florida and Ca d' Zan. There, with his nurse and a few servants, John watched his diet carefully, tried to regain his health, and lived like a recluse except for visits from Haley, the accountant, and an occasional call from an old crony. He still went to the museum to look at the paintings, and now and then rode over to St. Armand's and Longboat keys.

The circus would soon be coming home, and, in a way, he would be looking forward to that, for with it would come his friend Fred Bradna. There'd be a few others, too, like Carl Hathaway, Merle Evans, Pat Valdo, and Roland Butler.

He could talk to them and perhaps invite them out for dinner and a chat. They wouldn't tell him much about the circus doings, of course, but they'd be companions for an hour or two, and he could unload his thoughts about how the show was being run.

The IRS agents, having concluded the case against the circus, next took out after him. They came to report that he owned $141,347.42 in income taxes for 1923 and part of 1925, plus $166,308.92 for the remainder of 1925 and part of 1926.

"Holy Jesus!" he hollered. "You mean the show owes all that money besides the other claims? You must be way off in your figurin'. I thought all those taxes had been paid—every last dollar of 'em.

"I was sure the government had collected a long time ago. Now I see the crooks have been takin' me for an awful ride; taking all the Ringlings for a cleanin'. You realize those dirty bastards have been workin' for me and gyppin' me at the same time, and I trusted them all these years. It's a dirty shame!"

"It's not against all the Ringlings," one of the agents informed him. "It's against you, personally; these are your income taxes, Mr. Ringling."

"Well, you can see how I've been gypped," John replied. "You'll just have to wait for your money."

There was another matter John had neglected; it was the $40,521.90 due on his bank stock. The government was pressing for this and John had been told that the default was serious, so he telephoned the U.S. District Judge's office in Tampa and asked for an appointment. He was told to come in on Thursday.

John was a handsome figure of a man when his huge hulk filled the doorway to the judge's chambers, his head and shoulders erect and owlish eyes blinking at the pretty blue-eyed secretary, Mrs. Allie May Maynard.

She escorted him into the chambers of Judge Alexander Akerman, a crusty, white-haired old jurist who would not countenance any dallying with the law. He nodded and ordered, "Sit down, Mr. Ringling."

What had happened, John told the judge, was that he had given his attorneys money which he thought applied to the note, but it never appeared in the records. He even produced receipts showing he had paid $18,000, but the court said this had gone to his lawyers and not to the government.

Judge Akerman insisted the debt belonged to Mr. Ringling personally, and not to his lawyers. He insisted it be paid without further delay. The court's patience, he warned, had been exhausted and if payment was not made within five days, the government would seize and sell enough of his property to settle the claim.

John went home in a fog of uncertainty. For once he could see no way out unless, when the circus came in, he could borrow the money, but he wondered who might have the cash to lend him.

A week later Walter Crumbley, a hardworking, conscientious U.S. deputy marshal from the Tampa office stood at the door of Ca d' Zan with papers to serve on Mr. Ringling. The circus king sent out word that he was not at home, but Crumbley knew what he was doing and said, "Tell him I'll wait."

John ate a leisurely dinner and, after letting the marshal cool his heels for a couple of hours, invited him in and turned on the charm. He insisted he hadn't known the officer of the court was outside, apologized for making him wait, and promised to give the matter his attention in the morning.

"Mr. Ringling, here is a copy of a legal notice we are inserting in the local newspaper, offering certain of your properties for sale at the court's order," Crumbley explained. "Judge Akerman has ordered this done."

On the night of November 4, 1936, the nurse handed him a copy of the *Sarasota Herald* for that day, opened to the legal notices back among the classified advertisements. There, in the customary small type, was a notice offering the following items of property for sale at public auction:

The John Ringling home and its furnishings, together

with the grounds consisting of 17.6 acres; 2.67 acres on Lido Beach and 136.9 acres on Longboat Key, the latter including the remnants of his Sarasota Ritz-Carlton Hotel.

"When is it?" he asked, folding the paper.

"Monday, the seventh of December."

"They'll never sell this place," John vowed. "I'll get. this thing squared up long before that time.

He arose from his chair and rambled about the house as if trying to think of some way out. That weekend he had a few friends in for dinner and some cards, and complained to them that he was being harassed, that the government was trying to confiscate his property.

"The buzzards are tryin' to take everything I've got," he said, "but they can't do it. If the lawyers hadn't clipped me for so much, this thing never would have come up. It'll take a little time, but I'll get it straightened out."

A little time! The man who had never lived by clock or calendar now was begging for more time. The very thing he had spent so freely all his life was running out.

Home didn't mean much to him any more, for there was no love or companionship there—only loneliness. Even so he hated to lose the gaudy old mansion and his other possessions that were free and clear. It would be humiliating and he felt a certain affection for the place and its memories of Mable.

"All I need is a little time to get my old mitts on the show," he told his cronies. "Business is commencin' to come back and this income tax thing ought to help me. The government can't be too rough on me after all the help I've been to them.

"If things were half like they used to be, I could pay

the whole damn thing off and never miss it. Once I
let Tex Rickard have fifty thousand cash. Now it looks
like I'll have to go to New York to raise any money.
Might even get enough to take the show out of hock.
Then, by God, I can come back with the whole thing
under my wing."

There was some reason for his optimism, for in spite
of the depression, John had skilfully protected his financial foundation, and this is how he did it:

The loan which he had cut to $316,000 carried 72
percent of the collateral and the other one carried 28
percent. Manufacturers Trust held the $700,000 loan
and so all he had to do was borrow the $316,000 from
Manufacturers Trust, pay off the balance of the $800,-
000 note, and let the bank have the collateral.

Another thing that made it simple to raise some cash
was a deal he made when he sold his railroad in Oklahoma. To win approval for the sale and take care of
any obligations the railroad might have, he deposited
with the Interstate Commerce Commission in Washington $400,000 worth of Santa Fe Railroad bonds,
plus other miscellaneous securities to bring the total to
well over $500,000.

John went over all this with Haley and discussed
his plans to regain control of the circus. He became enthusiastic because the show was closing in Tampa on
Armistice Day and he almost felt as if it were coming
home to him.

When the show came in the following morning he
rode out to winter quarters to see some of his old friends.
He felt stronger and more confident than he had in years
and appeared in better health and spirits than he had
since Mable died. His hair was darkened and he was

dressed in his favorite brown suit, with shirt, tie, hat, and shoes to match.

But John had no luck raising money, either in town or among the circus folk, and a week later he told the nurse, "Pack your things. We're going to New York tomorrow."

A. B. Edwards went aboard the Jomar to pay a social call the afternoon the train pulled out. John greeted his old crony warmly and displayed unusual optimism.

"You're lookin' fine, Mr. Ringling," Edwards said.

"Feelin' pretty good, A. B., thank you. Gettin' better all the time. Figure I'll be all right soon as I get a few things ironed out. I might make a deal this trip that'll take care of everything."

He stiffened to his full height, like a proud old elk, bristling with courage and confidence. The sun slanted through the thick glass window like a shaft of bright gold—a big, square spotlight focussed on him.

Expansive and baronial, he stood like the game old warrior of other years and times—erect, alert, mind full of ideas and heart full of hope. Once again he was the powerful, imposing, amazing John Ringling, the last of his kind.

"You know, A. B.," he said, lifting his glass and sipping the Scotch. "I'm going to get hold of some cash this trip and then, by God, I'll take over the circus and take it out in the spring under my command—like it used to be and like it's got to be."

Edwards smiled approval. He had always considered it John Ringlings's circus and he was happy to see his old friend talking about a comeback. Naturally, Edwards didn't know John's financial condition but he shared his hopes.

"I'd like to see you get it all straightened out this winter and take over again," Edwards said, sincerely.

"I'm goin' to, A. B. Why, you know the bastards thought they had me down for the count, but they didn't. Some of 'em would like to see me down and out, but I'm not that kind of a man, and you know it. Gumpertz and them know it, too. I'll sure as hell be back in the saddle before the bluebirds sing."

"I'm mighty glad to hear it," Edwards assured him. "Hope it all turns out the way you want."

"I'll be back to sing Christmas carols at my house. You must plan to come out, A. B."

John loved children, though he never fathered any of his own. Many a time he sent clowns and other entertainers to hospitals to entertain, or saw to it that orphanages were emptied when the circus came to town, and drinks and ice cream were provided.

This not only provided an outing and entertainment for the children but was good public relations for the circus.

Some of John's happiest moments came during the holiday season when young people gathered at Ca d' Zan to sing Christmas carols. Leading them in his fine voice, with verve and enthusiasm, was the old circus king himself. When it was over he would order out favors and the flowing bowl. Christmas at John's house was an occasion to be anticipated and cherished.

When John arrived in New York late in November, he went to his suite in the Marguery Apartments. His nurse was with him and so was a friend, Frank Hennessy. A few years earlier his arrival in the big town meant meeting entertainment and business leaders but this was

1936 and no one knew better than he that times had changed.

He went out to dinner a few times and transacted a little business but the weather turned rainy and cold, so he stayed indoors. Even so, he came down with fever and a heavy cold.

A doctor was called but his condition did not improve and on the last Sunday in the month he was a very sick man. His sister was called and she hurried up from Florida. When she arrived he was fighting bronchial pneumonia.

He rallied on the first of December and those on watch at his bedside hoped that he might pull through. He was a big hulk of a man and showed a stubbornness not to surrender, but his slight improvement was more hope than progress and at midnight he slipped into a coma.

Then, quickly, like striking the Big Top after the final performance, John Ringling died at 3:00 o'clock on the morning of Wednesday, December 2, 1936. With him were his physician, Dr. Maurice Costello; his friend, Hennessy; his sister, Ida; his nephew, John Ringling North, and his nurse, Ina Sanders.

The body was taken to the Campbell Funeral Home where brief and simple funeral services were said at four o'clock the following afternoon. The remains were taken to the Brookside Mausoleum at Englewood, New Jersey, to be laid beside those of Mable.

John's expressed wish that they might be buried in the grove of stately royal palms overlooking the bay at the foot of his art museum in Sarasota never came to pass.

"We hope to bring the bodies back and bury them

there, but this is not the proper time," a prominent Sarasotan said not long ago. "We hope to do it eventually.

To which John would have snorted, were he alive, "Eventually can be a damn long time."

The Historical Association of Southern Florida offered to bring the bodies "home," as a public service, and Mable's sister gave her prompt and complete approval. However, relatives objected and said removing the bodies to Sarasota for final burial was "a private, personal matter."

The astounding luck that followed John all his life was with him to the very end. He died just six days before his home was to be sold at public auction to satisfy a government claim.

The same newspaper that had carried the final notice of sale told of his passing in bold, black headlines and columns of type, and it eulogized him editorially.

The death stunned Sarasota, as expected. Over sprawling winter quarters flags flew at half-staff. Workingmen went about their tasks of shunting railroad cars, putting baggage wagons and cages in the shops for overhauling and getting animals bedded down in outdoor dens and corrals. One after another paused in his work to pass the word.

"Did you hear the news?"

"About Mr. John?"

"Yeah. What's going to happen now?"

Heads shook wonderingly. Nobody knew who might gain control of the circus, or who might raise the cash, take it out of hock, and return it to the Ringling family.

For many months there had been rumors that Mr. John was coming back; that he was making plans to take over the circus once more, and that he would be at the helm in the 1937 season.

There were hundreds of old troupers who brushed aside their tears and swallowed hard that day, in their mourning and grief, for there were countless circus folk all over the land who, despite John's faults as a human being, admired him as brilliant leader and fearless promoter, one of the foremost figures in the circus world.

Rivals knew the Ringlings as hard and ruthless competitors, but all conceded they ran a great show and more than once tried to give all circuses a reputation for respectability. Some of the brothers were not loved in a business that is harsh and intensely competitive, but they were respected.

And so there were many among the great old show's employees and friends who sincerely hoped that some day Mr. John might again take over the reins and restore his circus to its former greatness and glory as America fought its way out of the depression and became prosperous once more.

These were not idle dreamings but were possibilities, and had he lived another ten, five, or even two years, it might have come to pass. But all this was out now; Mr. John was dead.

CHAPTER THIRTY-ONE

The Show Goes North

THE MAIN PERFORMANCE was over; it was time now for the concert, the aftershow—every bit as intriguing and exciting as the big show; a rousing family ruckus that was to last for twenty years.

Out of the blare of trumpets and roll of drums stepped dashing young John Ringling North, a vest-pocket edition of his fabulous old "Uncle John," who portrayed many of his uncle's habits and mannerisms and who felt he was qualified by talent, temperament, and training to carry on the family tradition under the Big Top.

Johnny North was Baraboo-born and bred to the circus, but where his uncles left school early to earn a living, he enrolled at the University of Wisconsin and at Yale. Marriage ended his college career in his junior year and North became a customer's man in New York, then a real-estate salesman for his uncle in Florida.

He had gone out with the circus as a concession vendor in 1916, at the age of thirteen, and the smell of the sawdust was in his nostrils to stay. Later he was cashier of concessions during summer tours, handling some circus finances and getting the "feel" of the whole operation.

Although in late years the circus king came to distrust his nephew, paid him precious little for his services, and cut him out of his will altogether, Johnny North was there to take command when John Ringling died, and suddenly his whole ambition was to gain control of the circus.

Thirty-three years of age at the time, North knew that John Ringling's affairs were in bad shape and he realized that quick, decisive action was necessary. So after the funeral he hurried to Sarasota, sold the old dredge and some other of John's belongings to raise a few dollars in cash which he added to the $286 his uncle left.

Johnny North knew there were wills and codicils, but the most important bit of paper among them was one stipulating that he and his brother, Henry, were to get nothing from the estate and their mother was to receive only five thousand dollars a year for life.

The important part of this document was that it named Mrs. North and John as executors and said all three were to be trustees of the estate.

Ida Ringling had never been active in the circus but led a rather sheltered life among her brothers until she ran off and married Henry Whitestone North, a railroad engineer several years her senior. He fathered John, Henry, and Salome before he died in 1920.

The family forgave Ida, of course, but she preferred her home and family to the life of a trouper, and although her brothers had a great deal of admiration for her, and always saw that her wants were fulfilled, she was never part of their circus.

She liked to cook and run her house and one of her greatest joys was to preside at a sumptuous meal, then play bridge or poker with her children and friends until far into the night, and join in their hilarity. Ida maintained a lively interest in everything until her death in 1950.

Henry North, born in the Presbyterian Hospital in Chicago in 1909, was educated at Yale and showed unusual talent as an executive. A tall, slender edition of his Uncle Charlie, Henry was a person of many interests and of unusual wit and charm. He made friends easily and could get along with people on or off the circus.

John and Henry North, anxious to prove themselves circus men, went to see Mrs. Gertrude Lintz in Brooklyn and bought from her a rather large and unusual gorilla. No announcement was made at the time and when the ape reached Sarasota on that pleasant Sunday afternoon in February, 1937, he created no more of a ripple than if a French poodle had come in from New York with his rich mistress on the Seaboard train.

The gorilla, confined in a stout wooden crate, was prodded awake by his keeper, Richard Kroener; hauled to winter quarters on the back of a truck, and placed in a corner of the hospital tent. There, the following morning, the life of Gargantua the Great had its real beginning.

Henry named him and the appellation was far more colorful and appropriate than the "Buddy" tag he had worn for most of his seven years. Besides, Henry North had been affectionately known as "Buddy" ever since his Uncle John called him that years ago, and he understandably did not wish to share his nickname with a gorilla.

The story was that a disgruntled sailor had thrown acid in the gorilla's face, giving him a permanent disfigurement that resembled an ugly scowl. Roland Butler, the astute press agent, soon convinced Kroener that "Gargantua the Great" was the meanest beast in captivity.

Looking over the animal in the hospital tent the morning after his arrival from the north, Butler observed:

"Pretty mean animal, ain't he, Mr. Kroener?"

"No, sir, Mr. Butler. He's very gentle."

"Gentle!" Butler thundered. "Why, he's the meanest monster ever captured by man. Make him mean! Feed him raw meat. Get him a tire to cut his teeth on—a great big truck tire.

"And forget that 'Buddy' stuff. He's Gargantua the Great!"

Gargantua found the tire an entertaining plaything and always had one in his cage, but instead of feasting on raw meat he consumed a steady diet of raw eggs, chocolate, bananas, and milk.

In the months between the time he arrived in winter quarters and the 1938 season when he went on tour, Gargantua became "The world's most terrifying living creature," and "The most fiendishly ferocious brute that breathes!"

Butler and his aides turned out reams of publicity showing Gargantua the Great with huge spiked teeth, slashing and snarling his way through the jungle, and called him "The mightiest monster ever captured by man."

As a moneymaking drawing card, Gargantua the Great was second only to the legendary Jumbo and surpassed any feature ever exploited by a circus in the twentieth century. His name, from the hero of a Rabelais romance, became a household word and his like-

THIS IS
CA D' ZAN,
THE
MANSION
IN
SARASOTA,
FLORIDA,
WHERE
JOHN AND
MABLE
RINGLING
LIVED

It is now a
state museum.

A COPY OF MICHEL-
ANGELO'S
"DAVID"
OVERLOOKS
THE JOHN
AND MABLE
RINGLING
MUSEUM'S
COURT-
YARD

There is a
fine stand of
royal palms
in the
background.

Photo by Robert Ford

WHEN JOHN RINGLING BUILT A FINE HOME IN SARASOTA, FLORIDA, HIS BROTHER CHARLES BUILT ONE NEXT DOOR

This is the Charles Ringling residence, now a part of New College.

ness appeared in print and on film throughout the world.

A reporter once asked John North how much he paid for the gorilla. North pondered the question a moment and replied, "He's worth a hundred thousand dollars."

Gargantua brought the circus far more than that in admissions, advertising revenue, and publicity. More than ten years after his death, pictures purporting to show "The Capture of Gargantua the Great" were being sold as collector's items.

The truth is that Gargantua was given to missionaries in Africa as a baby and found his way to America as the pet of a ship's captain.

Three years after Gargantua made his first tour with the circus, North arranged for Mrs. Marie Hoyt to bring over her pet gorilla from Havana, Cuba, and staged an elaborate "wedding" of the gorillas, complete with a bouquet of flowers for the bride.

They were housed in glistening glass and steel air-conditioned cages and although the marriage was never consummated, they attracted big crowds year after year until Gargantua died in Miami the night the tour ended in 1949, a trouper to the end.

Acquiring and exploiting the gorillas stamped the North brothers as master showmen but they had to find their way out of a jungle of lawsuits to claim the prize.

John North retained Jim Haley, the accountant, to handle paper work on the Ringling estate and put the late circus king's properties in some sort of order. His aim was to settle the tangled affairs as quickly as possible, make final disposition of the museum, and turn his attention to gaining control of the circus and running it.

Haley and William L. Van Dame, a Sarasota real-estate man, made a detailed inventory of the Ringling home and art museum, evaluating every item, something that had never been done. They listed every painting, piece of statuary and china; all the silverware, glassware, books, rugs, and furniture; all the real estate, bonds, and personal property in the estate.

They reported the art museum and its contents were worth $12,000,000; the house and its furnishings, $1,-500,000; and the remaining Sarasota real estate worth $4,000,000. John's share of the Ringling Bros. and Barnum & Bailey Combined Shows, Inc., was $650,000. His other circus holdings were listed at $616,000; oil lands and stock at $2,000,000, and railroad properties $1,600,000—a grand total of $22,366,000.

The art museum had been willed to the state, but it took some clever maneuvering to carry out the bequest. John North flew to London and when he returned he brought minutes showing the Rembrandt Corporation had held a meeting in the Savoy Hotel. Corporation officials were John and Mable Ringling and Julius Boehler, the art dealer, the only one of the trio still alive.

The minutes showed John North had been elected president and Henry North secretary-treasurer of the corporation. Young Johnny North's trip was a financial success, too. He sent Gargantua the Great over by steamer and put him on display while he conducted the Rembrandt Corporation's business.

The state of Florida, said North, should get the art museum and its contents "as soon as possible," in accordance with his uncle's wishes. He also stated publicly that he would not fight the codicil but would probate that with the will.

All of which put state officials on his side, although some of Florida's leading citizens were only mildly receptive and the legislature as a body wanted no part of it.

"We should not touch any part of the property until it is free and clear of all incumbences, including those tax claims," said a legislative leader.

Some Sarasotans also wanted the museum, contending that since the state was hesitant about taking it, the city should press its claim.

The federal government had whopping claims against the estate as well as the circus, in all approximately $13,500,000, and could take over the property but it wanted no part of that. Once Uncle Sam had seized a circus for taxes but soon discovered that circuses must keep moving to make a profit and must have expert management to stay alive.

Thus it wasn't difficult to convince government tax authorities they should compromise their claim of $3,-753,138.01 and settle for $850,000.

North scraped together $325,000 and the state of Florida gave him permission to borrow $525,000 from Manufacturers Trust to pay up. Later, he got a loan of $300,000 from the Florida National Bank in Jacksonville, added some cash from the estate, and paid back the $525,000. Thus, by 1942, the estate's debt had been trimmed to $649,240.

Numerous lawsuits and claims kept North and his attorneys in and out of court and appearing before the state cabinet for more than a dozen years. One of these was Emily's divorce, which she contested until 1943, when the court awarded her one dollar.

There were suits questioning validity of the wills, the codicil, and asking the courts to determine if, when the circus king took his nephews out of his will, he also in tended to drop them as executors and trustees. The court ruled that he did not.

Edith and Aubrey Ringling signed an agreement placing John Ringling North in charge of the circus for five years, which was perhaps the greatest single job of salesmanship he ever did. Leonard G. Bisco, a New York attorney representing Manufacturers' Trust and a close friend of North, bought eighteen shares of circus stock held by New York investors and eighty-two owned by Allied Owners for $28,000 at a bank-rupt sale.

This was another break for North, who acquired 70 of those shares while the others went to Edith and Aubrey, giving them 300 shares each, with 300 belonging to the estate and voted by North as trustee. There were 100 shares of treasury stock not voted.

North's agreement with his Aunt Edith and Cousin Aubrey entitled them to name three directors and he was to name three. William P. Dunn, Jr., of the Manufacturers Trust, was the seventh and deciding vote. That was how John Ringling North became president of the circus and his younger brother, Henry Whitestone Ringling North, became vice president and assistant to the president in April, 1937, less than six months after their uncle died.

The first full season the Norths were in command, in 1938, was a disastrous one, starting with a labor dispute at the opening in Madison Square Garden.

Sam Gumpertz, who resigned when the Norths took over, had signed a contract with the American Federation of Actors, which represented the workingmen, doubling their pay of thirty dollars a month and keep.

The pay scale was considerably lower in winter quarters, and in past seasons this had prevailed in New York and Boston, or until the show went under canvas.

Union leaders demanded full pay immediately and when North told them arrogantly to "go to hell," everybody walked out, leaving only management, performers, freaks, and animals.

The spec featured Frank (Bring 'Em Back Alive) Buck as the Maharajah of Nepal with his court, Merle Evans and his band dressed in Bengal Lancer uniforms—a glittering pageant built around Gargantua the Great and featuring the best of Broadway and the circus.

The spec came in on foot, and instead of riding an elephant, Frank Buck walked around the arena, a pet cheetah on his arm.

It was a wild night, with North digging in like a common workingman, along with Arthur Concello, newly appointed general manager; Pat Valdo, personnel director; Clyde Ingalls, sideshow manager; Jack Earle, the circus giant; Harry Doll, the midget; leapers, equestrians, and many from the audience.

The strike lasted through the next day, then was settled temporarily to finish out the New York and Boston dates.

There was sporadic labor trouble in Brooklyn and Washington, but the circus went on to Baltimore, Philadelphia, and Newark, with diminishing business. Then it swung through Pennsylvania and into Ohio and New York.

Organized labor was picketing and boycotting; North said he was losing $40,000 a week and couldn't meet salary demands. He gave notice of a 25 percent cut for everybody while the show staggered on to Rochester,

Watertown, Syracuse, Binghamton, and into Scranton, Pennsylvania.

There, on June 22, 1938, came the blow that put Ringling Bros. and Barnum & Bailey Circus off the road for the remainder of the season and probably marked the beginning of the end for the Big Top.

The North brothers were holed up in the Casey Hotel while the circus sat on the lot, surrounded by pickets in this strongly unionized community.

The water was shut off, there was no food or ice, and no show. The mayor of Scranton assured the pickets he was behind them, and he ordered the circus to get out of town. When North asked him how, the mayor replied, "That's not my problem, son."

The pathetic monster lay helpless for two tense days and nights. Performers were jeered at and stoned, even in the backyard. Airplanes bearing news photographers flew low overhead and one crashed, killing its two occupants.

Performers voted not to join the strike, and the crippled giant limped off toward winter quarters at Sarasota.

North leased some of his better known features and a trainload of equipment to the Al G. Barnes–Sells-Floto Circus, which was part of the Ringling combine, and finished out the season in the West and South, starting July 11 at Redfield, South Dakota.

North claimed he finished the season with a $400,000 profit, but he signed an agreement with the union that fall and the show went out in the spring as usual and had a profitable season.

That year the tour lasted from April 5 to October 30, covered more than 17,000 miles and took in more than $2,600,000, but in 1940 James C. Petrillo and his musicians' union pulled a strike that took Merle Evans and his band off the show for most of the season. The circus used "canned" music but the following year Evans and his band were back with a contract.

Trouble continued to travel with the Ringling Circus, however, and in the fall of 1941, while the show was nearing the end of its tour, eleven elephants were mysteriously poisoned and died.

A year later, on August 4, 1942, fire leveled the menagerie tent while the circus was on a lakeside lot in Cleveland, Ohio, burning to death two score animals which the show said were worth $200,000.

By this time America was embroiled in World War II, all able-bodied men were being called to bear arms or seek jobs in war plants. North was finding it difficult to get help and buy essential materials.

Arthur M. Concello, star of the flying trapeze, was general manager and gave North expert help and advice, but the going was rough.

North's five-year contract was about to expire and Edith and Aubrey Ringling agreed to vote their majority stock together. When the board of directors met, it was the two Ringling widows, Edith's son, Robert E. Ringling, and William P. Dunn, Jr., on one side. On the other were John and Henry North and George D. Woods.

North proposed two possible plans—to operate the circus for the war's duration as a nonprofit organization, playing for war bond drives and the entertainment of servicemen, with the government's approval and support, or stay in winter quarters on a caretaker basis.

Directors turned down both suggestions, and voted

North out, naming Robert E. Ringling as president, James A. Haley as first vice-president and assistant to the president, and Dunn as treasurer, reelected.

Robert was a recognized opera singer of considerable talent but he was no circus man. However, he was popular during his brief regime if for no other reason than that many troupers considered him "a good sport."

Robert proved to be an exciting individual who carried over some of North's theatrical productions, opened the show with an old-time circus parade, and made money.

During leisure hours performers often would call upon Robert in his private car and ask him to sing for them.

"Would you really like to hear me sing?" he would ask.

"Oh, yes sir; we sure would."

As many as could would crowd around and into Robert's car to listen, then to enjoy the beer and sandwiches he served. Robert had a fine baritone voice and was one of the most accomplished performers in the history of the Chicago Opera Company, where he sang 104 roles.

The circus had a prosperous season in 1943 and that same year Haley married Aubrey Ringling. The following spring it made an auspicious beginning in Madison Square Garden on April 5 and played there through May 21.

After that it moved into the Boston Garden for two weeks, then to Philadelphia, Waterbury, New Haven, Bridgeport, Worcester, Fitchburg, Manchester, Portland and Providence.

After that it went into Connecticut, where it had a date with disaster.

CHAPTER THIRTY-TWO

Fire and Finance

IT WAS HOT and sultry in Hartford on that afternoon of July 6, 1944. The spectators had just seen and applauded the performing wild animals, the first display on the program. Then, while waiting for the Wallendas to "shake hand with death at dizzy heights," horror struck with the swiftness of an atomic bomb.

A tiny tongue of flame suddenly appeared above the side wall at the entrance to the 520-foot-long Big Top. It leaped up the seams and grew to great volume as it raced toward the peak, gnawing at poles and licking the canvas like a hungry monster.

The horrified crowd of 6,789 scrambled for the exits—a pushing, shoving mob of screaming people, all trying to get out in one massive wave of wild confusion. Guy ropes burned quickly; poles became gigantic torches, crashing down among the frenzied, panicky men, women, and children.

Merle Evans and his band played "The Stars and Stripes Forever," traditional circus signal of disaster, until the last of six center poles began to sway dangerously, giant trees of flame with no lines or canvas to support them.

Then the world's largest single spread of canvas settled to the ground like a cloud of fire, smothering and burning everything beneath it.

Within ten terrifying minutes the scene had changed from one of gaiety and laughter to solemn death and ugly ashes; nothing was left but the smoking circus rings, scorched seats, and the awful stench of charred and blistered bodies.

The toll of dead, mostly women and children, on that tragic afternoon was one hundred and sixty-eight. Four hundred and eighty-seven others had been burned or injured.

There was quick and angry reaction, with press and public demanding investigations and jail sentences for those responsible for the greatest single catastrophe ever to strike the circus.

The Ringlings claimed that in sixty years they had never caused a single person's death by fire, but that did not pacify Hartford and the nation. Someone had to pay, not alone in money but in time spent behind bars.

For days the great amusement giant lay helpless, its officials under technical arrest and all its funds surrounded by legal barbed wire, guarded by the courts. Not a single train, wagon, truck, or even an elephant, could move.

Six of the circus' key men were charged with criminal negligence but Robert E. Ringling, the president, was not among them; he had been at home in Evanston, Illinois, that day.

Two things helped free the circus from bondage in Hartford. One was a $500,000 cash reserve fund it carried for emergencies and the other was a $500,000 insurance policy which James A. Haley, in his capa-

city of executive vice-president, had taken out only
months before.

By putting up that million dollars, the circus was
able to leave Connecticut and limp home to winter quarters in Florida nine days after the fire to rehabilitate and
plan its future. Even so, some of the circus' key men,
including Haley, had to remain in Hartford, where they
faced charges of involuntary manslaughter.

These included George Smith, the general manager;
James Caley, the seat boss; Edward R. Versteeg, superintendent of the light department; and David Blanch-
field, the tractor man whose home was in Hartford.

Leonard Aylesworth, the boss canvasman, was conferring with Ringling in Evanston at the time of the fire
but when he reached Hartford a warrant was served on
him.

Damage suits came in droves, prompting Karl Loos,
legal adjuster for the circus, to call in Daniel Gordon
Judge, of New York, to help work out a plan for handling the claims.

Loos, Judge, and attorneys representing the Hartford
Bar Association drew up what was known as the Hartford Arbitration Agreement, whereby the circus as-
sumed full responsibility and left to a committee the
task of fixing the amount of damages to be paid.

Less than a month later, on August 4, the circus
opened again in the Rubber Bowl at Akron, Ohio, giving tentless exhibitions in open-air stadia, fairgrounds,
and ball parks for the remainder of the season, ending
the 1944 tour at New Orleans in early October.

The circus executives came to trial in late 1944.
Robert E. Ringling was called as a witness and he testified Haley was a help ·to him but Johnny North told

the court none of the men was indispensable. Five of the six brought to trial were convicted and sentenced to short prison terms.

They were permitted to go to Sarasota and get the show ready for the 1945 tour, then report back to Hartford authorities.

Meanwhile, counsel for the men filed motions for suspension of sentence, claiming they were indispensable to operation of the circus. North sued Robert Ringling and Haley for five million dollars, alleging mismanagement.

His friends in Sarasota and many on the show felt that Haley was the "goat" at Hartford, and when he came home the following Christmas they gave him a rousing welcome at a civic dinner. Soon they elected him to Congress and he has been there ever since.

North busied himself settling the John Ringling estate but he never for a day relaxed his efforts to divide the family and gain control of the circus. This wasn't too difficult, with a cluster of cousins who had other interests and did not always agree.

North had to consult frequently with the Florida cabinet, whose members often were in disagreement. With each new administration came cabinet changes; attorneys moved in and out like the changing of the guard; there was sharp division among them and often a clash of personalities or politics.

"The Ringling estate is the most involved I ever heard of and it is a delicate situation," was the way Secretary of State Robert A. Gray described it. "There are many suits pending and there have been numerous differences. We have had a series of attorneys in this case."

By 1945, North had reduced outstanding claims

against the estate to $584,000, with salable property worth an estimated $5,796,973. A year later the executors reported they were ready to turn over the museum and mansion to the state, and it was formally accepted February 9, 1946.

In view of events connected with the Hartford fire, Haley had no love for North, but he had even less for Robert Ringling. Of course North was fully aware of this and made the most of it.

So when circus directors held their annual meeting in April, 1946, Haley voted his wife's share of stock, Edith Ringling voted hers, and North the remainder, which included his 7 percent and the estate's thirty.

Haley was named president and North went back in as first vice-president. There followed a blizzard of charges, countercharges and lawsuits, but the circus went out as usual.

North's mismanagement suit was still to be heard; Robert went to court to demand the salary he claimed was due him as president, and his mother, fed up with the whole mess, brought suit to have the election of Haley and North declared illegal.

The lower court decided in Edith's favor, and her son went back in as president, but only until North and Haley secured an injunction and took over again. Whereupon Robert suffered a stroke.

John Ringling North, who had organized a syndicate of executors called Ringling Enterprises, Inc., pushed for a final settlement of his uncle's estate. Florida was enjoying a postwar boom and North wanted to sell the Ringling real estate. He also saw a chance to pick up a bigger slice of the circus pie.

He offered the state of Florida $350,000 cash for the

remaining property and agreed to waive his claim for executors' fees. Under law, a fee of 2 percent may be paid for settling estates in Florida worth more than $100,000 and, using this formula, North figured he was due $1,900,000.

Would the state cabinet accept this offer, which by North's accounting would come to $2,250,000? The answer was "no." It was the same for John L. Sullivan, of Keerville, Texas, who bid $1,200,000.

Soon North was back with another offer—$500,000 cash and a mortgage for $750,000 on everything except the art museum and mansion, and eleven acres facing the museum and home which was to be set aside as a landscaped park with driveways.

In exchange, North and his associates, Leonard G. Bisco and Sydney R. Newman, would get 30 percent of the circus stock, oil wells in Oklahoma and Texas, a part interest in the Ringling Theater in Baraboo, the John Ringling Hotel, the old Jomar, the Whitaker House on Bird Key, and half the silver and china in Ca d' Zan.

That 30 percent of the circus stock was what North really wanted; then he'd need only fourteen more to have a controlling 51 percent.

He made an agreement with his Aunt Edith that if she would vote with him, he would drop all lawsuits and pay Robert a salary as chairman of the board, provided he got the job as president and was allowed to run the show.

That left the Haleys out, so there was nothing for them to do but sell, for a reported $435,000. North took 14 percent of the stock owned by Aubrey B. Haley and her husband, which gave him the majority. Edith and Robert acquired the remainder, thus keeping control in the family and splitting ownership 51 and 49 percent.

Thus busy, energetic, ambitious, and shrewd John Ringling North became, at the age of forty-four, the first individual in amusement history to hold a controlling interest in the "Big Show."

Directors named him president; his brother, Henry, vice-president and assistant to the president, and Robert E. Ringling chairman of the board.

When Johnny North ascended the circus throne in November, 1947, with his younger brother in the role of prince and second in command, it was a sharp and resounding retort to their robustious old luxury-loving, poker-playing Uncle John, whose avowed intention just before he died was to "cut them off without a Goddamn cent."

Robert Ringling lived only two more years, and his mother took his place as board chairman, serving until her death in 1953 at the age of eighty-three, proudly bearing the title "Queen Mother of the Circus" to the end.

Her estate included 400 shares of circus stock, a 33,000-acre spread in Sarasota County, several other parcels of real estate, and a plush pink mansion overlooking Sarasota Bay, just north of John's place. Principal beneficiaries were her daughter, Mrs. Hester Ringling Sanford and her two sons, Charles Ringling Lancaster and Stuart G. Lancaster; and Robert's two sons, James and Charles.

John Ringling North, following the pattern of his uncle who had given him his first job with the circus, traveled aboard the Jomar in kingly comfort, slept late, and was attended by a valet.

During the infrequent times when he was at winter quarters, he would ride one of the spirited circus horses for a hour, then confer with executives on plans for the approaching season.

In the evening he would review circus acts in the ballroom of the John Ringling Hotel, which spectators paid to see.

Once on the road, the circus operation was left largely to Henry and top executives, many of whom had worked for the Ringlings.

CHAPTER THIRTY-THREE

Au Revoir

ARTHUR M. CONCELLO, star of the flying trapeze, came in as general manager and began a program of modernization. He patented a portable steel grandstand that could be erected in less than an hour and provided dressing rooms underneath.

He also designed aluminum side poles and quarter poles, mechanizing where possible and giving the gigantic operation all his energy and executive ability to keep it going.

Concello had the backing of the North brothers and an executive staff of seasoned circus men. These included Frank McClosky, manager; Willis E. Lawson, assistant manager; Waldo T. Tupper, general agent; Theodore Forstall, treasurer with the show; and Lloyd Morgan, lot superintendent.

Herbert Duval was legal adjuster; Walter Rairden, assistant; Roland Butler, head of the press department; Frank Braden, his lieutenant; Pat Valdo, director of performance; Antoinette Concello, aerial director.

Merle Evans was director of the band that played everything from ragtime to grand opera; F. A. Boudinot was traffic manager; Dr. J. Y. Henderson, veterinarian; George J. Blood, superintendent of the cookhouse; and

William Yeske was in charge of the mechanical department.

The Ringling Bros. and Barnum & Bailey Combined Circus exhibited in Cuba for the first time, opening a thirty-two-day indoor engagement at the Sports Palace in Havana on December 8, 1949.

Personnel was flown to the island while a train loaded with animals and equipment made the trip by boat. All acts and features had to be crammed into the one-ring arena but this report came back: "Havana went wild over the performances and gave The Greatest Show on Earth the warmest reception it ever accorded a visiting amusement organization."

The 1950 show was produced by John Ringling North and staged by John Murray Anderson. The menagerie featured "Mrs. Gargantua the Great, world famous giant gorilla mate of the late Gargantua, and her adopted baby gorillas, Gargantua the Second and Mlle Toto, imported from the wilds of West Africa."

The program opened with performing bears, billed as "Superb Himalayan, Syrian and Polar bears—postgraduate prodigies of Europe's foremost schools of advanced animal education, presented by Albert Rix."

Paul Jung with his magic washing machine was next, followed by the Ugo troupe, leaping from springboards over the backs of massed elephants. The congress of aerialists included the three Hemadas, La Norma, the Les Reinyrs, Lilo Juston and the three Margas, followed by Peterson's jockey dogs in the center ring, flanked by Bostock's ponies and Eldridge's pony-riding chimpanzees.

The theme that year was "When Dreams Come True," with music by John Ringling North. It was called

"The most prodigious production in circus history," and described as "the inconceivably magnificent new musical super spectacle of 1950, designed in humor and fantasy for children from nine to ninety and two to toothless."

Unus was in the center ring, standing upside down on a forefinger atop a streetlamp with its lighted globe, while the Adus troupe of acrobats performed in one ring, Franklin and Astrid in the others.

Baptiste Schreiber and his springboard elephants were followed by comedy numbers by Gran Linona, Guti's gorilla parody, and the Boginos. Liberty horses were presented by Czeslan Mroczkowski, Gena Lipowska, and Andre Fox.

Then came a ballet of sixty stunning girls, featuring Pinito del Oro, with Bobby DuBrueil and Elsie Davis. A clown promenade preceded the backward somersault drop of Leon de Rousseau, followed by bareback riders, the Ringling clown contingent, headed by Emmett Kelly, Otto Griebling, Paul Jung, and many more.

There was Francis Brunn in the center ring, flanked by Miss Loni and Realles Trio, followed by the aerial act of the Geraldos, hailed as "the most desperate deeds of daring that ever chilled a spine."

Wedding day in Clownville was next, then acrobatic acts by the Chaludis, Freddi and Bokara troupes; another clown number and a display of horsemanship by Luciana and Freidel, Cilly Feindt and Claude Valois, titled "Old Vienna."

Antoinette Concello appeared as "the triple somersaulting goddess of flight," with the Flying Antonys and Comets.

After the "battalion of buffoons" came novelty numbers by the Hasleys, Idnavis and Rodolphos; Lou Jacobs and his midget automobile; the Alzanas in their chilling high wire act, featuring Harold Davis "the most daredevilish human ever to skirt eternity's brink."

The grand finale was "Jungle Drums," hailed as "a weird, wild, tom-tomic jubilee in the fantastic land of mumbo jumbo, with native girls, boys, and elephants."

On its mid-century tour, the circus traveled 15,932 miles, gave 430 performances in 217 days from April 5 through November 19, and entertained 3,179,000 customers, according to its literature.

But this was not the old Ringling Bros. and Barnum & Bailey Combined Circus. It had changed and was changing every year. The midway had lost its saucer-lipped Ubangis, the menagerie its pygmy elephants; the program itself the two Zacchinis shot from a cannon.

There were more trained animal acts, acrobatic and equestrian numbers embellished with singers and dancers; scores of pretty girls singing and swinging on long colored ribbons—a program combining beauty and melody.

America was changing, growing up, maturing; the circus had to change, too. Now it had become what some called a "girlie show," or a "hybrid"—part outdoor entertainment, part theater, and part nightclub—in a circus setting and still with the old circus music and flavor. One season the spotlight shone on a child playing a xylophone!

"How else could anyone compete with free radio and television, nightclubs, baseball and football day and night, and meet union demands?" North and others wanted to know. It was a big question; one not easily answered.

Down through the years, many of America's greatest
writers contributed to the circus' magazines and programs—Clarence Budington Kelland, Robert Lewis
Taylor, Rubye Graham, Richard Casper, Ned Roberts,
Spencer Tracy, Lauritz Melchoir, Ezra Stone, Don Mc-
Neill, Dr. Hugh Grant Rowell, Art Buchwald, and
many more.

"The circus is the only ageless delight that you can
buy for money," wrote Ernest Hemingway, one of the
greatest writers of our time, in the 1953 program.
"Everything else is supposed to be bad for you. But the
circus is good for you. It is the only spectacle I know
that, while you watch it, gives the quality of a truly
happy dream."

The smell of horses and elephants and all the other
animals in the menagerie was still the same; Merle Evans
and his band played the same old stirring marches and
lively waltzes.

Inside, the Big Top had been painted a royal blue,
with air-conditioning to make it comfortably cool and
there was fresh, clean sawdust on the floor. The sideshow men still gave the same spiels; candy butchers and
program hawkers were everywhere.

The ringmaster's whistle still had the same shrill
sound, the seals barked as usual, and the elephants
clanked their chains just as Babylon and Queen had done
sixty years before.

But the circus had changed, along with the times,
and the old days when circus folk came over the hill
and down the road "laughing and scratching" were no
more.

Automobiles, trucks, and buses had forced the circus parade into oblivion in the 1930's; now lots large

enough to accommodate the acres of canvas and props and trappings were no longer available within reasonable distance of downtown.

And if they were, most upper and middle classes had moved to the suburbs and were watching first-rate entertainment on television screens in living-room comfort, free.

The grand old institution carried on until it reached Pittsburgh. There on Monday, the sixteenth of July, 1956, came the end of what millions of Americans for three generations had known as the greatest circus of them all.

A handful of what had once been a happy, working family of 1,500 persons of all colors, creeds, and nationalities loaded all that was left of the old Ringling Bros. and Barnum & Bailey Combined Circus aboard sixty railroad cars for the 1,100-mile journey home.

The trip was a funeral procession. Performers and workingmen alike expressed anger and bitterness at the turn of fortune. Many went without food or funds on the long ride to winter quarters while those more fortunate managed to buy sandwiches and soft drinks along the way.

In Sarasota, a pickup band led by a minister played lilting tunes while the trains rolled slowly past the downtown station and on out to winter quarters. A few boosters from the chamber of commerce held aloft hastily-lettered banners saying, "Welcome home, Circus!"

But the crowd of a few hundred watching through the hours were seeing amid their tears the end of a glorious era. The muggy night air was charged with uncertainty and each hiss of steam and grind of wheels against rails emphasized doubt and bewilderment.

For thirty years these homecomings had been filled
with happy reunions and high hopes for next season and
the next, but this was a death march, without a coroner.
By the time the last train pulled in at three o'clock in the
morning, the townspeople had seen all they could take
without weeping openly and all but half a dozen had
gone home to bed.

With the mountains of canvas, props, and trappings
had come less than a score of American performers and
seventy-nine from foreign lands, plus ninety workingmen.

They were a sad, long-faced lot, burning with hunger
and aching with uncertainty, terribly neglected even
for basic human needs but not crying, not talking of
despair and disappointment, for these were circus folk
and they were strong.

Next day winter quarters was a scene of utter confusion. Many of those from across the sea could not speak
English and stared blankly at each passerby, wondering
with tired eyes how long they might be allowed to stay in
America, and how they would survive.

Strong, bronzed young men inquired anxiously if jobs
were to be had in the community or in the state—any
job so a man could eat and buy a pack of smokes now
and then. Older men sat silent and forlorn, staring at
their gnarled hands, still hoping but terribly unsure.

John Ringling North had announced in Pittsburgh
the Big Top was going down and the show returning to
winter quarters. Doubtless the decision came after long
deliberation and was painful to him, for he went into se-
clusion aboard the Jomar and would see no one.

Relief agencies stepped in to help provide food for

the most needy circus people; others found jobs so they could make it through that fall and winter.

Concello, an ingenious little man, devised steel supports for rigging so the acts could go on in auditoriums and convention halls, now rising in many cities. Finally, North announced that the circus would open in Madison Square Garden in the spring.

This gave the old-timers heart and hope, and many now insisted the show would rise again, as it did from the ashes of Hartford. Pat Valdo, a performer since 1904 and later personnel director, had this to say:

"Certainly we'll go out in the spring. As long as there is a child, a horse and a clown on earth, there'll be a circus."

The circus went north in that spring of 1957 aboard fifteen railroad cars. After New York and Boston, it traveled by train, bus, and automobile; hauled equipment by truck and trailer over roads unfamiliar to drivers. Detours often caused long delays and many engagements were missed. One truck en route from Montreal to Denver wound up in St. Louis!

North and Concello had other troubles, too. AGVA charged unfair labor practices and the 49'ers demanded that North be kicked out as president. They also filed suit for twenty million dollars.

As a circus, it had no menagerie, no midway or Big Top; no pink lemonade or calliope; no fresh sawdust or pungent odors; no backyard with drying clothes, sleeping workingmen, pets and children playing amongst the props and wagons.

Personnel had to find eating and sleeping accommodations, working only five, four, or even three days a week—sometimes less—and drawing pay for time put in. Star performers and whole acts left the show; many who stayed on barely made expenses.

The circus stayed on the road nearly all year, which meant winter quarters were abandoned. Animals were sold or loaned to zoos. The few left at Sarasota lived in the wild state, roaming amongst the pine trees and palms, hiding in the rank weeds and grass, finding shelter in rotting buildings and boxcars.

Dozens of railroad cars and acres of props and equipment lay peeling and rusting behind the stout wire fence, guarded by one man with two vicious dogs at his side.

And so the circus kept going, fighting competition and adversity every step of the way. Fighting among the stockholders continued, too, with John Ringling North and his brother the 51's and the other side of the family the 49'ers.

North added fuel to the flames in 1959 when he cashed in on his Uncle John's leavings in spectacular fashion. He sold considerable real estate and the John Ringling Hotel in Sarasota for $13,500,000, and let the 156 acres in circus winter quarters go in a separate deal for $350,000.

Sarasota County, which had welcomed the circus in 1927 and was a partner in the winter quarters deal, thought it was entitled to the money those 156 acres brought. The Board of County Commissioners instructed its attorney to see what could be done.

"There is nothing in the public records to indicate the land belongs to anybody but the Ringling estate," he reported after months of searching deeds, minutes, and agreements written thirty-two years before, and interviewing everyone he thought might be able to help. "I can find absolutely nothing to give the county any claim to it."

A. B. Edwards, sole survivor of the trio who "forgot" the mortgage so John Ringling could use the fairgrounds acres and buildings, suggested depositions might help.

"There is nothing you can do; absolutely nothing," the attorney assured him and the commissioners. "These papers make no mention whatsoever of revertment to original owners or the county. And I find this provision, written in, that the land and buildings thereon, 'shall belong to John Ringling or his heirs, forever.' "

No circus representatives were in the room at the time, or any members of the family. John Ringling North was in Europe and Concello was busy closing down the old winter quarters and negotiating an agreement with the town of Venice, eighteen miles to the south, to set up there.

Such relics as wagons, cages, stockcars, and a railroad coach went to the Circus World Museum at Baraboo; other props and rolling stock went to buyers all over North and South America, to end up in circuses, carnivals, and amusement parks.

Finally, the buildings were burned and the land scarified, erasing the last remnants of the circus. All that was left was a rotting old billboard half hidden amongst the weeds and bushes half a mile down the road, its paint peeling away and a faint arrow pointing to what had been the circus' winter home.

Ten years after the Big Top went down and out, the Ringling Bros. and Barnum & Bailey Circus was in what it called the ninety-sixth season, which would take it back to the time Al and his brothers put on their first performance in the barn at Baraboo.

The 1966 circus traveled aboard a twenty-eight-car train, with equipment and most performers aboard, but some others used automobiles and house trailers. The show boasted 18 elephants, 45 horses, and a varied assortment of dog acts, lions, tigers, llamas, zebras, and a gorilla billed as Gargantua II.

There were some three hundred in personnel, about one-fourth the number on the big show in its prime. John Ringling North, pictured impeccably dressed as usual with gloves, cane, Homburg, and cigarette in holder, was listed as president and chairman of the board, and Henry Ringling North, vice-president.

Other officers were Rudy Bundy, vice-president and treasurer; Mrs. Robert D. Bon Siegneur and Charles Ringling Lancaster, vice-presidents; Francis W. Kelly, assistant vice-president, and Robert Thrun, secretary.

Harold D. Genders was general manager; Dean McMurray, assistant; Lloyd Morgan, manager, and McCormick Steele, general agent. Robert Dover was performance director and coordinator, and Antoinette Concello, former star of the flying trapeze, was director of the aerial ballet. Harold Ronk was ringmaster and soloist.

Pat Valdo, a circus man for more than sixty years, was listed as general director but he spent most of his time at Venice winter quarters or at his Sarasota home.

Merle Evans, the great and enduring bandmaster, completed his forty-fifth year, still holding his silver cornet with his left hand while directing with his right.

There were reports that Madison Square Garden or one of the big television networks would buy the show. North was quoted as saying his 51 percent could be had for $5.1 million. The same reports said the 49'ers would sell for $4.9 million.

Nothing came of it but exactly twenty years after John Ringling North ascended the circus throne, on Saturday, the eleventh of November, 1967, he announced from his home in Rome, Italy, that ownership was passing to the Hoffeld Corporation of Delaware.

Two days before, Circuit Judge Lynn Silvertooth at Bradenton, Florida, had approved Dan Gordon Judge's request for permission to sell the 490 shares of minority stock. Judge was trustee for 315 shares under the will of Mrs. Edith Conway Ringling and 175 shares under that of Robert Edward Ringling.

North held 450 shares of his own and with his brother controlled 60 shares as executors of the estate of their mother, Mrs. Ida Ringling North.

Judge Silvertooth noted that all parties were in agreement and that in the sale of property such as a circus, "Where so much of the value is centered in good will, the court is careful that interests of the beneficiaries are protected."

Under terms of the sale, the Hoffeld Corporation— Judge Roy Hofheinz of Houston, Texas, and the brothers Irvin and Israel Feld, of Washington, D.C.—took over the 1,000 issued and outstanding shares of circus stock on payment of eight million dollars in cash.

The new owners announced that the circus' office would be moved from New York City to Washington; that Hofheinz, who built the Astrodome in Houston and had many other interests there, would be chairman of the board; that Irvin Feld would be president and chief executive officer and Israel Feld executive vice-president and treasurer.

North said the new owners "indicated their concern and their dedication to maintain the concept, tradition and artistic standards of the circus."

So the show is likely to go on, through adversity and prosperity, as it has through all the years because the circus can never die.

The new owners of the "big one" announced that John Ringling North would remain with it as producer and his brother as a vice-president. Hofheinz added, "The ownership by our family will bring additional worldwide acclaim to the city of Houston."

No matter, American children of all ages will never again be privileged to see and explore and enjoy the wonderful world of the circus, as generations knew it— great stretches of canvas to house and feed a city; a forest of props and trappings; wagons and trucks and trains to move it, and an army of men with strength, skill, and endurance to set it up and take it down in any weather in any city or town.

Never again shall we marvel at the vast menagerie with its huge collection of strange and exotic birds and animals from all corners of the globe; listen to the loud and lilting music of great brass bands and the calliope in street parades and while the mammoth Big Top is filling up; or shall we thrill to those magnificent productions of magnitude and splendor Alf T. Ringling created to amaze and amuse human beings of every race, color and creed.

Never again in this changing universe shall all the people be privileged to see and enjoy as children again, in an utterly carefree atmosphere, a day like Thanksgiving, Christmas, and the Fourth of July all rolled into one—a day at the beautiful, breathtaking and beloved circus the Ringling Brothers gave to the world.

Epilogue

IN CIRCUS HEAVEN

In Circus Heaven, here I rest,
    A wagon wheel with memory blest.
Care-free—wandering many lands;
    Happy children, clowns and bands;
Sun-drenched streets and gleaming tents;
    The Spieler's voice—"Ladies and Gents."
I never dreamed that there could be
    The riches that have come to me.

COURTNEY RYLEY COOPER

Index

INDEX

INDEX

INDEX